D0890286

# Bit by Bit

# BIT by BIT

## An Illustrated History of Computers

Stan Augarten

TICKNOR & FIELDS    NEW YORK    1984

*Library of Congress Cataloging in Publication Data*

Augarten, Stan.
  Bit by bit.

  Bibliography: p.
  Includes index.
  1. Computers—History.  I. Title.
QA76.17.A94      1984      621.3819′5′09      84-2508
ISBN 0-89919-268-8
ISBN 0-89919-302-1 (pbk.)

K 10 9 8 7 6 5 4 3 2 1

Acknowledgment is gratefully extended to the following:

    Arthur W. Burks for excerpt on page 99 from his speech "Who
Invented the General-Purpose Electronic Digital Computer?"
    IBM Corporation for IBM song on page 69; for quotations of
Thomas Watson, Sr., on page 167; for CTR song on page 179; and for IBM
song on page 180.
    W. W. Norton & Co., Inc., for excerpt on page 195 from *Science for
the Citizen* by Lancelot Hogben. Published by W. W. Norton & Co. in
1957.
    Ziff-Davis Publishing Company for excerpt on pages 273–74 from
editorial by Arthur Salsberg, reprinted from *Popular Electronics*, January
1975. Copyright © 1975 by Ziff-Davis Publishing Company.

*Illustration on title page:* A wafer of memory chips manufactured by
American Microsystems, Inc., of Santa Clara, California (photo courtesy
of American Microsystems, Inc.)

O dear Ophelia!
I am ill at these numbers:
I have not art to reckon my groans.

— Hamlet, act II, scene 2

# Contents

# Preface

No machine, no matter how extraordinary, is as interesting as its maker. When Wilhelm Schickard, a German professor at the University of Tübingen, invented the first mechanical calculator in 1623, he was giving expression to an imagination much richer, much stronger, than any collection of gears and axles. "History," declared the British historian and essayist Thomas Carlyle, "is the essence of innumerable biographies," and this book is as much, if not more, about the people whose work led to the invention of computers as it is about computers themselves.

Bit by Bit is also about ideas — in particular, the ancient and great idea that intellectual work can be performed by machines. The notion apparently originated with the invention of the abacus in Babylonia about five thousand years ago and evolved, in ever more potent forms, into the slide rule, the mechanical calculator, the punch-card tabulator, the first electronic calculating machines, and finally, in the United States and Great Britain in the late 1940s, the electronic digital computer.

The invention of the computer was one of the greatest technological achievements of the twentieth century, but it wasn't until the development of the personal computer, in the mid-1970s, that the magnificent promise inherent in this machine was fulfilled. We have reached a new stage in the evolution of the great idea that began with the abacus, and it is only fitting that we now pause to trace the long history of the ultimate machine, the reflection of our minds, the computer.

*Bit by Bit*

## CHAPTER 1

# The First Mechanical Calculators

There is no greater mistake than to call arithmetic an exact science. There are . . . hidden laws of number which it requires a mind like mine to perceive. For instance, if you add a sum from the bottom up, and then again from the top down, the result is always different.

*Maria Price La Touche, 1824–1906*

. . . I submit to the public a small machine by my invention, by means of which you alone may, without any effort, perform all the operations of arithmetic, and may be relieved of the work which has often times fatigued your spirit. . . .

*Blaise Pascal, 1623–62*

*In this nineteenth-century Chinese abacus, numbers are entered by sliding beads toward the crossbar. The upper beads represent fives; the lower ones, units. The number shown is 7,230,189. The instruction board above the abacus is turned on its side.*

The history of computers has two starting points. In one sense, it began during World War II, when a team of scientists and engineers at the University of Pennsylvania, in Philadelphia, invented a general-purpose electronic digital *calculator* known as ENIAC, or Electronic Numerator, Integrator, Analyzer, and Computer. Consisting of 18,000 vacuum tubes, occupying most of a large room, and adding 5,000 ten-digit decimal numbers a second, ENIAC was a revolutionary development, light years ahead of any other calculator. But it was not a *computer* in the strict meaning of the term. It could not store a program — a list of instructions that tells a computer what to do — and its operation was controlled by the physical rearrangement of thousands of wires and switches. Whatever a computer is — and we shall go into that later in this book — it must be able to store a program; otherwise, it isn't all that different from a calculator. Although ENIAC wasn't a bona fide computer, it quickly led to the invention of one, and today's computers are its direct descendants.

In another sense, however, the history of computers commenced with the invention of the abacus, probably in Babylonia (now Iraq) five thousand years ago. This humble tool was one of the first, and certainly one of the most effective, embodiments of a momentous idea — the notion of using a machine to help us perform intellectual work. However obvious this idea may seem today, its discovery initiated a long chain of technological developments that led, by way of countless wrong turns, dead ends, and technological breakthroughs, to the invention of ENIAC and the stored-program computer. The history of computers is the story not only of a certain kind of machine, but of the progress of a great idea from sliding beads on a frame to a machine that could retain a program. Our history, then, properly begins with that most humble of mathematical instruments, the abacus.

No one knows exactly where the abacus, or counting board, came from. The word *abacus* comes from the Greek *abakos* or *abax*, which means "board" or "tablet," and in turn may have descended from the ancient Hebrew word *ibeq*, which means "to wipe the dust." In its earliest form, the abacus was merely a row of shallow grooves or lines traced in the ground, with pebbles, stones, or bits of bone used as counters; the rows stood for units, tens, hundreds, and so on, and the quantity of counters in the rows represented a number. Unfortunately, there are no surviving examples of the first abaci, since they were made out of sand or wood; but counters, or round stones that apparently were used as counters, have been unearthed from ancient Babylonian ruins.

The Babylonians and most early civilizations had written number systems, although as a rule these systems were not designed for reckoning. In general, the symbols were complex and awkward to write, and the systems lacked the all-important concepts of zero and fixed numerical places for tens, hundreds, and so on. However, these inadequacies didn't prevent many early peoples from carrying out extraordinarily complicated calculations, and the reason is simple: the first number systems were not really intended for computation but to *record the results of calculations worked out on the abacus.* Such was also the case with Roman numerals: it's very difficult to divide MDCCLVI by LIX on paper or in your head, but it isn't hard to do with an abacus. Without the use of zeros or numerical places, Roman notation was inappropriate for pen- or mental-reckoning, but the Romans weren't at a great disadvantage as long as they relied upon the abacus.

Moreover — and this is the great beauty of the abacus — you don't have to know any number system to use it. Regardless of whether you can read or write, you can use it to solve most practical numerical problems, which means that even uneducated

*An advertisement for Hindu-Arabic math from a sixteenth-century English book,* Margarita Philosophica. *The smiling man has discovered Hindu-Arabic numbers; the frowning man is still using Roman numerals.*

Counting boards were widely used in Europe between A.D. 1200 and 1800. Unfortunately, few survive. This one was made in sixteenth-century Strasbourg.

A seventeenth-century French jeton, *front and back.*

merchants or traders could carry out the kinds of mathematical transactions involved in business, from keeping accounts to calculating interest. As a result, the abacus became one of the sine qua nons of the Western world, a commonplace and indispensable tool until the adoption of Hindu-Arabic numbers and the gradual spread of numeracy and literacy led to its extinction; you don't need an abacus if your numerical notation is conducive to pen- or mental-reckoning. All this may come as a surprise to most of us, since Westerners think of the abacus as an exclusively Oriental tool, yet it was widely used in Europe, chiefly in the form of a wooden board with metal counters, until a few hundred years ago.

Hindu-Arabic math entered Europe with the great Moorish invasions of the eighth and ninth centuries, and it spread with snail-like slowness. (Old habits die hard, even in modern times; witness the persistence of the English system of weights and measures in the United States, Great Britain, and other countries.) Depending on the region, the transition to Hindu-Arabic numerals occurred between the thirteenth and seventeenth century. They appeared first in Italy and Spain, which, being on the Mediterranean, were closest to the Arab world, and much later in France, England, and Germany. The switch also occurred in different social classes at different times, with the educated upper classes learning the new notation long before the unlettered lower ones. In general, the Hindu-Arabic system was commonly employed throughout Europe by the end of the sixteenth century.

The change created a great deal of confusion and consternation. Strange as it may seem to us today, most people were puzzled by the alien notions of zero and place and didn't understand their functions. For a time, the two systems were even used interchangeably, which created some amusing numerical bedfellows, a mathematical mixing of oil and water; for instance, one set of *jetons*, (metal tokens minted by the French government for use as counters on counting boards) show the date as MCCC94. For most Europeans (those who were numerate, anyway), it was like learning a new language. The symbols took some getting used to and there was a strong feeling — a feeling that's still with us — that you could prove anything with them. Indeed, some people were outraged by the whole thing. In 1299, to cite the best-known case of public antagonism to Hindu-Arabic math, the merchants of Florence were forbidden to use these strange new symbols in their accounts.

Although Hindu-Arabic notation made pen- or mental-reckoning fairly easy, most people still had a hard time with basic arithmetic, and the counting board hung on. As Europeans grew increasingly adept with the new math, however, the board gradually fell by the wayside and had all but disappeared by the end of the seventeenth century, when only the old-fashioned and the ignorant continued to use it. (Such people were referred to derisively as "counter casters.") Yet there was no practical reason for tossing the age-old abacus aside; it is a useful tool regardless of your number system, and it still thrives in Japan, China, and other parts of Asia. But the Western world has always been partial to "progress," no matter how painful or inconvenient it may be, and it was Hindu-Arabic math, not the abacus, that stood for progress. And progress is exactly what came.

*John Napier (1550–1617), in an engraving from a painting in the collection of the current Lord Napier.*

*Opposite:*
*The rent rolls of Bristol, England, document the switch to Hindu-Arabic. The figures on the page at the left, compiled in 1599, are in a stylized form of Roman numerals; those on the right, written in 1640, are Hindu-Arabic. The third line from the bottom on the 1599 rent roll says: "Sume of this side ——— xxxii^li v^s [32 pounds, 5 shillings]."*

In 1614, John Napier (1550–1617), baron of Merchiston, Scotland, published one of the most important papers in the history of science. A highly original mathematician, Napier announced the invention of *logarithms,* or *logs* — a series of numbers that enabled multiplication and division, the two most difficult arithmetic operations, to be reduced to addition and subtraction. Instead of multiplying or dividing natural numbers (1, 2, 3, etc.) on paper or in your head, you simply looked up the numbers in a table of logs and added or subtracted the given figures; then, to get the final answer, you converted the sum of the logs back to a natural number by referring to a table of *antilogs.* The principle of logs is quite simple, and is based upon the fact, now taught to schoolchildren everywhere, that numerical powers can be added or subtracted: $x^2 \times x^4 = x^6$ or $x^6 \div x^2 = x^4$.

In their original version, Napier's logs weren't useful for ordinary figuring, so Henry Briggs (1561–1630), a geometry professor at Gresham College, London, took up the grueling job of calculating the logs for thousands of natural numbers. In 1617, Briggs published a small table giving the logs for the numbers from 1 to 1,000 and, seven years later, a much larger one for 2,000 to 29,000 and 90,000 to 100,000. At a time when most people had trouble with basic arithmetic, Brigg's tables were a mathematical godsend and were circulated widely. Other mathematicians gradually filled in the gaps in his tables, providing, for example, the logs for frequently used mathematical functions, such as sine and tangent, which made Napier's invention an increasingly indispensable tool for navigators and surveyors.

The creation of logs was one of the seminal achievements in the history of mathematics, with a great deal of influence on the development of computers. Aside from its many practical applications, the invention led mathematicians to take a closer look at numerical powers, and the development of exponents was one result. Unlike most great scientific discoveries, Napier's work wasn't preceded by decades of lesser labors along the same lines by other mathematicians, and there isn't even a hint in earlier mathematical writings of the feasibility of abbreviating such basic operations as multiplication and division. The invention was entirely Napier's doing, the work of a determined genius in out-of-the-way Scotland, a rather primitive place compared to London, Paris, and the other intellectual centers of seventeenth-century Europe.

The wealthy lord of a castle outside Edinburgh, Napier re-

In 1614, Napier's Mirifici Logarithmorum Canonis descriptio, *one of the great papers in the history of science, was published. It introduced logarithms and contained ninety pages of tables.*

garded mathematics as a hobby. He attended Cambridge University for a few years but, apparently at the suggestion of an uncle who didn't think much of English schools, finished his education on the Continent, probably at the University of Paris. Living in a time of intense religious strife — the Protestant Reformation was underway — Napier, who did not seem to do anything halfheartedly, got caught up in the general fanaticism. He became a zealous anti-Catholic, a leader in the campaign against Popism, and spent five years writing a long religious tract called *Plaine Discovery of the whole Revelation of Saint John,* which he composed in English instead of Latin so that "hereby the simple of this Iland may be instructed" in the Protestant way. With the peculiar shortsightedness of the zealot, Napier was certain that he would be remembered above all else for his *Plaine Discovery.*

Napier was also a resourceful inventor, especially in defense of God and country. He devised a large hydraulic screw for draining flooded coal mines and a small arsenal of weapons for Scotland's defense against an anticipated invasion by the dreaded King Philip of Spain, a Catholic. (And he described these weapons in a curious document entitled *Secrett Inventionis, proffitabill and necessary in theis dayes for defence of this land, and withstanding of strangers, enemies of God's truth and religion.*) He drew up plans for mirrors that could set fire to ships at a distance; a cannon that could rain shot in a circle; and a round metal chariot — a forerunner of the tank — that could carry musketeers. According to a witness, the cannon was particularly fearful, destroying several sheep and cattle (of the Catholic faith, no doubt) in a test on a plain outside Edinburgh.

In his autobiography, William Lilly, a seventeenth-century astrologer, relates an amusing story, possibly apocryphal, about the first meeting of Napier and Briggs. Lilly apparently heard the tale from a witness, John Marr:

> When Merchiston [Napier] first published his Logarithms Mr Briggs . . . was so surprised with admiration of them that he could have no quietness in himself until he had seen that noble person whose only invention they were. He acquaints John Marr therewith who went into Scotland before Mr Briggs purposely to be there when these two so learned persons should meet. Mr Briggs appoints a certain day when to meet at Edinburgh; but, failing thereof, Merchiston was fearful he would not come. It happened one day as John Marr and the Lord Napier were speaking of Mr Briggs, "Oh! John," saith Merchiston, "Mr Briggs will not come now"; at the very instant one knocks at the gate, John Marr hasted down and it proved to be Mr Briggs to his great contentment. He brings

Mr Briggs into my Lord's chamber, where almost one quarter of an hour was spent, each beholding the other with admiration, before one word was spoken.

In the last years of his life, Napier developed another ingenious arithmetic trick — hardly as significant as logs but rather a clever little gimmick. Employing an ancient numerical scheme known as the Arabian lattice, he laid out a special version of the multiplication tables on a set of four-sided wooden rods; there was a rod, or numbered stick, for each of the ten digits, including zero. Napier's rods, or bones, as they came to be called, were essentially a multiplication table cut up into movable columns. For example, to multiply 1,952 by 4, you picked up the rods numbered 1, 9, 5, and 2, and placed them on a wooden board outfitted with a vertical index labeled from 1 to 9. You moved your eye down to index number 4, and added up the two numbers, or partial products, that appeared in the fourth row of each of the rods. That was your answer. By repeating these operations, you could multiply and divide large numbers and find square and cube roots.

*Napier's rods were fashioned in many different forms and sizes. The set on the right was made in the seventeenth century and came in a leather case; the one on the left dates from the eighteenth or nineteenth century and came in a wooden box. The rods on the left have been set up to multiply 746,159 by any number from 2 to 9. To multiply by 2, you simply read the figures in the first horizontal row, moving from right to left and adding the numbers in each parallelogram. Hence 746,159 × 2 = 1/4/8+ 1/2/2 + 1/1/8 or 1,492,318.*

Napier's rods were enormously popular and constituted the Scotsman's chief claim to fame among his contemporaries. They were used all over Europe, testimony to the poor state of numeracy at the time, when even the lower rungs of the multiplication table taxed the ability of well-educated people. (Arithmetic ordinarily wasn't taught in school.) The rods were available in basic, middling, and deluxe versions; in an especially fancy edition,

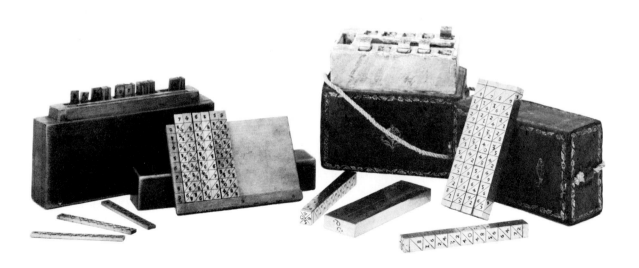

they might be carved out of ivory and set in a carrying case made
out of fine leather, with an addition table, pasted to the lid,
thrown in for good measure. In later versions, the rods were
turned into cylinders and mounted inside wooden boxes; instead
of laying out the rods on an index board (to set up the multiplicand), you simply rotated them in their places in the box. In any
event, Napier's rods fell out of fashion after several decades, as
people gradually got the hang of Hindu-Arabic math.

Napier's work had many practical offshoots. In 1620, three years
after Napier's death, the English mathematician William Gunter
(1581–1626) developed a physical analog of logarithms. Gunter, a
colleague of Briggs's at Gresham College, drew a grid of lines on a
sheet of parchment and multiplied and divided numbers by adding and subtracting lengths with a compass. As with logs, the op-
erative principle is the exponent, and each point on Gunter's

*Some versions of Napier's
rods were cylindrical. Here,
the cylinders have been set
to multiply 3,100,768,129 by
any multiplier from 1 to 9.
An addition table is
engraved on the lid.*

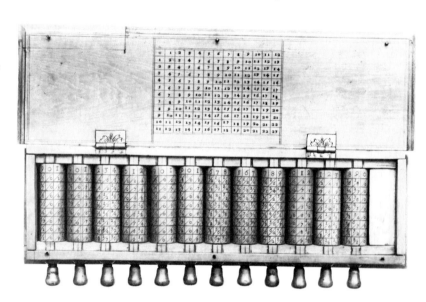

*Below: Gunter's scale, front
and back. It is two feet long
and two inches wide.*

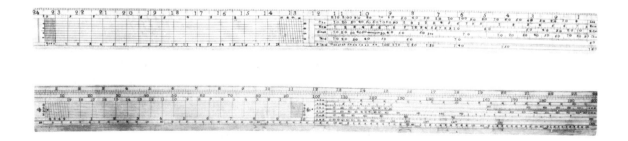

scale, or line, is exponentially distant from the others. The "Gunter" became a popular navigator's tool. Two years later, another English mathematician, William Oughtred (1574–1660), rearranged Gunter's lines into a pair of circles, refigured their numbers, and came up with a device that found a warm spot in the hearts of scientists and engineers for hundreds of years — the slide rule, which enables you to perform rough but rapid multiplication and division by sliding a numbered stock between two fixed slats.

*William Oughtred (1574–1660), in an engraving from his* Clavis Mathematicae *(1631)*

Oughtred was one of those brilliant country clergymen who dabbled in mathematics. A deeply religious man, he wavered between a career in academia and the church; but he decided to follow his heart and, after serving as a fellow for several years at Cambridge, his alma mater, joined the ministry. He wound up as rector in Albury, Surrey, where he continued his research and corresponded with mathematicians all over Europe. He gained a considerable reputation as a mathematician and attracted many students. (Albury, which lies just south of London, wasn't far from Oxford, Cambridge, and the other intellectual centers of England.) There, Oughtred tutored the sons of the local nobility and taught promising young mathematicians for free.

One of his more imaginative students was a fellow named Richard Delamain, who went on to become a mathematics teacher in London and who, in 1630, published a paper describing a circular slide rule. Oughtred, claiming to have invented the circular rule eight years earlier, accused Delamain of stealing his idea. The two men and their supporters fought it out for years, in print and in person; one of Oughtred's wittier defenders described Delamain as "the pickpurse of another man's wit." Oughtred finally freed himself from his shyness for the printed word and issued a paper on the circular rule in 1632 and another on a rectilinear version in 1633. Meanwhile, Delamain, thanks to his newfound fame as the creator of the circular rule, was appointed quartermaster general and mathematics tutor to King Charles.

It appears that Delamain invented the circular rule later than, but independently of, his teacher, who is the undisputed creator of the more useful and popular rectilinear version. In any event, the first rectilinear rule consisted of two wooden scales, marked with logarithmic lines, that were held in the user's hands and slid back and forth against each other; in 1654, the rectilinear rule as we know it today — a sliding stock between two fixed slats — appeared. As time went by, both types of rule were modified and improved, and various mathematical scales, in addition to the original ones for multiplication and division, were in-

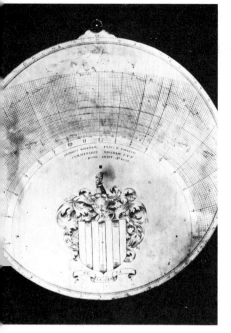

The first circular rules consisted of a series of concentric logarithmic scales whose values had to be added and subtracted with compasses.

cluded. Many special-purpose rules were also developed, in various shapes and sizes, for the use of scientists and engineers.

With their numerical scales engraved or printed on wood or ebony, slide rules were accurate only for computations to the second or third decimal place. (Plastic slide rules came along in the 1950s.) However, because many practical problems in science and engineering don't require exact answers, the thumbnail computational ability of slide rules wasn't necessarily a drawback, and the slide rule enjoyed a long and fruitful life. By the late nineteenth century, the need for faster and more accurate figuring led to ever bigger and more complicated rules and, by the middle of the twentieth century, the device reached preposterous dimensions. In 1952, for instance, an engineer at the Northrop Aircraft Company, of Hawthorne, California, created a circular rule that was about the size of a tabletop. It was quite possibly the largest rule ever made.

Incidentally, the invention of the slide rule wasn't Oughtred's only contribution to mathematics. In the early seventeenth century, there was little consensus on the kind of notation to use for even the most basic arithmetic operations, and Oughtred is credited with introducing the times sign ( × ) for multiplication and the double colon (::) for expressing ratios, a symbol now rarely used. Napier also did his part to standardize numerical notation, giving us a simple and unambiguous way to write decimals — the decimal point.

Right: The first rule with a sliding stock (top) was made by Robert Bissaker in 1654. Below are rules made in 1689 and 1742.

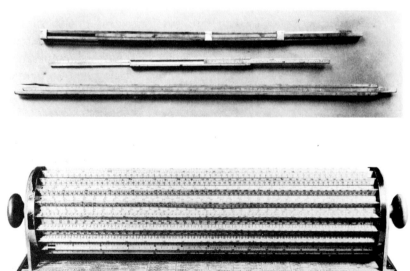

Below right: In 1881, E. Thacher, a New York inventor, patented a huge cylindrical rule. It contained two logarithmic scales, each divided into forty sections engraved on the edges of twenty triangular bars. By adding and subtracting the values with a compass, you could perform computations that were accurate to four places.

*Richard Bemis, a Northrop engineer, holds an enormous circular rule that he had designed in 1952 for aerodynamic calculations.*

At this point in our account, it's important to explain the difference between the terms *digital* and *analog*, one of the most crucial distinctions in the lexicon of computers. The words describe different methods of counting or measuring various phenomena, and the distinction between them is best illustrated by two gadgets that are found in almost every car: a speedometer and an odometer. As a recorder of miles traveled, an odometer is a digital device, which means that it counts discrete entities; as a measurer of miles per hour, a speedometer is an analog device, because it keeps track of velocity. When we count things, regardless of what those things may be, we are performing a digital operation — in other words, using numbers that bear a one-to-one correspondence to whatever it is we're enumerating. Any device that counts discrete items is a digital one. By contrast, when we measure things, whether to find their weight, speed, height, or temperature, we are making an analogy between two quantities. Any gadget that does this is an analog one.

Scales, rules, speedometers, thermometers, slide rules, and conventional timepieces (the kind with hands) are all analog instruments, whereas odometers, Napier's rods, mechanical calculators, and the overwhelming majority of electronic computers are digital devices. The line between digital and analog is quite distinct, even though some instruments, like watches and thermometers, are manufactured in both digital and analog forms. In general, when an operation calls for measuring something, an analog device is employed; similarly, when it calls for counting things, a

*By X-raying the Antikythera mechanism, a salt-encrusted portion of which is shown above, historians were able to deduce its structure and function.*

*Opposite: A reconstruction of the Antikythera mechanism. The device is about as big as a mantelpiece clock.*

digital machine is used. The speedometer-odometer illustration is a simple way to remember the analog-digital contrast.

Analog computers have been around for thousands of years. The ancient Greeks, for example, developed an astonishingly sophisticated clocklike mechanism that could register and predict the motion of the stars and planets. The device, found in an ancient shipwreck off the southern Greek island of Antikythera near Crete, in 1901, consisted of metal gears and pointers encased in a box that opened up like a book. The Antikythera mechanism is by far the most sophisticated scientific instrument from antiquity, and it seems scarcely possible that it was made in the first century B.C. rather than in the seventeenth or eighteenth century. Despite the rapid proliferation of digital electronics, the world is still thickly populated with analog gadgets, and the evolution of these machines is closely linked with the invention of the computer.

For hundreds of years, historians believed that the great French mathematician and philosopher Blaise Pascal invented the first mechanical calculator in approximately 1642. Pascal's machine was a small metal box equipped with a set of interlocking metal gears; by turning the numbered dials on the outside of the box, you could add and subtract. As it turns out, however, the first calculator wasn't invented by Pascal but by an obscure German professor named Wilhelm Schickard. Schickard's calculator was built in 1623 — the year Pascal was born. This fortuitous discovery was made in 1935 by an alert German historian by the name of Franz Hammer, and it led to the reconstruction of Schickard's machine and to the historical resurrection of its inventor.

Schickard was born in Herrenberg, a small town near Stuttgart, in southwestern Germany, on 22 April 1592. Not much is known about him. His father, Lukas, was a carpenter; his mother, Margaret, the daughter of a Lutheran minister. A precocious child, he won a scholarship to a monastery school in the nearby town of Tübingen. (The scholarship was awarded by the government of Württemberg, then a quasi-independent state.) After graduating from the monastery, he entered the seminary at the University of Tübingen, where he studied theology and prepared for the ministry. He received a B.A. in 1609 and, two years later, an M.A. In addition to theology, he specialized in what were then known as the Oriental languages — Arabic, Hebrew, Persian, and Syrian. From 1613 to 1619, he served as a pastor or deacon in several

*Wilhelm Schickard (1592–1635) in a portrait at the University of Tübingen*

*A prolific scholar, Schickard wrote dozens of books and monographs, including a Hebrew grammar, published when he was twenty-two, and a dissertation on ancient Hebrew coins.*

nearby towns, and then returned to his alma mater as a professor of Hebrew and Oriental languages.

Schickard was a polymath, with a wonderful talent for languages. He was also a skilled mechanic, cartographer, and engraver whose published writings span an extraordinarily wide range of subjects — mathematics, astronomy, optics, meteorology, cartography, Semitic studies, and theology. Even at a time when the extent of knowledge in any field was considerably smaller than it is today, and a determined individual could master several diverse disciplines, the range and variety of Schickard's achievements are impressive. He was a universal man — the first of many in the history of computers — with a rare mixture of scientific and artistic ability.

In the winter of 1617, Schickard met Johannes Kepler, the great mathematician and astronomer. Kepler was passing through Tübingen on his way to Leonberg, the Württemberg town where his mother had been accused of being a witch. The old woman, whom the mathematician had once described as "thin, garrulous, and bad-tempered," faced torture and trial (in that order), and Kepler was on his way to Leonberg to arrange for her defense and eventual acquittal. Imperial mathematician to the Holy Roman Emperor, Kepler was a famous and controversial man, much persecuted for his religious beliefs; he was a Lutheran with strong Calvinist leanings, and his faith ran counter to the prevailing dogma. Ironically, his religious stand caused him infinitely greater grief than his revolutionary scientific achievements, which

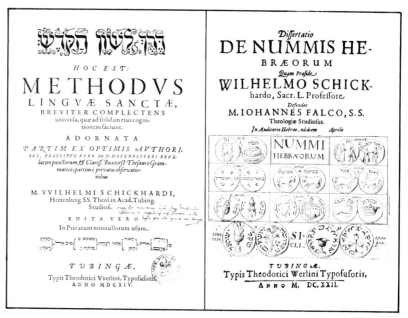

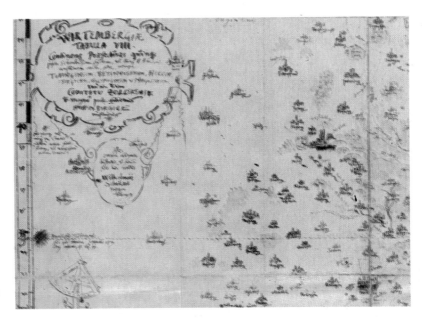

*A detail of one of Schickard's maps, showing a section of Württemberg*

most people didn't understand and, therefore, were less well known.

It is believed that Michael Maestlin, an astronomy professor at the university, introduced Schickard to Kepler. Although Kepler was twenty-four years older than Schickard, the two men had much in common, professionally and personally — the same religion, the same alma mater, the same home province, the same scientific interests — and they became friends. Their relationship speaks well of Schickard, who was only a twenty-five-year-old deacon at the time, not only because the great Kepler was interested in him but because Schickard himself was willing to risk the general disgrace that surrounded a man whose family had been touched by the devil and whose religious beliefs contradicted the church's. Kepler was impressed with the multitalented Schickard and later asked him to draw the tables of figures for his great work, *Harmonice Mundi (World Harmony,* 1619). The two men corresponded with each other for several years, and Schickard looked after Kepler's son when the young man attended the University of Tübingen. (And he took over Maestlin's chair when the professor died in 1631.)

In their letters and conversations, Schickard and Kepler discussed the latest mathematical and scientific achievements, including logarithms and Napier's rods. Schickard's calculator appears to have been an outgrowth of these discussions, although it seems that he conceived of the machine on his own. In any event, Schickard, who liked to work with his hands, designed and built the Calculating Clock, as he called his invention, sometime in 1623.

On 20 September 1623, Schickard wrote Kepler a letter that described, in Latin, the result of his labors. "What you have done in a logistical way (i.e., by calculation)," Schickard announced,

> I have just tried to do by way of mechanics. I have constructed a machine consisting of eleven complete and six incomplete (actually "mutilated") sprocket wheels which can calculate. You would burst out laughing if you were present to see how it carries by itself from one column of tens to the next or borrows from them during subtraction.

Schickard's next letter, written on 25 February 1624, brought bad news:

> I had placed an order with a local man, Johann Pfister, for the construction of a machine for you; but when half finished, this machine, together with some other things of mine, especially several metal plates, fell victim to a fire which broke out unseen during the night. . . . I take the loss very hard, now especially, since there is no time now to produce a replacement soon.

At this point, the Calculating Clock disappears into the sands of time. In 1618, the Thirty Years' War erupted in Prague, and half of Europe was swept up into the madness. For three decades, the armies of Germany, Austria, Sweden, France, and Spain marched to and fro across the Continent. The majority of the soldiers were mercenaries with a professional interest in prolonging the war; they ravaged the countryside for food and plunder, and left ruin, starvation, and disease in their wake. Germany, the main battleground, lost about 40 percent of its population, mostly through starvation and plague; in some regions, such as Württemberg, which the war reached in the late 1620s, more than half the populace perished. Schickard died of bubonic plague on 24 October 1635, and his family passed away at about the same time. In all likelihood, his house and possessions were burned, looted, or given away.

With the death of Schickard's family, no one was left to memorialize his achievements. Aside from an occasional reference in obscure sources, the Calculating Clock was forgotten. But, against all odds, some of Schickard's papers were preserved in the Stuttgart Landesbibliothek and the two letters quoted above wound up in collections of the astronomer's works. The first letter was included in a collection of Kepler's papers that came to rest in the Pulkovo Astronomical Observatory outside Leningrad, while the second was published in a volume of Kepler's works entitled *Lit-*

In Schickard's calculator, carrying and borrowing was accomplished with "mutilated" gears positioned between the number wheels.

| 1 | 2 | 3 | 4 | 5 | 6 | 7 | 8 | 9 | 0 |
|---|---|---|---|---|---|---|---|---|---|
| 0/2 | 0/4 | 0/6 | 0/8 | 1/0 | 1/2 | 1/4 | 1/6 | 1/8 | 0/0 |
| 0/3 | 0/6 | 0/9 | 1/2 | 1/5 | 1/8 | 2/1 | 2/4 | 2/7 | 0/0 |
| 0/4 | 0/8 | 1/2 | 1/6 | 2/0 | 2/4 | 2/8 | 3/2 | 3/6 | 0/0 |
| 0/5 | 1/0 | 1/5 | 2/0 | 2/5 | 3/0 | 3/5 | 4/0 | 4/5 | 0/0 |
| 0/6 | 1/2 | 1/8 | 2/4 | 3/0 | 3/6 | 4/2 | 4/8 | 5/4 | 0/0 |
| 0/7 | 1/4 | 2/1 | 2/8 | 3/5 | 4/2 | 4/9 | 5/6 | 6/3 | 0/0 |
| 0/8 | 1/6 | 2/4 | 3/2 | 4/0 | 4/8 | 5/6 | 6/4 | 7/2 | 0/0 |
| 0/9 | 1/8 | 2/7 | 3/6 | 4/5 | 5/4 | 6/3 | 7/2 | 8/1 | 0/0 |

Schickard installed a modified set of Napier's rods in the upper half of his calculator. The multiplication table shown above was laid out on each of the calculator's six cylinders.

*Working from Schickard's letters and drawings, Dr. Bruno Baron von Freytag Löringhoff reconstructed Schickard's calculator in 1960. Below is a view of the completed machine, showing, from top to bottom, Napier's rods; the addition and subtraction dials; and the independent number wheels, used for storing numbers. Above is the back of the machine, revealing the rods.*

*terae ad Kepplerum* (1718). (Catherine II of Russia acquired most of the astronomer's manuscripts, bound in eighteen volumes, in 1773.) Unfortunately, the many scientists, historians, and archivists who pored over Kepler's literary remains failed to recognize the importance of Schickard's letters, which is quite understandable given the size of Kepler's papers. And there wasn't much reason to pay any attention to the dusty Schickard material in Stuttgart.

In the early 1930s, the German Research Union and the Bavarian Academy of Sciences decided to publish a complete edition of Kepler's works. Max Caspar, Kepler's noted biographer, and Franz Hammer, another Kepler expert, were the co-editors of the series. One day in 1935 Hammer was sifting through copies of the astronomer's papers at the Pulkovo Observatory when he came across a curious slip of paper about the size of a postcard. The paper contained a rough drawing of a gadget of some sort. In the letter to Kepler published in *Litterae ad Kepplerum*, Schickard describes his invention in detail and refers to an enclosed sketch, but the drawing had been lost. Fortunately, Hammer remembered that letter, and linked the drawing to it. Although he realized that he had found documentary evidence of the invention of a mechanical calculator, Hammer, burdened with a great deal of work and hampered by the outbreak of World War II, didn't publicize his discovery.

Twenty-one years later, Hammer was examining Schickard's papers in Stuttgart when, as luck would have it, he found another drawing of the calculator along with a small piece of paper containing instructions for a mechanic. The drawing jarred his memory, and he decided to announce his findings. In 1957, at a Congress on the History of Mathematics at a mathematical institute in Oberwolftach, in the Black Forest, he presented what he had found. One of the people in the audience was Dr. Bruno Baron von Freytag Löringhoff, a mathematics professor at the University of Tübingen and, in a manner of speaking, Schickard's spiritual descendant. Since Hammer didn't understand how Schickard's device worked, Professor von Freytag, who knew a bit about old mathematical methods, studied Schickard's documents and deciphered the puzzle. Back in Tübingen, Professor von Freytag embarked upon the reconstruction of the machine, and completed a working version in 1960.

Schickard's calculator, which resembles a mechanical cash register, was actually two machines in one; the top half was simply a version of Napier's logs, minus the oblique line, laid out on six cylinders suspended in a wooden box. The face of the box was

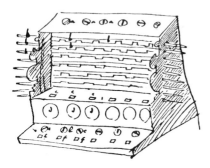

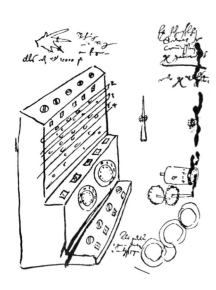

*The Schickard sketch that Franz Hammer discovered at the Pulkovo Observatory in 1935 is shown at the top and, below it, the one that he found at Stuttgart twenty-one years later.*

composed of nine wooden slats with little windows cut out of the slats to show the numbers on the rods. If, for example, you wanted to multiply 332 by 5, you turned the first three rods to 332, slid the fifth slat to the left, and added the products that appeared in the windows of that slat. As long as the multiplications were simple enough, you could get the final result by toting up the numbers on the logs in your head. But if your multiplier had several digits, you were better off entering the product of each multiplier on the mechanical adder that Schickard installed in the bottom of the machine, underneath the rods.

There are six numbered dials on the face of that adding and subtracting mechanism. Those dials are connected to six axles in a box behind them. The chief technical problem in building a mechanical calculator is the design of a device for carrying or borrowing tens, and Schickard apparently solved the problem by equipping each of the axles with a single-toothed gear. (These are the mutilated gears mentioned in his letter.) Each single-toothed gear was linked to an intermediate gear, which in turn meshed with a gear on the adjacent axle. When, for example, you turned the first numbered dial past zero, the single-toothed gear nudged the intermediate one, which moved the adjacent axle a notch. As a result, a ten was added to that axle's numbered dial. (Much the same way automobile odometers work.) Subtraction was accomplished by turning the dials in the opposite direction, and all the results showed up in little windows above the dials.

With typical German thoroughness, Schickard outfitted the base of the machine (directly under the adding and subtracting mechanism) with six independent numbered wheels, which enabled the user to store a number while he or she fiddled with the rods or adding dials. And he installed a bell, or what Professor von Freytag believes may have been a bell, in the machine to notify the user when an addition or subtraction exceeded the calculator's capacity; the bell was rung whenever the sixth main gear

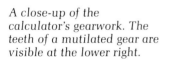

*Dr. Bruno Baron von Freytag Löringhoff in the early 1970s.*

*A close-up of the calculator's gearwork. The teeth of a mutilated gear are visible at the lower right.*

attempted to carry a ten forward or backward. Despite its numerical limitations, the machine (or Professor von Freytag's reconstruction) worked quite well. Schickard had created the mathematical equivalent of the wheel, but his invention, swallowed up by the Thirty Years' War, had no effect on the technology of mechanical calculation.

*Blaise Pascal (1623–1662)*

In the eyes of the world, the first mechanical calculator was invented by Blaise Pascal. Born in 1623 in Clermont-Ferrand, in the Auvergne region of France, Blaise was the son of a well-heeled lawyer who served as the deputy president (judge) of the local tax court — a position that he had, in the tradition of the time, purchased from the government. Étienne Pascal was an intelligent man with a wide range of intellectual interests; he was especially devoted to science and mathematics and seems to have been a fairly talented mathematician. He was also a determined social climber and a loyal officer of a severely oppressive government; the France of Louis XIII and Cardinal Richelieu, the foreign minister, was rocked by savage peasant revolts, and officers of the state like Étienne occasionally were assassinated. In 1626, when Blaise was three, his mother died, and Étienne, who had become rich through quasi-official graft, resigned his judgeship and moved to Paris, where he devoted himself to the education of his son and two daughters.

Blaise's brilliance surfaced early. As a child, he discovered several fundamental mathematical theorems (at least according to one of his sisters, whose account may be exaggerated). At sixteen, he wrote an essay on conic sections that proved a fundamental theorem about geometric shapes inscribed in conic sections. He supposedly derived four hundred corollaries from the theorem — which has come to be known, in what is certainly a unique honor for a teenager, as Pascal's mystic hexagram. (His *Essai pour les coniques* has been lost, but a broadside, written several years later, survived.) Most mathematicians couldn't believe that the essay was the work of a boy; René Descartes, one of the seventeenth century's most important mathematicians and philosophers, at first suspected that Étienne was the real author of the essay, and it took him a while to acknowledge Blaise's genius.

Blaise's short life was full of accomplishment. In his twenties, in addition to inventing a calculator and producing several mathematical treatises, he demonstrated the existence of atmospheric pressure and of vacuums. In his thirties, he invented the syringe and the hydraulic press, and enunciated the basic princi-

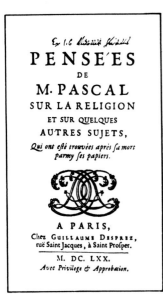

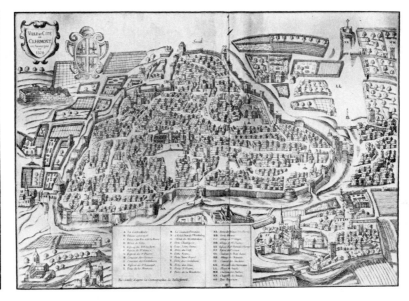

*Pascal's Pensées, a collection of notes and manuscript fragments, was published a year after his death.*

*Right: Clermont-Ferrand, Pascal's birthplace, in the early seventeenth century*

ple of hydraulics — a principle now known as Pascal's law. (Briefly, it states that any pressure applied to a confined liquid will be transmitted with equal force in every direction, regardless of where the pressure is applied.) And along with Pierre de Fermat, the Swiss mathematician, he laid the foundations of the theory of probability, a project that began as a favor for a card-playing nobleman who wanted to know more about the odds of the draw. Blaise was also interested in the affairs of the world; shortly before he died, in great pain, of ulcers and stomach cancer at the age of thirty-nine, he and a group of farsighted Parisians established one of the earliest public transportation systems in Europe, a bus line in central Paris.

Blaise is one of the greatest might-have-beens in science. There's no telling what he might have accomplished had he not died so young and had he not, at the age of thirty-two, entered a Jansenist convent outside Paris. To a large degree, Blaise's extreme religiosity was fueled by agonizingly poor health and a pent-up sexuality — he apparently was a homosexual — and he flagellated himself for more than his share of sins. At the request of the Jansenists, Blaise generally abstained from scientific pursuits and devoted himself to the castigation of the Jesuits and the atheists. He wrote two philosophical works, *Les Provinciales* and the *Pensées*, which were considered masterpieces of expository writing and which established him as one of the founders of modern French prose.

The origin of Blaise's calculator is rooted in both political and personal matters. In 1635, France declared war on Spain and marched into the Thirty Years' War. Short of money, the French government reneged on part of its internal debt and stopped paying interest on certain government notes. Étienne, who had invested heavily in municipal bonds, suddenly found himself without an income. On the verge of bankruptcy, he joined four hundred investors in a tempestuous confrontation with the French chancellor, Peter Seguier, in a meeting in Paris in 1638. Richelieu was outraged by the protest and ordered the arrest of the more outspoken investors, and Étienne fled, alone, to his native Auvergne. Thanks to the intercession of influential friends and the help of one of his daughters, who charmed the cardinal with a performance in a children's play, Étienne was restored to favor. The state needed able men like him, and he was allowed to prove his loyalty and recoup his fortune as the tax commissioner for Upper Normandy, based in the thriving port of Rouen.

At first, Étienne, who assumed his new post in 1639, was buried with work. He and his son were often up until two or three o'clock in the morning, figuring and refiguring the ever-rising tax levies with the help of counting boards. In the course of their labor, it occurred to Blaise that it might be possible to mechanize their calculations with a device that counted numbers much as a timepiece marked the passage of time. "The calculating machine," wrote a reviewer in *Le Figaro Littéraire* in 1947, "was born of filial love flying to the rescue of the tax man." With his father's encouragement — Étienne was nothing if not forward looking — Blaise went to work designing an apparatus that could do the job. It was 1642 and Blaise was nineteen.

*A five-digit Pascaline with its carrying case*

A high-strung perfectionist, he labored on the machine for two or three years, experimenting with many different designs, components, and materials. Étienne hired workmen to make prototypes under his son's direction, but the going was slow, partly because of Blaise's fastidiousness, partly because of the primitive state of metalworking at the time; it was very difficult to cut precisely toothed gears. Blaise finally came up with a feasible design — a five-digit calculator about the size of a shoe box, with dials on the front for entering the numbers and crown-type gears on the inside for calculating the answers, which appeared in little windows on the face. A practical engineer, he tested the solidity of the gadget by taking it on bumpy carriage rides in the country. Although the machine seemed sturdy enough, its five-digit capacity was plainly inadequate, and Blaise went on to develop six- and eight-digit models.

The Pascaline or Pascale, as the elegant contraption came to be called, looked much better than it worked. It was really good only for basic addition. Addition was performed simply enough — you dialed in the numbers and the answers appeared in the little windows on the face — but subtraction was a rather tedious procedure. As Pascal designed the device, the gears could turn in one direction only — we'll see why in a moment — which meant that subtraction had to be carried out by a roundabout method known as nines complements. An ancient trick, nines complements transforms subtraction into a form of addition. As for multiplication and division, the Pascaline accomplished them, maddeningly enough, by repeated addition and subtraction.

The nines complement method is worth a closer look, since it is also used in many computers. Say you wanted to subtract 600 from 800 on the Pascaline. First, you pulled down a thin horizontal slat that masked the regular answer windows. A new set of numbers was revealed on the drums — the nines complements. Then you dialed in 600, which produced a nines complement of 399, or the difference between 600 and 999. Next you returned the slat to its regular position and added 800 and 399, which gave 1199. Finally, you mentally performed an *end-around carry*, adding the leftmost digit in 1199, or 1, to 199, which yielded the answer, 200. A nines complements is merely the difference between a given figure and a row of nines, the size of the row being determined by the number of digits in the figure. By using nines complements, or a variant known as tens complements, a computer can perform addition and subtraction, and therefore multiplication and division, with the same circuits.

Inside, the Pascaline consisted of five to eight axles. There

were three crown-type gears on each axle, with a fourth perpendicular gear linking the axles to the dials on the face of the machine. The axles also held the numbered drums. Whenever a ten was carried, a weighted rachet between the main gears nudged the adjacent gear, or next highest power of ten, around a notch, and so on down the row. In theory, the weighted rachets were supposed to make it easier for the Pascaline to perform carries; but, in practice, the rachets tended to jam — the machine's major technical drawback. Moreover, the rachets prevented the gears from turning in more than one direction, necessitating a roundabout approach to subtraction.

With its weighted rachets and eight-digit capacity, the Pascaline was conceptually more ambitious than Schickard's Calculating Clock. But the German's six-digit machine, with its simple carrying mechanism, worked perfectly, while Pascal's creation did not. (By the way, the clock's capacity for multiplication and division derived from the unmechanical strategems of Napier's rods and any user of the Pascaline could have compensated for its multiplying and dividing deficiencies by buying a set of rods.) Nevertheless, the Pascaline was a historic achievement, for it demonstrated that an apparently intellectual process like arithmetic could be performed by a machine. (Of course, the Calculating Clock was also a cogent demonstration of the power of machines, but it had no historical impact.)

Despite its shortcomings, the Pascaline was an instant sensation. Rouen's elite trooped through the Pascals' drawing room for free demonstrations, and Étienne and his son took their mechanical wonder to Paris, where they showed it off to royalty, businessmen, scientists, and government officials. Pierre de Rob-

*Opposite: A six-digit version of the Pascaline, built in 1654. Below is a frontal view of the device, showing the number dials and answer windows. Above is the back of the machine, revealing the gears.*

*Right: The Pascaline's inner workings were quite complicated. The weighted ratchet (labeled c) is the little gadget in front of the numbered drums. It looks like the handle of a shovel.*

erval, a family friend and a mathematics professor at the Royal College of France, agreed to demonstrate the contraption to prospective customers in his apartment at the College Mâitre Gervais every Saturday morning and afternoon. He would sell the machine — on commission, of course — and teach buyers how to use it. Blaise went to work writing advertising flyers for the invention and asked another friend, the poet Charles Vion Dalibray, to compose a publicity sonnet:

> Dear Pascal, you who understand with your subtle insight
> What is admirable in mechanics
> And whose skill gives us today
> A lasting proof of your marvelous genius,
>
> After your great intelligence, what is the point of having any?
> Calculation was the action of a reasonable man,
> And now your inimitable skill
> Has given the power to the slowest of wits.
>
> For this art we need neither reason nor memory,
> Thanks to you, each of us can do it without fame or pain
> Because each of us owes you the fame and the result.
>
> Your mind is like that fertile soul
> Which runs everywhere inside the world,
> And watches over and makes good whatever is lacking in all
>      that is done.

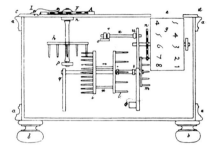

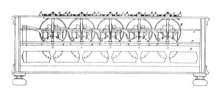

Cross sections of the Pascaline

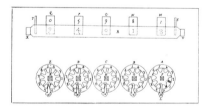

By raising or lowering a long, thin slat (above), the user set up the machine for subtraction.

Perhaps inevitably, counterfeit versions of the Pascaline appeared on the market. Blaise was furious. "I have seen with my own eyes one of these false products of my own idea," he wrote in one of his publicity broadsides, "constructed by a workman of the City of Rouen, a clockmaker by profession. . . .

> After being given a simple account of my first model, which I had constructed several months previously, he was bold enough to attempt another, and what is more, with a different kind of movement; but since the fellow has no aptitude for anything except the skillful use of his own tools and does not even know whether there is such a thing as geometry or mechanics, the result was that (though very competent in his own line of business and very industrious in various ways unconnected with it) he simply turned out a useless object, nice enough to look at, to be sure, with its outside smooth and well-polished, but so imperfect inside that it was no good for anything; but owing simply to its novelty it aroused a certain admiration among *people who knew nothing at all about such things,* and not withstanding the fact that all the basic defects came to light when it was tested, it found a place in the collection of one of the connoisseurs of this

same city which was filled with rare and interesting things. The sight of this little abortion was extremely distasteful to me and so chilled the enthusiasm with which I was working at the time to perfect my own model that I dismissed all my workmen, fully intending to abandon the enterprise owing to the fear I rightly felt that others might set to work with the same boldness and that the spurious objects they might produce from my original thought would undermine both public confidence and the use that the Public might derive from it.

Blaise applied for a patent, or privilege as it then was called, but it was slow in coming. Unluckily for him, the issuing of patents was controlled by the office of Chancellor Seguier, who had presided over the boisterous investors' meeting of 1638. Seguier had a long memory. Although the Pascals' had attempted to appease the chancellor by dedicating one of their first calculators to him, Seguier didn't act on their patent application until 1649, four to five years after the Pascaline's debut.

Patented or not, the machine failed to sell, even though there obviously was a need for it, given the poor state of numeracy in seventeenth-century France. There were several reasons for its failure, including its tendency to malfunction and its limited mathematical ability, which didn't make it very helpful to bookkeepers, clerks, and businessmen who could have used a good adding machine. The Pascaline was also very expensive, going for 100 *livres*, or pounds, apiece, which was enough to keep a seventeenth-century Frenchman in modest comfort for a year. Moreover, people were suspicious of a machine that could count; if a scale or a roulette wheel can be fixed, so can a calculator, and more than two hundred years were to pass before most people could place their trust in nuts and bolts. At the very least, the

*Pascal gave this eight-digit calculator to Chancellor Seguier.*

Pascals expected that they'd be able to sell the machine to royalty, but the aristocrats disdained arithmetic and intellectual matters in general; bookkeeping was for servants. It's not known how many machines were sold but the total was probably no more than ten or fifteen.

*Gottfried Wilhelm von Leibniz (1646–1716), in a portrait at the Royal Society in London*

The third great calculator inventor of the seventeenth century was Gottfried Wilhelm von Leibniz. The range and richness of his intellect was nothing less than phenomenal. Leibniz was a master of almost a dozen disciplines: logic, mathematics, mechanics, geology, law, theology, philosophy, history, genealogy, and linguistics. His greatest achievement was the invention of differential calculus, which he created about twenty years later than Newton but in a much more practical form. Indeed, the stubborn refusal of English mathematicians to adopt Leibniz's notation retarded the development of mathematics in England for more than a hundred years. Leibniz was driven by a monumental obsession to create, to build, to analyze, to systematize — and to outdo the French. A bibliography of his writings would go on for pages; many of his manuscripts have still not been published and his letters may be measured by the pound.

Born in 1646, two years before the end of the Thirty Years' War, Leibniz was the son of a notary (a minor judge) and professor of moral philosophy at the University of Leipzig. His father died when he was six and he was raised by his mother, a pious Lutheran who passed away when he was eighteen. Like Pascal, he was a prodigy, and his mother gave him the run of his dead father's library — not an easy decision in those days, when children were brought up on a very tight leash and their reading restricted to approved books, lest their minds be contaminated by impure thoughts (of which Leibniz undoubtedly had many). He had a natural aptitude for languages and taught himself Latin when he was eight and Greek a few years later. At thirteen, he discovered one of his lifelong passions, the study of logic. He was, as he later wrote, "greatly excited by the division and order of thoughts which I perceived therein. I took the greatest pleasure in the predicaments which came before me as a muster-roll of all the things in the world, and I turned to 'Logics' of all sorts to find the best and most detailed form of this list."

He entered the University of Leipzig when he was fifteen, majoring in law. He was by nature a weaver of grand systems, and in 1666 he wrote a treatise, *De Arte Combinatoria (On the Art of Combination)* offering a system for reducing all reasoning to an ordered combination of elements, such as numbers, sounds, or colors. That treatise is considered one of the theoretical ancestors of modern logic, a primitive form of the logical rules that govern the internal operation of computers. That same year, all his requirements for the doctorate in law having been completed, Leibniz proudly presented himself for the degree. He was only nineteen, and the elders in charge of the gates of the bar turned him down on account of his age. Furious, he went to the University of Altdorf, in Nürnberg, where his dissertation *(De Casibus Perplexis, or On Perplexing Cases)* immediately won him a doctorate and an offer of a professorship.

However, Leibniz disliked the stuffiness and pettiness of academia and sought a diplomatic career. One of the most important diplomats of the time, Johann Christian von Boyneburg, took him under his wing and secured a post for him at the court of the archbishop of Mainz, the Prince Elector Johann Philipp von Schönborn. (The electors chose the Holy Roman Emperor, who ruled over the states encompassing Germany and most of Central Europe.) Leibniz was put to work codifying and revising the laws of Nürnberg — hardly a reforming effort, since the many codifications of the period were designed to solidify the power of the ruling classes. For the rest of his life, the broad-shouldered, bandy-legged Leibniz served in one or another capacity as an official in the courts of the German princes, a genius in the service of mediocrities.

France was the greatest power in seventeenth-century Europe, and the Holy Roman Empire feared that she would invade Holland and, possibly, Germany. Hoping to distract Louis XIV, Leibniz and the archbishop's advisors tried to interest him in a military campaign in the Mideast. In terms full of religious emotionalism, they recommended that France launch a holy crusade against Egypt and Turkey. In 1672, the archbishop dispatched Leibniz on a solitary mission to Paris to discuss the plan with the king. Not surprisingly, the trip was an utter failure; Louis XIV didn't even bother to acknowledge the young German's arrival, let alone grant him an audience. But Paris proved to be a muse of the highest order, and it was there, between 1672 and 1674, that Leibniz built his first calculator (or, rather, had a craftsman build it for him).

He explained the genesis of the Stepped Reckoner, as he called his invention, in a note written in 1685:

> When, several years ago, I saw for the first time an instrument which, when carried, automatically records the num-

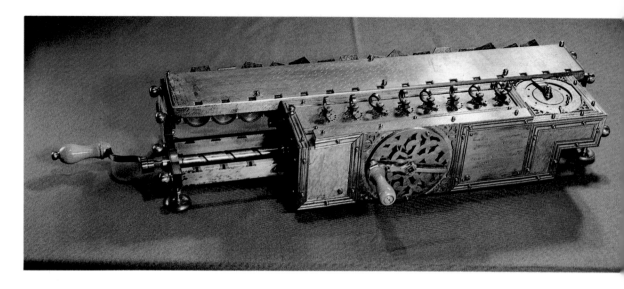

*A reconstruction of Leibniz's Stepped Reckoner*

bers of steps taken by a pedestrian [he's referring to a pedometer, of course], it occurred to me at once that the entire arithmetic could be subjected to a similar kind of machinery so that not only counting but also addition and subtraction, multiplication and division could be accomplished by a suitably arranged machine easily, promptly, and with sure results.

The calculating box of Pascal was not known to me at that time. I believe it has not gained sufficient publicity. When I noticed, however, the mere name of a calculating machine in the preface of his "postumous thoughts" [the *Pensées*] . . . I immediately inquired about it in a letter to a Parisian friend. When I learned from him that such a machine exists I requested the most distinguished Carcavius by letter to give me an explanation of the work which it is capable of performing. He replied that addition and subtraction are accomplished by it directly, the other [operations] in a round-about way by repeating additions and subtractions and performing still another calculation. I wrote back that I venture to promise something more, namely, that multiplication could be performed by the machine as well as addition, and with greatest speed and accuracy.

Conceptually, the Stepped Reckoner was a remarkable machine whose operating principles eventually led to the development of the first successful mechanical calculator. The key to the device was a special gear, devised by Leibniz and now known as the Leibniz wheel, that acted as a mechanical multiplier. The gear was really a metal cylinder with nine horizontal rows of teeth; the first row ran one-tenth the length of the cylinder, the second two-tenths, the third three-tenths, and so on until the nine-tenths length of the ninth row. The Reckoner had eight of these stepped wheels, all linked to a central shaft, and a single turn of the shaft rotated all the cylinders, which in turn rotated the wheels that displayed the answers.

Say you wanted to multiply 1,984 by 5. First, you entered the multiplicand (1,984) through the numbered dials, or pointers, on the top face of the machine. Then you put a metal peg in the fifth hole of the large dial on the far right; the peg served as a built-in reminder that the multiplier was 5 and prevented you from entering a larger figure. You next took hold of the wooden handle on the big dial on the front — this was the multiplier dial, which was linked to the central shaft — and turned it once. The answer appeared in the little windows behind the numbered pointers. If the multiplier contained more than one digit — say, 555 — you had to shift the Reckoner's movable carriage one place to the left for every decimal place, and turn the multiplier handle once for every digit. (Along with the stepped cylinder, the movable carriage ended up in many other calculators, not to mention the typewriter.)

*Two views of the Stepped Reckoner without its cover. The Leibniz wheels are the cylindrical gears underneath the numbered dials. The pentagonal widgets at the back of the machine were used for carrying and borrowing digits.*

Although the Reckoner could process fairly large numbers — multipliers of four or five digits, multiplicands of up to
eleven or twelve digits — it wasn't fully automatic, and you had
to fiddle with a row of pentagonal widgets at the back of the machine to help it carry and borrow digits. Nevertheless, it was far
more sophisticated than the Calculating Clock or the Pascaline,
capable of all four arithmetic operations and much closer to what
we would consider to be a calculator. But the Reckoner suffered
from one great drawback, much more serious than its inability to
carry or borrow numbers automatically — it didn't work. Leibniz's ambition outran his engineering skill, and the only surviving
version of the calculator, on display at a museum in Hannover,
West Germany, is an inoperative relic.

In 1764, forty-eight years after Leibniz's death, a Reckoner
was turned over to a clockmaker in Göttingen for overhauling.
The job wasn't done, and Leibniz's pride and joy wound up in the
attic of the University of Göttingen, where a leaky roof led to its
rediscovery in 1879. Fourteen years later, the university gave the
machine to the Arthur Burkhardt Company, the country's leading
calculator manufacturer, for repair and analysis. Burkhardt reported that, while the gadget worked in general, it failed to carry
tens when the multiplier was a two- or three-digit number. The
carrying mechanism had been improperly designed. It's unknown
whether Leibniz, who worked on the Reckoner off and on for
twenty years, built more than one calculator — one that was
flawed and one (or more) that worked. In all likelihood, given the
high costs of fashioning a device as complicated as the Reckoner,
Leibniz made only one and never managed to perfect it.

Endowed with boundless intellect and curiosity, Leibniz was one
of the first Western mathematicians to study and write about the
*binary system* of enumeration. There are only two digits in binary
math — 0 and 1 — but any number, no matter how large, may be
expressed with them. For example, a decimal 2 is 10 in binary; 3
is 11; 4 is 100; 5 is 101; 6 is 110; 7 is 111; 8 is 1000, and 9 is 1001.
Each digit to the left represents a greater power of 2. It's the simplest possible numerical system and it had enormous influence
on the development of computers. To Leibniz, however, binary
math had more religious than practical significance, and he regarded it as a sort of natural proof of the existence of God, arguing
that it demonstrated that the Lord, the all-knowing *one*, had created the universe out of *nothing*. At one point, Leibniz, in a bril-

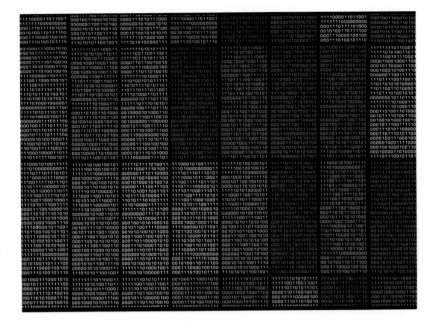

*Any information can be encoded in the 0s and 1s of binary math, including music. These are the first four notes of Beethoven's Fifth Symphony.*

liant flash of insight, considered making a binary calculator but, unfortunately, nothing ever came of the idea.

(Incidentally, the term used today to refer to a single binary digit — a *bit* — inspired the title of this book. The word is an acronym of the first letter of "binary" and the last two letters of "di*git*." Every operation in a computer is the result of the interaction of bits.)

An enormously energetic man, Leibniz was in constant motion. He established the German Academy of Sciences; formulated an enormously influential philosophy which held that the universe was made out of irreducible, ever-changing substances called monads; worked as a mining engineer in the Harz Mountains, where he invented a windmill-driven pump and theorized that the earth was originally molten; sought the reunification of the Catholic and Protestant churches; founded the science of topology; was appointed an advisor to the Holy Roman Emperor and made a baronet; and died in 1716, at the age of seventy, poor and friendless, ignored by the noblemen he had served.

## CHAPTER 2

# The Engines of Charles Babbage

One evening I was sitting in the rooms of the Analytical Society, at Cambridge, my head leaning forward on the table in a kind of dreamy mood, with a table of logarithms lying open before me. Another member, coming into the room, and seeing me half asleep called out "Well, Babbage, what are you dreaming about?" to which I replied, "I am thinking that all these tables (pointing to the logarithms) might be calculated by machinery."

— *Charles Babbage, 1791–1871*

*Charles Babbage completed only a small part of his Difference Engine. Twenty-four inches high, nineteen inches wide, and fourteen inches deep, it was a fraction the size of the machine he envisioned.*

Whether or not it really worked, the Stepped Reckoner was one of the greatest inventions of the seventeenth century. It inspired a host of imitators, and almost every mechanical calculator built during the next 150 years was based on Leibniz's device. Between 1770 and 1776, for example, a German vicar named Mathieus Hahn built a drumlike calculator containing eight Leibniz wheels (but no sliding carriage). And in 1775, the Englishman Charles, the third Earl Stanhope, designed a machine with eight Leibniz wheels and a sliding carriage. Unlike the Reckoner, both of these devices worked well, and gained a small measure of fame for their inventors. Although Stanhope's device was simple enough for mass production, the idea of manufacturing machines en masse was only beginning to set in during his day, and the first mass-produced calculator didn't appear until about 1820.

The Arithmometer, as it was called, was invented by the Frenchman Charles Xavier Thomas de Colmar (1785–1870). Thomas ran an insurance company in Paris, where the mathematical nature of his work led him to contemplate the rich possibilities of mechanical calculation. His machine was a first-rate piece of practical engineering — compact, reliable, easy to use, and, like Hahn's and Stanhope's, based on the Leibniz wheel (but without a carriage). Although the first Arithmometers were limited to six-digit results, they were semiautomatic, being driven by a spring-loaded belt that the user pulled before every operation. In later models, the belt, which tended to wear down, was replaced by a

*Mathieus Hahn and his son, the court mechanic in Stuttgart, constructed several calculators. This one, built in 1809, could produce twelve-digit products.*

*Thomas de Colmar (1775–1870)*

metal crank, and the Arithmometer's capacity was expanded to a much more useful twelve digits. About fifteen hundred models were sold over the next thirty years, chiefly to banks, insurance companies, and other businesses.

As the first mass-produced calculator, the Arithmometer attracted a good deal of attention. Thomas built a giant version for the 1855 Paris Exposition, and the machine, which resembled a fancy upright piano, won a gold medal; another Arithmometer captured a medal at the International Exhibition in London eleven years later. Like the Reckoner, the Arithmometer had many imitators, and *arithmometer* passed into the language as a generic term that referred to any Thomas-type calculator. The term survived until the early 1900s, when arithmometers fell out of use, replaced by keyboard calculators, which were much easier to use.

The Arithmometer was only one of hundreds of mechanical inventions ushered in by the industrial revolution, which inspired an unprecedented appreciation of the power of machines — an appreciation that was celebrated in the many international industrial exhibitions of the nineteenth century. By the early 1800s, the industrial revolution was in full swing in Great Britain and spreading to the Continent, particularly France. The rapid expansion of industry and commerce, and the growth in population and education, sent a torrent of statistics through science, industry, business, and government. The world was moving on a faster and bigger track. For the first time, there was not only a pressing need for calculators like the Arithmometer, there was also a need for the systematic manufacture of numerical tables.

Since the advent of logs, the tools of the trade of anyone

who worked with figures, whether bankers or navigators, were mathematical tables. These lists of figures were indispensable in science, finance, navigation, engineering, surveying, and other fields. There were tables of square roots, cube roots, interest rates, hyperbolic and exponential functions, mathematical constants, like Bernoullian numbers, and the price of meat per pound at the butcher's. Many mathematicians devoted the greater part of their careers to tabular calculation, and the need for accurate tables was a matter of national concern. In 1784, for instance, the government of France decided to draw up new tables of logs and trigonometric functions (such as sine and cosine). Six distinguished mathematicians devised the mathematical methods and supervised the enterprise; seven or eight human computers served as foremen and another seventy or eighty performed the calcula-

*Like all early calculators, the Arithmometer was difficult to use. If you wanted to multiply, say, 3,042 by 234, you had to turn the crank on the lower right once for every digit of the multiplier and slide the narrow upper plate one step to the right for every decimal place (10s, 100s, and so on) in the multiplier.*

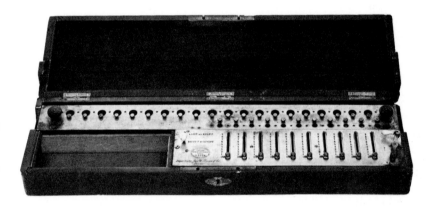

*Six Leibniz wheels (the thick cylinders in the center) were used in this version of the Arithmometer, built by Arthur Burkhardt, the German calculator manufacturer, in about 1880.*

*Charles Babbage (1792–1871) at fifty-six, in a painting at the National Portrait Gallery in London*

tions. The project took two years and the results were two hand-written copies of seventeen volumes of tables. Known as the *Tables de Cadastres (Surveyors' Tables)*, they were never published for fear of typographical errors and were stored at a library in Paris, where anyone could consult them.

Despite all the cost and effort that went into the making of tables, they inevitably were full of errors. In 1835, an informal survey of one scientist's library turned up 140 books of tables, and an examination of only some of the figures in forty of the books uncovered 3,700 inaccuracies. Even the British *Nautical Almanac* — the navigators's bible — was sprinkled with mistakes, and more than one ship was said to have run aground or been lost at sea as a result of the miscalculations. Maddeningly enough, some of the slip-ups were even deliberate, inserted by publishers as traps for would-be plagiarizers. Given the importance of tables in navigation, their fallibility was an overriding concern in Great Britain and other seafaring nations.

Mathematicians were at a loss for a remedy. And then a young Englishman by the name of Charles Babbage came up with a solution. The son of a wealthy banker, Babbage was a gifted mathematician with the eye of a seer. He was a student at Cambridge University, in 1812 or 1813, when the first glimmer of the solution came to him. As he recalled in his autobiography, *Passages from the Life of a Philosopher* (1864), he was sitting in the quarters of the Analytical Society, an undergraduate mathematics club, gazing at a table of logs, when it suddenly occurred to him that the figures might be calculated by machine. It was a great idea and none of his contemporaries seemed to have thought of it; Babbage wasn't thinking of using a run-of-the-mill calculator like Stanhope's but a machine specially designed to manufacture tables.

Babbage was only a sophomore or junior at the time and the idea soon faded from his mind. But it recurred to him several years later. Once again, the muse was a mathematical table and the circumstances a chance conversation. In 1820 or 1821, Babbage and John Herschel, an astronomer and a close friend from Cambridge, were checking a set of tables they had helped prepare for the Astronomical Society. (Herschel was the son of Sir William Herschel, the great astronomer and founder of cosmology.) As usual, there were several errors. "I wish to God these calculations had been executed by steam," said Babbage. Herschel, a talented mathematician, thought the idea was sensible enough. "It is quite possible," he said. The two men discussed the notion, and Babbage later drew up plans for a machine that could do the job.

The Difference Engine, as he called the gadget, was an ambitious conception. Powered by falling weights raised by a steam engine, it could calculate tables by the method of constant differences (which we'll discuss in a moment) and record the results, figured to the twentieth place, on metal plates. By printing the tables directly from these plates, or from plates made from the originals, it would eliminate the table-makers' worst gremlins, typographical errors. Babbage hired several workmen to make a prototype and, after ironing out the inevitable bugs, produced a working model in 1822. It was a six-digit calculator made of toothed wheels and run by a hand crank. Only a kernel of the machine he had in mind, it proved the feasibility of his conception.

The method of constant differences is a simple but powerful technique for calculating consistent numerical progressions. Table-makers often used it, and the process can be best illustrated with a task that the Difference Engine was designed to handle — the calculation of the cubes of all the numbers from 1 to 100,000.

Since the engine needs a set of initial values to get started, we have to do some preliminary paperwork, setting up a table of the first few numbers and, by a process of subtraction, searching for the various numerical differences. First, we subtract the cube of 1 (which is, of course, 1) from the cube of 2 (which is 8). The result, 7, is the *first* order of difference. Then we subtract the cube of 2 from the cube of 3 (27), and the answer, 19, is another first order of difference. Now we have to find the *second* order of difference. By subtracting 7, the first result, from 19, the second result, we get 12 — and that's the second difference. It should be obvious from the table below how we obtained the *third*, and in the case of cubes, the *constant*, order of difference:

| Number | Cube of Number | Order of Difference Between Numbers | | |
|---|---|---|---|---|
| | | FIRST | SECOND | THIRD |
| 1 | 1 | | | |
| | | 7 | | |
| 2 | 8 | | 12 | |
| | | 19 | | 6 |
| 3 | 27 | | 18 | |
| | | 37 | | 6 |
| 4 | 64 | | 24 | |
| | | 61 | | 6 |
| 5 | 125 | | 30 | |
| | | 91 | | |
| 6 | 216 | | | |

etc.

All this boils down to a basic mathematical principle: Any consistent numerical progression may be calculated by a process of repeated addition. Since the method of constant differences is a repetitive process, it lends itself quite nicely to the actions of a machine. As Babbage planned it, an operator would feed the various differences into the Difference Engine, which would add them to each other again and again and record the answers with a printer of some kind. Because each addition is based upon the preceding one, the method contains a built-in check: if the last numbers in a table are correct then all the numbers must be correct. A human computer, on the other hand, may slip up at any point.

Babbage believed that he was the first person to conceive of a Difference Engine, but he was wrong. There is very little new under the sun and his invention was no exception. In 1786, one E. Klipstein, of Frankfurt, Germany, published a small volume called, roughly, *Description of a Newly Invented Calculation Machine.* The book gives an account of a calculator invented by a J. H. Müller, a captain of engineers in the Hessian army, and includes an appendix that, astonishingly, describes a Difference Engine (although Müller used another term). The machine, which Müller hoped to build if he could raise the necessary funds, was designed to calculate tables by the method of constant differences and print out the results directly on paper. (The Difference Engine's printing process was superior, since Babbage's machine was designed to punch out plates that could be used to print any number of copies.) Unfortunately, Müller failed to raise the money and nothing came of his proposal.

Babbage realized that a full-fledged Difference Engine would require thousands of precisely engineered gears, axles, and other parts and would cost thousands of pounds. Even if he possessed his father's considerable fortune, which he was bound to inherit, the project would undoubtedly strain his resources. Moreover, it would benefit England, not him, and he therefore believed that it should be financed with outside support, preferably from the government. So Babbage wrote an open letter to Sir Humphrey Davy, president of the Royal Society of London, Britain's pre-eminent scientific organization. The missive, dated 3 July 1822, described the Difference Engine, explained its many applications and, in the understated tones of an English gentleman, requested external funds.

Babbage's letter was widely circulated and a copy reached the exalted hands of the Lords of the Treasury, who were interested in any machine that might ease their work and improve the

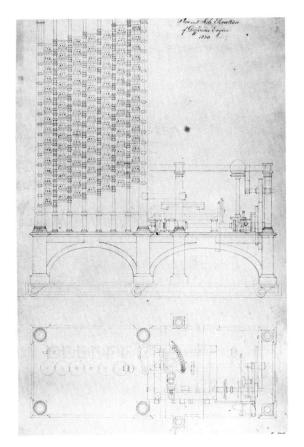

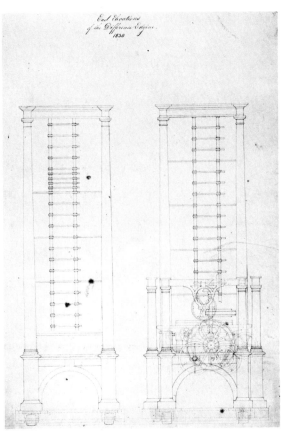

*Two of Babbage's meticulous engineering plans for the Difference Engine, depicting the machine from the side (left) and from both ends (right)*

state of British navigation. On 1 April 1823, the Lords wrote the Royal Society, requesting an assessment of Babbage's proposal. Davy appointed a committee to study the matter, and the organization issued its offical verdict about a month later: "Mr. Babbage has displayed great talent and ingenuity in the construction of his Machine for Computation, which the Committee think fully adequate to the attainment of the objects proposed by the inventor; and they consider Mr. Babbage as highly deserving of public encouragement in the prosecution of his arduous undertaking."

On 27 June, Babbage was summoned for an interview with John Frederick Robinson, chancellor of the Exchequer. "I had some conversations with the Chancellor of the Ex$^r$ who treated me in a most liberal and gentlemanlike manner," Babbage wrote Herschel. "He seems quite convinced of the utility of the machine and that it ought to be encouraged. At present he is to procure for me £1000, and next session, if I want more to complete it, he is willing that more should be granted or that I should have a committee of the house if a larger sum were wanted than the fund could be charged with." The chancellor's offer was unprecedented; the British government didn't normally support private scientific or technical projects, but the condition of the *Naval*

*Almanac* and other tables inspired it to take a chance. Babbage got his money, and one of the most extraordinary episodes in the history of science had begun.


Charles Babbage was a genius of the first order. He was one of the most original and versatile scientists in history, and we can't hope to touch on all of his activities here. He was a mathematician, an engineer, a politician, a professor, a writer, an inventor, a cryptographer, a man about town, a founder of scientific organizations, and an expert on industry. His pioneering book, *On the Economy of Machinery and Manufactures* (1832), was cited repeatedly by Marx in *Capital* and by John Stuart Mill in *Principles of Political Economy*. He was a human dynamo who needed only five or six hours of sleep a day and who was driven by a millennarian vision of man and machine that brought him within a hair's breadth of the invention of the greatest of machines, the computer.

Born on 26 December 1791, in London, he was the oldest son of Benjamin and Betty Plumleigh Babbage. Benjamin was a hard-nosed, no-nonsense banker who had started out as a goldsmith in the small town of Totnes, a picturesque port in Devonshire, on the River Dart, about 200 miles southwest of London. Benjamin parlayed his capital into a successful business as an independent banker, and he and his wife moved to London the year before Charles's birth. He became a junior partner in an up-and-coming London bank, accumulated an impressive fortune, and retired to Totnes in 1803, when Charles was eleven. Benjamin could have been a character out of Dickens — stern, reserved, domineering, with a sharp temper and an excessive fondness for money. There was no love lost between Charles and his father, although his mother was a kind, loving, and patient woman, and he was always close to her.

Charles grew up much as any other well-to-do English boy. He attended small private schools near Totnes, where he studied mathematics, navigation, accounting — subjects that made up the bulk of the curriculum in the schools around the ports of Britain. Math was his favorite discipline; as Babbage recalled in his autobiography, he and a like-minded student used to "get up every morning at three o'clock, light a fire in the schoolroom, and work until five or half-past five" studying algebra. He also had an inventive frame of mind. One of his most memorable creations was a pair of wooden boards, linked together with hinges, for walking on water; he tested it on the Dart one day and almost drowned.

Charles entered Cambridge in 1810. Hardly a bookworm, he

*Totnes, Babbage's hometown, as seen from the River Dart in a watercolor by J. M. W. Turner, about 1824*

was a charming, gregarious, and athletic young man, with a fondness for whist and sailing. Even his serious pursuits bore a lighthearted touch. During his years at Cambridge, for example, the school was caught up in a controversy over the format of the Bible. Should the book be printed with or without explanatory notes? One side sought to make the word of God more comprehensible to the masses, the other to preserve its literal purity. Cambridge, which took its religion seriously, was littered with posters and broadsides advocating one or the other side of the issue.

At the same time, however, the university was less than zealous in its cultivation of the intellect, and the school, Newton's alma mater and once the guiding light of European mathematics, had lost its luster. English mathematicians were trained in an inferior notation of calculus — the confusing dots of the Newtonian version as opposed to the clearly defined d's of the Leibnizian system — and the rift between Britain and the Continent had widened to a point where most English mathematicians couldn't decipher the publications of their Continental counterparts. English mathematics was falling by the wayside, and Babbage, Herschel, and most of the country's bright young mathematicians and scientists were unhappy with the quality of their education.

Nothing might seem more petty and inconsequential to us today than the controversy between the dots and the d's, but it was a significant matter in the history of science, residue of the great quarrel between Newton and Leibniz over the invention of calculus.

One spring day in 1812, Babbage picked up a broadside that demanded, in absurdly exaggerated terms, the publication of the unelaborated word of God. He couldn't resist a parody. So he wrote out a plan for the establishment of a society for the propagation of "the principles of pure *D*-ism in opposition to the *Dot*-age of the university." The satire struck a sympathetic chord with his mathematically minded schoolmates. Over the objections of the university authorities, who frowned on independent student organizations, Babbage and his friends established the Analytical Society. The group was dedicated to the overthrow of the Newtonian way, and Babbage, the intellectual rabble-rouser who founded it, was on his way to making his mark in the world.

Like most undergraduate clubs, the Analytical Society was more talk than action. It had about a dozen active members and issued only one publication, *Memoirs of the Analytical Society* (1813), consisting of mathematical papers written in the Leibnizian style by Babbage and Herschel, before disbanding in 1814. (Herschel, the society's president and Cambridge's best undergraduate mathematician, graduated in 1813 and Babbage came down the following year.) But the spirit of the group lived on. In 1816, two years after Babbage had left college, he, Herschel, and George Peacock, another ex-Analytical, launched a more mature sally against the Newtonian dots with the publication of their translation of a popular French textbook on calculus. Four years later, the three men wrote a two-volume calculus workbook complete with solutions. The books accomplished what the Analytical Society had not. They were adopted by Cambridge teachers, and helped steer British mathematicians back to the mainstream.

In July 1814, the newly graduated Babbage married Georgina Whitmore, the youngest daughter of a prosperous family in Shropshire, and began looking for a job. He didn't want an academic career, since he disliked academia and regarded universities as fatally dull and stuffy places. (At times, however, Babbage sought a professorship to supplement his income, and in 1827 he was named to Newton's chair — Lucasion Professor of Mathematics at Cambridge. Busy with his own work and uninterested in teaching, he did not deliver a single lecture during his ten-year tenure and ignored most of the post's other duties.) And he was bored by banking, his father's business. In fact, he wasn't sure what he wanted to do. He considered something in mining, and asked a friend of his father's, a rich country gentleman with extensive mining interests, for help. He (or so he wrote Herschel) also ran employment ads in several country newspapers. But nothing came his way. Even in the England of the industrial revolution, suitable positions for college-educated men were hard to find.

In 1815, Babbage was given a small house in London (most likely a wedding gift from his father) and wasted no time entering the local scientific scene. He gave a series of lectures on astronomy at the Royal Institution and joined Herschel and Peacock in translating the French text on calculus. He published several mathematical papers in *The Journal of Science* and in *The Philosophical Transactions of the Royal Society of London,* and was elected to the Royal Society in 1816, only two years after he had left Cambridge. Anybody who was anybody in British science belonged to the society, as did many nonscientists; the group was more like a good club than a bona fide scientific association, and the nonscientists often held sway. The situation annoyed Babbage to no end, and he eventually became one of the organization's sharpest critics. In reaction to the society's mixed membership, Babbage, ever the joiner, helped establish three competing organizations — the Royal Astronomical Society, The London Statistical Society, and the British Association for the Advancement of Science.

The late 1810s and early 1820s were the happiest time of Babbage's life. His scientific reputation was growing — he published ten papers between 1815 and 1821, as well as the books on calculus — and his marriage was a joy. A sociable pair, he and Georgina liked to entertain and often visited friends and relatives in the country. Georgina gave birth to a child in 1815, and seven more offspring arrived during the next twelve years (but only three children survived into maturity). The family's financial situation improved with the death of Georgina's father, who left them a tidy inheritance that complemented Babbage's allowance from his father. He had one or two servants and enough money to finance his research. Yet he was only a gentleman scientist, without a worthy position, a great goal, or high status.

He found all three in the Difference Engine.


The project to build the Difference Engine began in August or September of 1823. Two rooms in Babbage's house were converted into workshops and a third into a forge. On the recommendation of a friend, Babbage hired Joseph Clement, a first-rate mechanical engineer, to serve as chief engineer and to fashion most

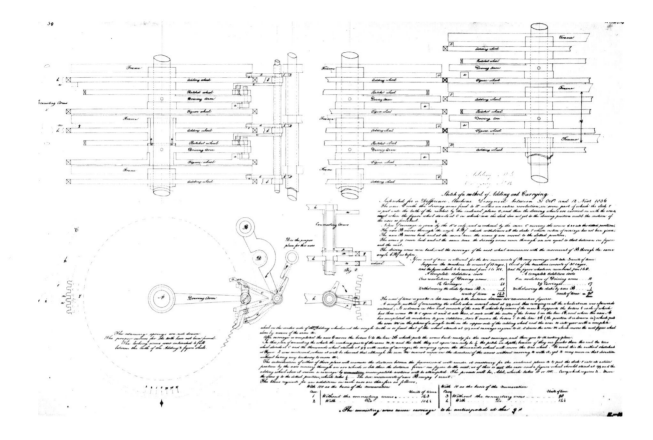

*A sketch of the mechanics of adding and carrying with the Difference Engine, drawn in October and November 1836*

of the parts in his own factory. Clement, who had worked for Henry Maudslay, one of Britain's leading engineers, was down on his luck when Babbage entered his life, with only one good lathe to his name. Clement and the draftsmen and workmen he hired played a pivotal role in the construction of the engine, and we shall hear a good deal more about him.

Next Babbage undertook a thorough investigation of the state of machine manufacture in British industry, going on a tour with Georgina of factories throughout England and Scotland. Machines were an uncommon sight in everyday British life at the time. Steamships had only begun to appear and the proliferation of the railroad was ten years away. The most common mechanical objects were clocks, watches, locks, guns, and pumps. There was, of course, a much wider range of machinery in industry: looms, lathes, stampers, turbines, shears, presses, boring engines, milling machines, and so on. The Difference Engine would be vastly more intricate than any of these — in fact, it probably would be the most sophisticated machine made up to that time — and Babbage, a perfectionist, demanded construction standards that the machine tools of the period simply could not meet.

The engine was designed to operate to the sixth order of

difference (Müller's would have handled only three orders); calculate numbers to the twentieth place; and print out forty-four digits a minute. It required hundreds of carefully machined components, all working in perfect coordination; any slack in the gears might throw the engine out of whack. As he got deeper into the project, however, Babbage realized that he couldn't hope to meet the engine's precise specifications without better machine tools, and he therefore redirected his effort, putting much sweat and ingenuity into the design of new tools. In general, he would design a part or series of parts for the engine, and then design and build the tools to make them. In the course of the process, he invariably conceived of a better way to make either the parts or tools, and the whole procedure had to be repeated. Although his ambitious, multilayered enterprise lifted the British machine tool industry to new heights, it also delayed the engine and greatly inflated its cost.

In 1827, four years after the project had begun, Babbage's father died. Babbage inherited about £100,000, the bulk of his father's estate, which made him a very rich man, with enough money to help finance the project and to support his family in style. Despite the government's financial help, he spent thousands of pounds on the Difference Engine and the grand conception that followed it, the Analytical Engine. Yet, at the very time that Babbage came into the means to enjoy his life to the fullest, death visited his family three more times within the year. His second oldest son died in July; his wife passed away the following month, apparently from complications caused by childbirth; and his newborn son died soon after.

Filled with sorrow, Babbage left England for a year-long tour of the Continent. Clement continued to work on the Difference Engine, but the endeavor fell into low gear. Fortunately, the trip did Babbage a great deal of good and he returned in better spirits. Although his famous charm, wit, and humor had been restored, Babbage had clearly changed. His family life was gone and an uncharacteristic tone of bitterness entered his public controversies — a tone that had not been there when Georgina was alive. (As he grew older, and his dreams fell by the wayside, the bitterness deepened.) Trying to forget his loss, Babbage threw himself into the engine project and his numerous social and political activities. He was an outspoken Liberal and managed one candidate's successful Parliamentary campaign in 1829. Three years later, he ran for Parliament himself, placing third in a field of five. If another woman entered his life, there is no record of it.

While abroad, Babbage had reviewed the project's accounts. In addition to the government's £1,500, he had spent £1,975 of his own money. As he understood the terms of his agreement with the government, the Treasury was supposed to reimburse him for any expenses above the original £1,500. Therefore, Babbage (and some of his influential friends) asked the Treasury to pay him back and authorize more funds. However, Robinson, who had since left the Exchequer, claimed that he had never committed the Treasury to more than the original sum and that he most certainly had not given Babbage a blank check. Since neither of them had put their agreement into writing, it was one man's word against the other's. Babbage appealed to the Duke of Wellington, the current prime minister, and Wellington ordered the Treasury to evaluate the entire project. The Treasury, in turn, asked the Royal Society for an appraisal of the engine, and once again the society endorsed Babbage unqualifiedly. Then Wellington decided to see the engine for himself.

It was November 1829, and Babbage had little to show for six years of labor. There was the first model of the engine, assembled by Babbage in 1822; Clement's superior machine tools, which had advanced the state of machine tooling and made the engine feasible; and hundreds of drawings and parts for the engine itself. The device was obviously several years and thousands of pounds from completion. Yet Wellington was persuaded. A military man, he had a fair amount of technical knowledge and a solid understanding of the engine and its potential benefits to science, technology, and England. At his order, the government disbursed £7,500 in late 1829 and early 1830, and the project resumed after a nine-month hiatus.

Babbage, meanwhile, faced another critical problem: Clement. Even before he had left for Europe, he had suspected the chief engineer of padding his bills. He also believed that Clement had built special lathes and other costly tools at the venture's expense, not so much to use them on the engine as to enrich his own shop. In those days, the law held that a workman had the right to his own tools, even if they had been constructed on an employer's time and with an employer's money. A holdover from medieval times, when a craftsman's tools were no more expensive or elaborate than hammers and files, the law was unreasonable in an era of expensive machine tools. But the law was the law, and Babbage couldn't claim Clement's tools for himself or for the government, the engine's legal owner. As long as he employed Clement, the issue of ownership was a moot point, although it surely would turn into a major dilemma if, for whatever reason, he decided to let Clement go. So Babbage took the only step open to him: he refused to pay Clement's bills until a three-man panel of engineers was appointed to inspect the work and to approve the bills. The arrangement was a common practice at the time, and it worked for a while.

Babbage also wanted Clement to move his workshop closer to his Dorset Street home. His house and Clement's shop were four miles apart, and Babbage, who often fretted about his health, wanted the engine (or, rather, the many parts that made it up), tools, and plans placed in a more convenient and comfortable setting. He also worried about the safety of his project, since fire was an ever-present hazard in nineteenth-century London and Clement's shop was not fireproof. Clement stoutly resisted the change; he knew that his freedom of action and profits would certainly shrink under Babbage's direct supervision. But the government went along with Babbage, and an architect was commissioned to build the appropriate facilities on Babbage's property. Although Babbage offered to loan Clement a small house next to his, Clement was not appeased.

In 1832, almost *ten years* after the project had begun, there

*A sketch of the Analytical Engine's driving and directive apparatus. The barrel, which contained the machine's internal operating instructions, is on the far right.*

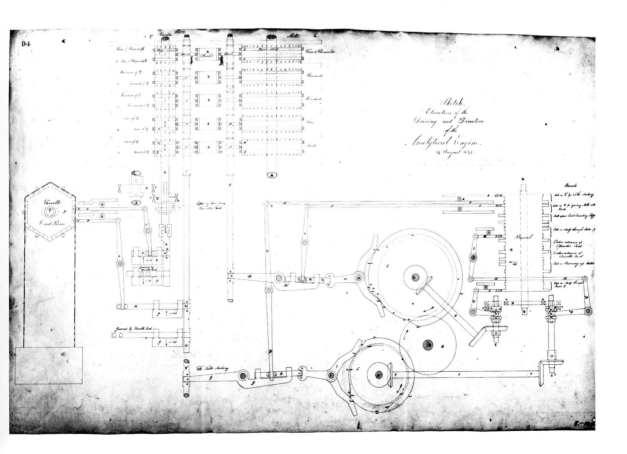

were enough parts to assemble a section of the engine. Consisting
of six vertical axles and a few dozen gears, the section was about
twenty-four inches high, nineteen inches wide, and fourteen
inches deep. It worked perfectly, solving equations to the second
order of difference and yielding six-digit results. It was a beautiful
piece of machinery, one of the finest and most sophisticated machines of its time — as solid as the Empire (back then!) and as de-
pendable as the pound (ditto). The Arithmometer was a toy by
comparison. The precious invention was moved to a new fireproof building adjacent to Babbage's house, where he showed it
off to his friends at his famous Saturday night parties. Wellington,
proud of his role in the project, was a regular guest.

Babbage's weekly soirées were the most popular parties in
London. His home was one of the most interesting in the capital,
with all sorts of amusing gadgets to play with. In addition to the
famous engine, on display in a glass and mahogany case, he had a
foot-high silver automaton of a dancing woman dressed in a fancy
gown. Babbage knew many of the most important people in England — writers, actors, aristocrats, and politicians, as well as scientists, engineers, and businessmen — and he often pops up in

*A plan for the operation of the Analytical Engine's variable-card counting mechanism. Among other things, the variable cards supplied the initial numerical values of the variables in an equation.*

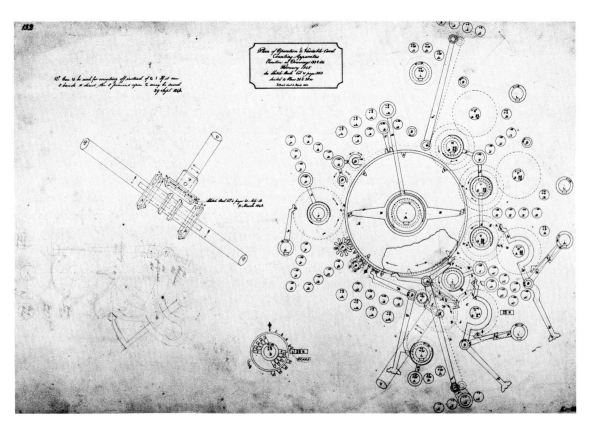

their diaries. Charles Darwin wrote: "I remember a funny dinner at my brother's, where, amongst a few others were Babbage and Lyell [Charles Lyell, the founder of modern geology], both of whom liked to talk. Carlyle however silenced everyone by haranguing during the whole dinner on the advantages of silence. After dinner, Babbage, in his grimmest manner, thanked Carlyle for his very interesting lecture on silence."

After the engine had been transferred to his property, Babbage continued to press Clement to make the move, too. But Clement put up a big fuss. He submitted a bloated estimate of his moving expenses and demanded £660 a year to maintain two homes and to run a divided business. Outraged, the Treasury refused his claims. Most of the £12,000 that had been spent on the engine so far had passed through Clement's hands and he had earned a great deal of money. He had also equipped his shop with thousands of pounds' worth of machine tools, designed by Babbage and paid for by the government, and which were, under the law, his property. "My Lords," the Treasury wrote, "cannot but express their surprise that Mr. Clement should have advanced so unreasonable and inadmissable a claim."

Clement's selfishness became a major obstacle to the completion of the engine, and it was all downhill from here. The chief engineer agreed to submit his claims to the arbitrators but, realizing that they were as unsympathetic to his cause as the Treasury, changed his mind and then simply refused to budge. Under the circumstances, Babbage declined to pay his bills (normally, Babbage paid Clement and the Treasury paid Babbage), instructing him thereafter to submit his chits directly to the Treasury — which meant that he would no longer be reimbursed promptly. In response, Clement, who seems to have been deeply jealous of Babbage's talent and wealth, fired his staff and refused to turn over the engine's plans or parts until his bills were paid. As a result, the project ground to a halt. Unfortunately, Clement had the upper hand and there was nothing to do but examine his accounts and pay him off, which the Treasury finally did. On 16 July 1834, more than a year after work had stopped, Clement finally relinquished the goods. Babbage wrote the Treasury: "The drawings and parts of the Engine are at length *in a place of safety* — I am almost worn out with disgust and annoyance at the whole affair."

Although Babbage tried to resurrect the project, his appeals fell between the cracks of British politics. There were several changes in administration in 1834 and 1835 — from Melbourne to Wellington to Peel and back to Melbourne — and Babbage's problems were lost in the shuffle. Moreover, he foolishly confounded the issue by informing the government that he had conceived of a far more powerful and versatile machine — an Analytical Engine — which rendered the Difference Engine obsolete. The Analytical Engine could do all that its predecessor could do, and a great deal more. Under the circumstances, he suggested it might be more prudent and less expensive to write off the Difference Engine and build the newer version. This was not what the government, which had shelled out £17,000 for a glimmer in an inventor's eye, wanted to hear.

For his part, Babbage, who had spent £6,000 of his own money on the endeavor, regarded the government as fatally shortsighted and ill-equipped to lead England into the industrial age. The criticism was uncannily astute, and in making it, Babbage was, as usual, ahead of his time. "I have . . . been compelled to perceive," he wrote his friend, Edward, duke of Somerset, in 1833, "that of all countries England is that in which there exist the greatest number of practical engineers who can appreciate the mechanical part whilst at the same time it is of all others that country in which the governing powers are most incompetent to understand the merit either of the mechanical or mathematical."

Not surprisingly, the government grew tired of Babbage's importunities. Wellington's successors lacked his grasp of science and technology and scoffed at Babbage's work. "What shall we do to get rid of Babbage's calculating machine . . . worthless to science in my view," Prime Minister Peel wrote to an associate. "If it would calculate the amount and the quantum benefit to be derived to science it would render the only service I ever expect to derive from it." In 1842 — nineteen years after Babbage, full of confidence and high spirit, had started the project — Peel got his way. The venture was officially canceled and the engine wound up on display at the Science Museum in London.

But one cannot blame the project's failure entirely on the government. Clement's selfishness, petty and indefensible, and Babbage's perfectionism, which brooked no shortcuts, were also responsible.

If the Difference Engine had been built it would have stood ten feet high, ten feet wide, and five feet deep, and weighed about two tons. Internally, it would have consisted of seven main vertical axles. Six of those axles represented an order of difference, the seventh the value of the function being computed. Each of the axles held twenty wheels, or gears, since the engine could process twenty-digit numbers or, in special circumstances, be readjusted

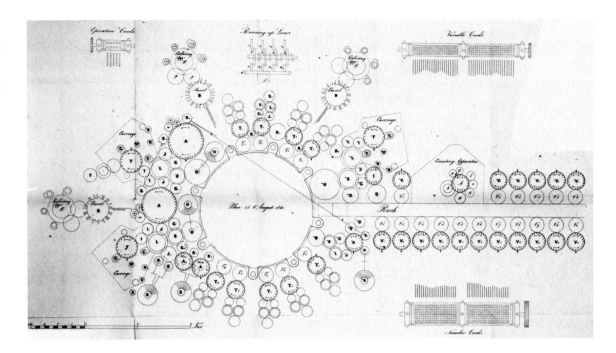

*The general plan of the Analytical Engine, as Babbage saw the machine in 1840. The number wheels on each side of the rack on the right constitute the store; the number wheels around the large circle on the left comprise the mill. The capacity of the store could be increased by building a longer rack and adding more number wheels.*

to use thirty-digit numbers. There were two sets of vertical axles behind the main ones, one for carrying or borrowing tens from one main axle to the next and another for engaging or disengaging the carrying axles. (If any of the gears fell out of place, a system of springs and pins forced it back into position, or, if the misalignment was bad enough, brought the apparatus to a halt.)

While the engine was designed chiefly to calculate constant progressions, it could also compute nonconstant ones like logs, in which the differences are exponential. In such cases, it calculated by approximation, employing a set of differences that applied to one series of logs and then figuring out the answers to the twentieth digit — but only printing out seven. Then it came to a stop, ringing a bell to notify the operator to enter a new set of differences. Obviously, this process was painfully slow and cumbersome, but it was preferable to pen-reckoning. Finally, the engine printed out results via a stamping mechanism attached to the seventh axle (which stored the result), producing negative molds that could be converted into positive printing plates.

The Difference Engine received a great deal of publicity, and it was only a matter of time before such a machine was built, if not by Babbage then by someone else. In 1834, Pehr Georg Scheutz, a technical editor, printer, and publisher in Stockholm, Sweden, read an account of the project in the *Edinburgh Review*. Fascinated, he built a small model of an engine out of wood, wire, and pasteboard. Babbage supplied the inspiration but Scheutz came up with his own design; the article in the *Edinburgh Review* did not contain a detailed description of the engine, and Scheutz, a paragon of self-reliance, did not write Babbage for more information. In 1837, Scheutz's son, Edvard, an engineer who had been trained in Sweden's Royal Technological Institute, joined his father's effort, and the two of them set out to build a full-fledged engine out of metal.

At this point, history repeated itself. Like Babbage, Scheutz and his son soon realized that the venture outstripped their resources and they appealed to the Swedish government for help. But the authorities, who did not wish to go down the same road as the British government, turned them down. The Scheutzes continued the project on their own and, by 1840, managed to produce a small machine that operated to the first order of difference. Two years later, they extended the machine to three orders of difference and, a year later, added a printing mechanism. Once again, father and son applied for government support. This time around, the Royal Swedish Academy of Sciences endorsed them, and the Swedish Diet advanced 5,000 *rix-dollars* (about $1,500) on the condition that the inventors finish the project by the end of 1853. Otherwise, the money would have to be returned.

Unlike Babbage, the Scheutzes were an eminently practical pair, and the Tabulating Machine, as they called it, was completed on schedule (though not within the budget). The Swedish engine was not as well built as Babbage's and, as a result, was prone to error. Nevertheless, it could operate to the fourth order of difference; process fifteen-digit numbers; and print out results, rounded off to eight digits, on molds from which metal printing plates could be cast. In operations involving constant differences, the device could generate more than 120 tabular lines an hour, and was only slightly slower in nonconstant operations, producing, in one test run, about ten thousand logs in eighty hours, including the time spent resetting the wheels for the twenty different equations used in the calculations. No human computer could have worked as fast or as accurately. The Scheutzes' difference engine was the first concrete demonstration of the enormous mathematical potential of machines.

In 1854, the Scheutzes brought their invention to London, where they demonstrated it before the Royal Society of London. Babbage, ever the gentleman, welcomed his fellow inventors with open arms. The following year, the Swedes entered the machine in the Great Exhibition in Paris and it won a gold medal — thanks, in part, to Babbage, who was a highly respected member

*Pehr Georg Scheutz (1785–1873)*

of the Institute of France and who had lobbied on their behalf. (Thomas's oversized Arithmometer, a Baroque throwback compared to the Tabulating Machine, also won a gold medal.) Pehr and Edvard were deeply grateful for Babbage's support. "Inventors are so seldom found that acknowledge the efforts of others in identical aims," the father wrote Babbage from Stockholm in 1856,

> that your liberality in this respect has, as we hear, made éclat in the French scientific world. Respecting me and son we would not have been so much surprised, having had occasion before, during our stay in London, to learn at your house the true character of an English gentleman; although our admiration of it can only be surpassed by our deep sense of gratitude. We came as strangers; but you did not receive us as such: conforming to reality you received us but as champions for a grand scientific idea. This rare disinterestedness offers so exhilarating an oasis in the deserts of humanity that we wished the whole world should know of it.

*Edvard Scheutz (1821–1881)*

The gold medal gave the Scheutzes the recognition they deserved. It also attracted a buyer, which the pair had been searching for almost from the day they had completed the machine. Dr. Benjamin Gould, director of the Dudley Observatory in Albany, New York, acquired the device for $5,000, and shipped it off to America in 1857. There it had a rather odd history. Dr. Gould put it aside for a year, and finally used it to calculate a set of tables relating to the orbit of Mars. But the observatory's trustees were unhappy with Dr. Gould's stewardship — among other things, they considered the purchase of the Scheutz difference engine as ill-advised — and fired him in 1859. After Dr. Gould's departure, the machine, which required a good deal of mathematical and mechanical skill to operate effectively, was never used again and eventually was donated to the Smithsonian Institution.

Several difference engines were constructed in Sweden, Austria, the United States, and England, where the British Register General, who was in charge of the collection and publication of vital statistics, had a copy of the Scheutzes' machine built in the late 1850s. The Register General used it to produce a new set of lifetime, annuity, and premium tables for the insurance industry, and it was more heavily used than any other difference engine. All in all, it calculated and printed out more than 600 different tables, including 238 tables for the insurance project. The machine made the Register General's work somewhat easier, but it required constant attention and often malfunctioned.

*The Scheutz Difference Engine was powered by falling weights. This is a photo of the second engine, built for the General Register Office in London in 1859.*

It was during his nasty quarrel with Clement, who had deprived him of his blueprints for a year and a half, that Babbage conceived of the Analytical Engine. Why not, he asked himself, build a machine that could solve *any* mathematical problem, in addition to those based on constant differences? Why not indeed? At the age of forty-three, Babbage had a vision of a computer, and he pursued it for the rest of his life; from the moment he began working in earnest on the Analytical Engine, he seems to have stepped straight into the middle of the twentieth century. He confronted technical problems that the first computer engineers faced a hundred years later, often coming up with the same solution as he — although most of them were unaware of his work.

Babbage revised his plans for the Analytical Engine many times, improving its structure and operation. As a result, it's difficult to pin down exactly what he had in mind. He created the first workable design by mid-1836 and overhauled it a year later. During the next twelve years, he refined the basic scheme of 1837 to 1838, putting the project aside in 1849. He took it up again in 1856 and tinkered with it until his death in 1871 at the age of seventy-nine. He produced six to seven thousand pages of notes, and he and his draftsmen (one or two men at any one time) created about three hundred engineering drawings and six to seven hundred charts illustrating, with a form of notation Babbage had developed for the Difference Engine, precisely how the machine operated. The drawings are more than meticulous engineering plans; part art, part dream, they are one of the greatest intellectual achievements of the nineteenth century.

At first, Babbage hoped that the government would finance the Analytical Engine. "The *constructor* of the *navy* might as well be required to *pay* for the building of a new ship he has devised as the inventor of the Anal[lytical] Engine to manufacture it," he wrote in his notebook in 1868. The Analytical Engine would serve England, not him, and he seemed to think that the government had a moral duty to support it. Of course, the government believed otherwise. Disgusted by the outcome of the first project, it refused to sponsor another of Babbage's ventures. Although Babbage eventually realized that neither the Difference nor Analytical Engine would be built during his lifetime, he continued to draw up plans for both machines at great personal expense.

The Analytical Engine was a thought experiment, an effort to prove, on paper, that such a machine was possible. When, toward the end of his life, Babbage gave up all hope of building the engine himself, he lived in the hope that someone else would take

*An assortment of printing molds produced by the second Difference Engine. The molds are made by the flat, perpendicular gadget in the center.*

*In the late 1860s, Babbage began building a scaled-down version of the Analytical Engine. A portion of the mill, including a built-in printing device, was assembled shortly before his death.*

up his dream after his death and construct the engine using his plans. Babbage was actually in the process of building part of the engine when he died, and his son, Henry, fashioned a section of it in about 1889. Unfortunately, his dream died with him. Eight years after his death, a committee of the British Association for the Advancement of Science looked into the feasibility of building the machine. Understandably cowed by the complexity of the task, it concluded that the venture was hopeless without Babbage. Of course, it would have been equally hopeless with him. A perfectionist, he probably never would have completed it.

The Analytical Engine was designed in the shape of a lollipop; the stick contained the *store*, where the numbers were kept, and the candy held the *mill*, where the numbers were operated upon. (In current computer terminology, the mill was the *central pro-*

*cessing unit,* or *CPU,* while the store was the *memory.*) Many times larger than the Difference Engine, the machine contained hundreds of vertical axles and thousands of wheels, or gears. The axles, which were about ten feet tall, represented a number, the wheels on the axles the digits in that number; since each axle contained forty wheels, the machine could process numbers up to forty digits long — twice the capacity of the Difference Engine. All told, the Analytical Engine would have been about fifteen feet tall and twenty-five feet long, or about as big and heavy as a small locomotive.

The mill contained nine main axles for performing multiplication and division and two accumulator axles for addition and subtraction; the accumulators also stored the results of all operations. As for the store, it held fifty primary axles and an equal quantity of adjoining secondary axles. Each of the store's axles had *two* sets of wheels; since the act of reading a number from the store erased it, the extra set of wheels enabled the machine to keep a copy of the original number — meaning that the store could contain one hundred forty-digit numbers. (And it could be enlarged by the addition of more axles.) When a number was entered into or taken out of the store, the primary axle holding the figure relayed it to the secondary axle, where it was passed on to a series of long horizontal toothed bars, or racks. Spanning the length of the store, the racks conveyed the number to an "egress axis" or an "ingress axis," which served as gateways into and out of the store.

The machine's internal operation was orchestrated by a barrel made up of metal slats with rectangular studs. The pattern of the studs could be varied, and each of the barrel's fifty to one hundred slats could hold as many as four studs. (The barrel served as the *control unit.*) It was these studs that told the engine when and how to execute a given operation. For instance, when the engine was directed to divide a number, the barrel turned to the slat, or slats, that governed division, and slid forward, pushing the studs against a group of levers that manipulated the appropriate axles in the mill and the store. By changing barrels, the operator could alter the engine's internal operations to suit the calculating needs of the moment.

Despite its size and complexity, the Analytical Engine was hardly a lumbering mechanical monster. The addition or subtraction of two forty-digit numbers took only three seconds, multiplication and division required two to four minutes — a pace that meant most of the calculations had to be performed by repeated addition and subtraction. Transferring a number between two ad-

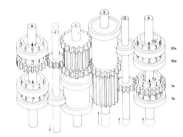

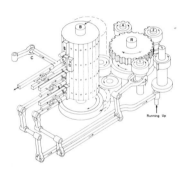

*By lifting a number from a lower to a higher set of number gears, the Analytical Engine could multiply by ten. In the upper diagram, a thick pinion (labeled S) is pushed upward, transferring a number to pinion L. Division may be accomplished by reversing the process. The Analytical Engine's internal operations were controlled by a barrel affixed with five rectangular studs (bottom). A group of levers (a, b, and c) read the studs and relayed the instructions to the rest of the machine.*

*In the 1880s, Babbage's son, Henry, designed and built a simple mill that printed a table of the multiples of π, but the gears tended to stick. The flat plate near the base of the mill is the printing mechanism, shown in greater detail in the second photo on the left.*

jacent axles took two and a half seconds, while a carry from the lowest wheel on an axle to the highest, or from the fortieth digit all the way through to the first, needed only a fourth of a second; Babbage, realizing that all the carrying to and fro would reduce the engine's speed to a crawl, devised an ingenious mechanism that triggered a carry before a number wheel actually turned to nine.

The Analytical Engine's external program was provided by punch cards — just like most of the computers of the 1950s and 1960s. Babbage got the idea of using cards from the textile industry. In 1801, the Frenchman Joseph-Marie Jacquard invented an automatic loom that was controlled by punch cards; as the cards, which were strung together into a kind of tape, moved through a mechanical reader, wooden plungers passed through the holes, orchestrating the machine's operation. The loom's ability was nothing less than amazing — Babbage owned a silk portrait of Jacquard sewn with instructions from about ten thousand cards — and Jacquard's invention, which had been based on an earlier, less-efficient loom invented by another Frenchman, had revolutionized the textile business.

The Analytical Engine employed three types of cards, each with its own mechanical reader: "operation cards," "variable cards," and "number cards." The first kind of card carried the instructions; the second held the symbols of the variables in an equation (x, y, and so on), the numerical value of the variables in that equation (1, 18, whatever), and certain numerical constants (like $\pi$); and the third contained entries from mathematical tables, such as logs and trigonometric functions. This three-pronged approach was cumbersome and complicated, and the programming side of the Analytical Engine was the least-developed aspect of the machine; Babbage wrote about two dozen programs between 1837 and 1840, but they are incomplete, segments of programs rather than entire lists of instructions.

Like a modern computer, the Analytical Engine had the ability to make decisions; that is, it could adopt one of two alternative courses of action based upon the results of its calculations. In the case of the Analytical Engine, this ability was quite limited, and the operation cards could only order the engine to add two numbers and, if the results were less than zero, to proceed to a specified card and carry out the indicated instruction (such as "add 10"). Known as a *conditional jump*, or *branching*, this is one

*A drawing of one of the Analytical Engine's punch cards.*

of the most important attributes of a computer — one of the characteristics that distinguishes it from an ordinary calculator. The operation cards could also instruct the machine to repeat a given set of instructions any number of times or to perform a sidestep within a general program; both of these tricks are important programming tools, the latter called a subroutine, the former a loop.

Much of what we know about the engine's programming potential comes from a remarkable article written by Augusta Ada Byron, countess of Lovelace, the daughter of Lord Byron, the poet. A talented amateur mathematician, Ada met Babbage in 1833 and was enthralled by the man and his work; at the suggestion of a mutual friend, she translated an article on the Analytical Engine written by an Italian mathematician. Ada added many pages of

*In a vivid demonstration of the power of his invention, Joseph-Marie Jacquard, using 10,000 punch cards, programmed a loom to weave a portrait of himself in black and white silk (above).*

*Right: A Jacquard loom*

explanatory notes and her translation, published in a popular scientific journal, became the most widely circulated account of the Analytical Engine, an astute analysis of the machine and of Babbage's ideas. Ada had a good deal of literary talent, and her notes are often quoted today: "We may say most aptly that the Analytical Engine *weaves algebraic patterns* just as the Jacquard-loom weaves flowers and leaves."

Was the Analytical Engine a computer? Obviously, the answer is a matter of definition. What is a computer? What is a calculator? Unfortunately, the words are almost impossible to define. Their meanings have changed over the years, and undoubtedly will continue to change. For centuries, *computer* designated a person who did calculations for a living; nowadays, it applies to a certain kind of machine with a broad range of attributes and capabilities; many years from now, it may refer to a device with substantially different characteristics and applications than today's computers. The same holds true for *calculator*, which was often employed as a synonym for *computer*. Since the late nineteenth century, *calculator* has referred to a small machine that people use to perform arithmetic; but it took on a much grander meaning in the 1940s, when it was enlisted to describe such "giant brains" as the Selective Sequence Electronic *Calculator*.

In its broadest sense, and in the modern meaning of the term, a *computer* is an information-processing machine. It can store data — numbers, letters, pictures, or symbols — and manipulate that data according to programs that also have been stored in the machine. The ability to retain data and programs gives computers a considerable degree of automaticity, and, equally important, the capacity to make decisions, such as the conditional jump, based on the results of its own computations. A calculator, on the other hand, can't do any of these things. It can only solve mathematical problems, and its operation must be directed every step of the way by the user. Unable to store data and programs, it cannot make decisions. Physically, calculators vary a great deal (as we shall see), but computers generally possess five basic parts — a structure that seems to have arisen more out of practicality than tradition (just as cars have four wheels). Those parts are a central processor, a central control, a memory, and input and output units.

On the one hand, the Analytical Engine resembled a calculator. It could only perform mathematical work and could not store programs. On the other hand, it also resembled a computer. It was programmable, and possessed a large degree of automaticity and a modest ability to make decisions. And it had a memory (a

*Augusta Ada, Countess of Lovelace, in a portrait painted in about 1835*

store), a central processor (a mill), and a control (the barrel). Neither fish nor fowl, it was a rudimentary form of computer known as a *program-controlled calculator*. Such a machine falls short of being a computer in at least one all-important respect: it cannot retain a program, and its instructions are forever frozen on punch cards, tape, or another medium. Although the Analytical Engine is as far removed from a computer as an open-air biplane is from a Boeing 747, it was a great, if unrealized, intellectual achievement — a magnificent glimpse of the future.

In the last years of his life, Charles Babbage was a lonely, cranky old man. John Fletcher Moulton, a Cambridge mathematician, visited him a few years before his death. As Moulton recalled in a speech at the Napier Tercentary in Edinburgh in 1914,

> In the first room I saw the parts of the original Calculating Machine, which had been shown in an incomplete state many years before and had even been put to some use. I asked him about its present form. "I have not finished it because in working at it I came on the idea of my Analytical Engine, which would do all that it was capable of doing and much more. Indeed the idea was so much simpler that it would have taken more work to complete the calculating machine than to design and construct the other in its entirety, so I turned my attention to the Analytical Machine." After a few minutes' talk we went into the next workroom where he showed and explained to me the working of the elements of the Analytical Machine. I asked if I could see it. "I have never completed it," he said, "because I hit upon the idea of doing the same thing by a different and far more effective method, and this rendered it useless to proceed on the old lines." Then we went into the third room. There lay scattered bits of mechanism but I saw no trace of any working machine. Very cautiously I approached the subject, and received the dreaded answer, "It is not constructed yet, but I am working at it, and will take less time to construct it altogether than it would have taken to complete the Analytical Machine from the stage in which I left it." I took leave of the old man with a heavy heart.

*Charles Babbage in his
sixties*

## CHAPTER 3

# The Bridge Between Two Centuries

Herman Hollerith is a man of honor
What he has done is beyond compare
To the wide world he has been the donor
Of an invention very rare
His praises we all gladly sing
His results make him outclass a king
Facts from factors he has made a business
May the years good things to him bring.

> — *Early IBM song, to the tune of "On the Trail of the Lonesome Pine"*

I was a student in civil engineering in Berlin. Berlin is a nice town and there were many opportunities for a student to spend his time in an agreeable manner, for instance with the nice girls. But instead of that we had to perform big and awful calculations.

> — *Konrad Zuse, b. 1910*

*The main office of the Prudential Insurance Company of America, Newark, New Jersey. By the turn of the century, when this picture was taken, big businesses were awash with paperwork.*

B y the late 1800s, the United States, which had emerged from the Civil War politically and economically united, was the world's greatest industrial power. Technologically, it had also begun to pull ahead of the rest of the world, its vast and unregulated market a great spur to invention. Patent applications poured into the U. S. Patent Office, once a drowsy government agency. In the decade before the Civil War, the office granted about a thousand patents a year. By the 1870s, the figure had risen to twelve thousand a year, and in 1890 alone it ballooned to twenty-five thousand. (By contrast, in 1890 Great Britain awarded only eleven thousand of these licenses to fame and fortune.) A vigorous spirit of invention was afoot in America, and it is to this colossus of innovation and industry that we now turn.

In 1884, an ambitious young engineer named Herman Hollerith filed the first of a series of patents for an electromechanical system that counted and sorted punch cards. In the Analytical Engine, punch cards contained numbers, variables, and processing instructions; in the Hollerith system, they contained statistics — any kind of statistics, whether gender, income, population, sales, or inventory. The cards were run through a sorter, which grouped them into specified categories, and then through a tabulator, which counted the perforations and displayed the totals. (The machines did not calculate or compute; they just collated and added.) Hollerith's system was the world's first data processor; suddenly, it was possible to count, collate, and analyze information by machine.

Herman Hollerith (1860–1929), the son of German immigrants, was born in Buffalo, New York, where his family owned a small carriage factory and repair shop. He attended the School of Mines at Columbia University, in New York City, not so much because he was interested in mining but because he wanted to be an engineer, and engineering schools were rare in those days. A bright, hardworking perfectionist, Hollerith graduated near the top of his class in 1879 and went to work as a special agent for the Census Office in Washington, D.C. One of his professors, William P. Trowbridge, who moonlighted for the Census as an expert special agent, got the job for him. The 1880 enumeration was about to begin, and the Census needed employees with mathematical and engineering ability.

Hollerith began as Trowbridge's assistant. He investigated the role of steam and water power in the iron and steelmaking industries and wrote a report on his findings. In his spare time, he helped Dr. John Shaw Billings, head of the division of vital statistics, compile his reports. Billings appreciated the young man's help, and invited him to dinner one Sunday night in August or September of 1881. Billings was a dynamic and innovative man, a first-rate administrator who established the Surgeon General's Library, one of the largest medical libraries in the world, and who became the first director of the New York Public Library, sketching the general plans for the great central library in Manhattan. The surgeon general's office had transferred him to the Census to supervise the compilation of vital statistics.

Billings and Hollerith's dinnertime conversation inevitably turned to their work. Although the 1880 headcount had taken only a few months, the chore of tabulating and analyzing the data promised to drag on for years. By the time it was done, the Census reports would be hopelessly out of date; the government would be lucky enough to finish in time for the next census. Since the country's population, swelled by immigration, was growing by the millions, the 1890 census undoubtedly would take even more time and money. The situation was getting out of hand and the Census was casting about for a solution. And Billings had an idea — a gem of an idea. As Hollerith recalled in a letter to a friend in 1919:

Herman Hollerith (1860–1929) in 1880, a special agent for the U.S. Census

One Sunday evening, at Dr. Billings' tea table, he said to me there ought to be a machine for doing the purely mechanical work of tabulating population and similar statistics. We talked the matter over and I remember . . . he thought of using cards with the description of the individual shown by notches punched *in the edge of the card*. . . . After studying the problem I went back to Dr. Billings and said that I thought I could work out a solution for the problem and asked him would he go in with me. The Doctor said he was not interested any further than to see some solution of the problem worked out. [Italics added.]

*The formidable John Shaw Billings (1838–1913), in a portrait at the National Library of Medicine, in Bethesda, Maryland*

Tackling the problem on his own, Hollerith studied the Census's procedures. In the first step of the count, enumerators called at every household and recorded the answers to their questions on large sheets of paper known as schedules. The completed schedules were sent back to Washington, where an army of clerks transcribed the answers to tally sheets. For example, for every native-born white male on a schedule, a slash mark was placed in a small box on a tally sheet, five slashes to a box. It was easy to add up the slashes on a tally sheet, since the form was divided into large boxes that contained a specific number of small boxes; the clerks totaled up the completed large boxes and noted the number of slashes at the bottom of the sheet. In the next step, the tally totals were transferred to consolidation sheets, whose figures were combined to yield the population of the states, and finally, the nation.

The 1880 enumeration required six tallies, one for every major statistical classification. In the first tally, the Census broke down the population by sex, race, and birthplace; in other tallies, it collated these statistics with literacy, occupation, and other characteristics. Every time a tally was called for, the clerks had to sift through the schedules all over again, and there were millions of schedules. The process was painfully slow and expensive, and prone to error. Moreover, it prevented the Census from performing sophisticated analyses of the data.

Everything was done by hand. The only mechanical aid was a simple contraption called the Seaton device, invented by Charles W. Seaton, the Census's chief clerk, and used in the 1870 and 1880 censuses. It consisted of a continuous roll of tally sheets wound on a set of spools in a wooden box. By zigzagging the roll around the spools, it brought several columns of a sheet, which measured seventeen by twenty inches, close together, making it easier for the clerks to enter the slashes. (If Seaton's solution seems backward — why not just make tally sheets smaller? — the reason was that, for purposes of recording and tabulating, the

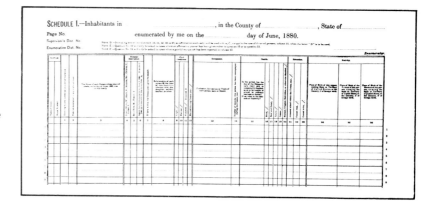

SCHEDULE I.—Inhabitants in ............................, in the County of ......................, State of ..............

Page No. ..................

Supervisor's Dist. No. ..................

Enumeration Dist. No. ..................

enumerated by me on the .......... day of June, 1880.

Right: The 1880 census schedule was divided into twenty-six statistical categories. Among other things, the government wanted to know whether the respondents were "idiotic" or "insane."

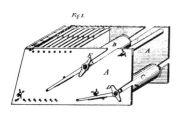

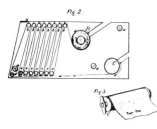

Clerks compiled the tally sheets with the help of the Seaton device.

sheets had to contain a certain amount of data.) Completed rolls were removed from the box, cut into separate sheets, and consolidated numerically. Although the Seaton device made the clerks a bit more efficient and accurate, it made only a small dent in the Census's problems. Nevertheless, Congress paid Seaton, a well-connected if not especially talented inventor, $15,000 for the rights to his invention. The size of the award was not lost on Hollerith.

In 1882, Hollerith became an instructor in mechanical engineering at Massachusetts Institute of Technology (MIT). Taking advantage of the school's workshops, he built his first tabulating system. For some reason, he decided to use punched tape instead of cards. The tape was run over a metal drum, under an array of metal brushes; whenever the brushes passed over a hole, electrical contact was made with the drum, advancing a counter. A separate counter was set up for each statistical category, and the totals were displayed by a number on the counter (as time is shown on a digital watch). The system was an improvement over tally and consolidation sheets; once the data on the schedules had been converted into punched tape, many items could be tabulated in a single, fast run of the tape, in contrast to the one, two, or three items that could be collated on a tally sheet at any time.

Although this system was a solid step forward, Hollerith soon realized that he had made a serious mistake: paper tape was a flawed medium, severely limiting the tabulator's speed and flexibility. For example, if you wanted to retrieve a particular piece of information, or related pieces of information, from a tape, you might have to sift through the entire reel. The data could be anywhere — at the beginning, in the middle, or, as these things often seemed to work out, at the end. Moreover, once you found the data, there was no way to isolate it for future reference — other than cutting the tape into pieces. (In modern terminology, this method of retrieving data is known as *serial access*.)

To solve the problem, Hollerith turned to punch cards, and

it's odd that he didn't follow Billings's suggestion in the first place. Most likely, Billings's idea didn't click in his mind until he had rediscovered it on his own. "I was traveling in the West," he wrote a colleague years after he had perfected his tabulators and sorters, "and I had a ticket with what I think was called a punch photograph. . . . The conductor . . . punched out a description of the individual, as light hair, dark eyes, large nose, etc. So you see, I only made a punch photograph of each person." (Punched photographs discouraged vagrants from stealing passengers' tickets and passing them off as their own.)

In effect, Hollerith cut the tape into sections, and the result was a quick and versatile tabulating system. Once you had transcribed the information on the schedules to the cards, you could manually or electromechanically isolate any card or class of cards. (This form of retrieval is known as *random access*.) For instance, you could set aside a pile of cards representing nothing but farmers and perform any statistical analyses of this group you wished. You did not have to sift through the schedules all over again. Therefore, if you wanted to know how many white male farmers owned more than five hundred acres and earned the bulk of their income from tobacco, you had only to run through the farmer cards, setting up the counters on the tabulator to match the appropriate holes in the cards.

The decision to use cards led Hollerith to redesign his system. He fashioned a special puncher — a pantograph punch — consisting of a template and two connected punches; when the

*Hollerith's first tabulator employed paper tape. Fig. 1 shows a tape pulley from above; fig. 2, a pulley with a punching template; fig. 3, a hole puncher; fig. 4, a punching template; and fig. 5, an electrical tape reader.*

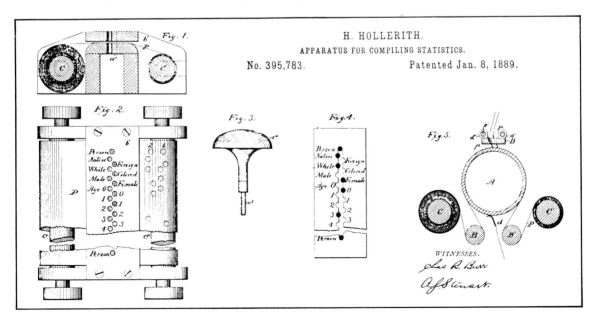

*The card puncher (upper left and right) consisted of an interchangeable template and a dual puncher. The first punch cards were blank, which made them difficult to read, but printed cards were introduced for the 1900 census.*

operator punched the template, the second puncher perforated the card. The card reader was a small press made up of an overhead array of pins and an underlying bed of tiny cups of mercury; when the operator slipped a card into the press and pulled down on the handle, the pins passed through the holes into the mercury, closing electrical circuits that advanced the counters, simple dials set into a wooden table that resembled an upright piano. (He had dispensed with digital counters.) As for the sorter, it was simply a box with several compartments; when a card with a desired set of characteristics passed through the press, a box on the sorter opened up, and the operator slipped the card into it.

Hollerith's use of electricity is worth special mention. Babbage had toyed with the idea of electrifying the Analytical Engine — by designing, for example, an electrical mill and store — but the nature and use of electricity was poorly understood in his day and he decided against it. By the 1880s, electrical equipment and electrical power networks were no longer figments of an inventor's imagination, and a forward-looking engineer could reasonably use electricity in his inventions. Hollerith intended to power his tabulators with batteries and recharge them through the local power company. His work possesses a distinctly modern air, with all the advantages that accrue to electrical, as opposed to mechanical, machines. His equipment was faster, smaller, simpler, and more reliable than mechanical machines could ever have been.

The Census was impressed with Hollerith's work, but it decided to conduct an official test of the system before making a commitment. The trial pitted Hollerith's machines against the "chip" system of Charles F. Pidgen and the "slip" system of William C. Hunt, both Census officials. In the chip system, data from the schedules were transcribed to colored cards; in the slip system, the information was written onto slips of paper in colored inks. In both cases, the cards and slips were counted by hand. The competition called for the transcription and tabulation of a thick sheaf of schedules, compiled during the 1880 census, covering 10,491 people in St. Louis. There were two parts to the trial: the time required to transcribe the schedules and the time required to tabulate the data.

Not surprisingly, Hollerith's system swept the boards. It showed its greatest advantage in the tabulation portion of the test, completing the job eight to ten times faster than the hand-counted slip and chip methods:

*A tabulator in use at the Census, probably in 1890.*

|  | Transcription | | Tabulation | |
|---|---|---|---|---|
|  | HOURS | MINUTES | HOURS | MINUTES |
| Hollerith cards | 72 | 27 | 5 | 28 |
| Pidgen chips | 110 | 56 | 44 | 41 |
| Hunt slips | 144 | 25 | 55 | 22 |

Pleased with the results, the Census ordered fifty-six tabulators and sorters (the machines were rented, not purchased), and Hollerith was in business.

THE NEW CENSUS OF THE UNITED STATES—THE ELECTRICAL ENUMERATING MECHANISM. [See page 132.]

*Hollerith's punch card system received a great deal of attention in the popular and scientific press and was featured on the cover of the 30 August 1890 issue of Scientific American.*

*Each counter kept track of a single statistical category.*

His machines went to work in July 1890, shortly after the completion of the headcount. The first task was a general tally of the population, and Hollerith devised a special counter for the job, a typewriterlike device equipped with twenty keys, numbered 1 to 20. The clerks read the schedules, which represented only one family per sheet, then pressed the key signifying the number of people on the schedule. Some operators handled 9,200 schedules, listing 50,000 people, in a single day. By August 16, only six weeks after the count had begun, the Census had a tally: 62,622,250. With great pride and fanfare, the figure was officially announced in October, and everyone was suitably amazed. Other statistics quickly poured out of Washington, the typical Census clerk processing an average of 7,000 to 8,000 cards a day. (The record was 19,071.)

Compared to the 1880 census, which had taken nine years and cost $5.8 million, the 1890 count was completed in fewer than seven years, but it had cost $11.5 million, almost twice as much. Under the circumstances, there was some controversy about the benefits of automation — an issue that still hasn't been settled. The Census, which had shelled out only $750,000 in rental fees for Hollerith's equipment, ascribed the financial dis-

In 1894, John K. Gore, an actuary for the Prudential Insurance Company, patented an automatic punch card sorter (in the background). It consisted of four circular platforms, each containing ten bins configured with a different arrangement of pins. A motor turned the platforms, and the cards dropped into the appropriate bins. Although Gore's invention could process about 15,000 cards an hour, it was built with Prudential needs in mind and wasn't used elsewhere.

parity to the expense of running a far more careful and thorough statistical analysis of the raw data; the 1890 census was more comprehensive than any previous headcount. Indeed, the Census estimated that it had actually saved about $5 million in labor costs. If, for the sake of argument, we assume that the disparity wasn't caused by bad management and political featherbedding, then Hollerith's system apparently possessed hidden costs — the great temptation to use the equipment to the hilt. All those millions of cards, those thousands of watts of electricity, those scores of statisticians, had run up a big bill.

Hollerith's system was adopted all over the world. In late 1890, Austria ordered several tabulators and sorters for its census, and Canada, France, and Russia also requested them. After much initial resistance, private industry began renting them too. Swamped with paperwork, large companies like the Chicago department store Marshall Field & Co., the New York Central Railroad Company, and the Pennsylvania Steel Company moved the equipment into their accounting and inventory departments. Soon they couldn't live without it. By the early 1900s, Hollerith's firm, the Tabulating Machine Company, had more customers than it could handle. However, because the firm leased rather than sold its equipment, which provided a steady and quite profitable stream of income but produced a thinner cash flow, the company was always short of capital. The best solution seemed to be a merger, and in 1911 Hollerith's firm joined with three other outfits to become the Computing-Tabulating-Recording Company (CTR), which eventually became the International Business Machines Corporation, or IBM.

When we last examined the state of mechanical calculation, Thomas de Colmar had invented and marketed a reliable four-function calculator, called the Arithmometer. Based on the Leibniz wheel, it was the first major advance in calculator technology since the late 1700s and Thomas's design was widely emulated. For decades, Thomas-type machines were the only truly useful calculators on the market. But the situation changed dramatically after 1875. As a result of advances in machine tooling and mechanical engineering, it became possible to do more with gears and axles than ever before. A veritable explosion in calculator design and manufacturing took place, as a growing number of inventors sensed a need and sought to fill it.

Once again, the major breakthroughs occurred in America. In 1872, Frank Stephen Baldwin, of St. Louis, conceived of a new kind of calculator mechanism, the pinwheel, which operated like the Leibniz wheel. When the operator entered a number — let's say, five — via a lever on the face of the machine, five spring-loaded pins, or sprockets, protruded from the edge of a wheel inside the device. The operator then turned a crank and the pinwheel rotated the relevant inner gears five notches. Baldwin's clever machine was the first major innovation since the Arithmometer, and it inspired a host of imitators. In 1875, he obtained a patent and set up a small factory in Philadelphia, inaugurating the American calculator industry. However, he failed to make a go at it until 1912, when he and Jay Randolph Monroe, an auditor for the Western Electric Company, established the Monroe Calculating Machine Company. By this time, poor Baldwin was seventy-four years old.

Incidentally, in 1878 a Swedish engineer named Willgodt Theophil Odhner developed a calculator very much like Baldwin's. Odhner had greater financial success than Baldwin and several European manufacturers produced his machines. Although both men have been credited with the invention of the pinwheel principle, the honor rightly belongs to Baldwin; in his first U.S. patent, Odhner didn't lay claim to the pinwheel idea.

At about the same time Baldwin came up with the pinwheel, other inventors managed to design calculators with the mechanical equivalent of built-in multiplication tables. The first of these machines, which greatly speeded up multiplication and division, was invented in 1878 by Ramon Verea, a Spaniard living

*In the early 1870s, Frank Baldwin invented a new calculating mechanism, the pinwheel, a set of nine spring-loaded pins at the base of the large circle in the patent drawing. An improved version of the patented machine is shown above.*

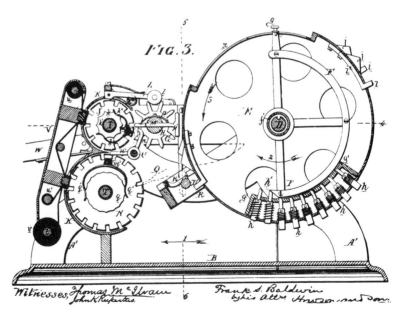

FIG. 3.

Witnesses, Thomas McIlvain
John K. Rupertus

Frank S. Baldwin
by his attorney Hnston and Son.

in New York City. His device "looked up" the product of two numbers on a pair of cylinders, and multiplied the inner gears accordingly. An interesting fellow, Verea had no commercial ambitions; he told a *New York Herald* reporter that he "did not make the machine to either sell its patent or put it into use, but simply to show that it was possible and that a Spaniard can invent as well as an American." Touché!

And the French were no less clever. In 1889, Léon Bollée, an eighteen-year-old mechanical genius, also invented a calculator with an internal multiplication table. His machine captured a gold medal at the 1889 Paris Exhibition, but Bollée, an energetic and restless man, soon went on to other things — such as constructing race cars and establishing the racetrack at Le Mans. It was left to Otto Steiger, a Swiss engineer, to design and market the first practical multiplication-table calculator. Known as The Millionaire, it was introduced in 1893 and found a welcome home in accounting rooms and universities all over the world. The Millionaire had an unusually long life for a machine: 4,655 were sold before it was taken out of production in 1935.

All of these machines operated on different principles, testimony both to the ingenuity of their inventors and to the anarchy of the state of the art of mechanical calculation. Although Baldwin's and Steiger's calculators could perform all four arithmetic functions, they failed to crack the mass market, and the reason was chiefly technical. Along with all their rivals, these calculators had at least two major limitations. First, they lacked a truly con-

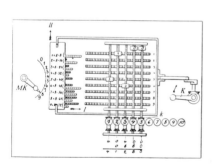

*The Millionaire contained a mechanism that represented numerical products by racks of different lengths.*

*Dorr E. Felt (1862–1930), perhaps the most prolific and original of the calculator inventors*

venient method for entering numbers, which made them somewhat awkward to use; second, they lacked a printer for recording results, which meant that you had to keep track of your results and write the answers down on a sheet of paper. There were too many opportunities for error.

In 1885, Dorr E. Felt, a veritable fountain of creativity who worked as a mechanic for the Pullman Company, in Chicago, made the pivotal breakthrough with the invention of a key-driven calculator. Felt's Comptometer was the epitome of convenience: all you had to do was tap in the numbers on a typewriterlike keyboard and the gadget did the rest. The mere act of pressing the keys, which were linked to springs, drove the device. Four years later, Felt solved the second drawback with a built-in printer that automatically recorded the entries and answers. He teamed up with Robert Tarrant, a Chicago businessman, and the Felt & Tarrant Manufacturing Co. started production in 1889. By 1930, when Felt died, the firm had $3.1 million in sales and 850 employees.

Without direct competition, Felt & Tarrant might have dominated the market, but the idea of a calculator with a numeric keyboard and a built-in printer also occurred to William S. Burroughs (1857–98). Burroughs, a clerk in a bank in upstate New York, knew from firsthand experience the inadequacies of the available calculators. When he was twenty-six, he moved to St. Louis and worked briefly in his father's model-making and casting shop, where he met many inventors, including Baldwin. Suitably in-

Never heard of the Comptometer.
TOO BAD.
Having trouble with that trial balance.

Saw our advertisement.
FEELING BETTER.
Has time for other work.

*An advertisement for the Comptometer, about 1900*

spired, Burroughs began tinkering with a calculator of his own. In 1884, he developed a version with a keyboard driven by a handle (not by springs, as in Felt's model, which was not yet on the market). With the substantial backing of three St. Louis merchants, Burroughs rushed his machine into production in 1887.

But his haste proved to be an expensive mistake; the machines didn't stand up to everyday use and had to be scrapped. Furious, Burroughs walked into the stockroom one day and tossed his machines out of the window, one by one. In 1892, he patented another keyboard calculator, this time with a built-in printer, and this model turned out to be a winner. It far outsold every other calculator on the market; about 2,000 were purchased in 1901, 3,000 in 1902, 4,500 in 1903. Unfortunately, Burroughs, who suffered from poor health, did not live long enough to enjoy his success; he died in 1898 at the age of forty-one. By 1913, the Burroughs Adding Machine Company, which had moved to Detroit, had some 2,500 employees and $8 million in sales — it was as big as all of its competitors combined.

Burroughs, Monroe, Felt and Tarrant, and the other calculator manufacturers found a ready market for their wares in banks, companies, accounting departments, and universities. By the 1920s, electric calculators were available; you just pushed some buttons and the machines did most of the work, printing out the results on neat rolls of paper. Although anyone with a couple of hundred dollars to spare could buy a machine that did basic arithmetic, these calculators weren't much good at more compli-

*Above: Compared to earlier calculators, the Comptometer was easy to use. All you had to do was push the keys; the machine did the rest. Later models contained built-in printers.*

*Right: In 1888, William S. Burroughs patented his first calculator. Like the Comptometer, it was really an adder-subtracter, but it could multiply and divide via repeated additions and subtractions.*

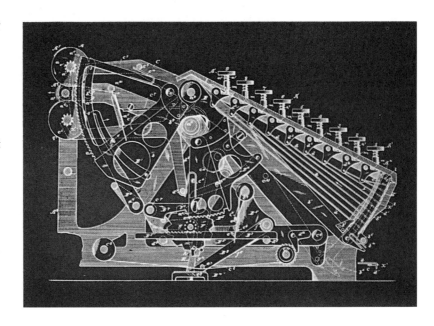

*A secretary with a portable Burroughs calculator, about 1922*

cated mathematical problems. Some scientists and engineers, thinking they had the seeds of a solution, ganged conventional calculators together in cascading rows; but such Rube Goldbergian contraptions were expensive and cumbersome. The computer demanded a completely different approach, from the composition of its innards to the nature of its number system.

Among the most important and widely used analytical tools in science and engineering are *differential equations*. A branch of calculus, these equations give us the power to predict the behavior of moving objects, like sailboats or airplanes, or of intangible forces, like gravity and current, by relating them to certain variables. The sound of a plucked violin string, the sway of a bridge in the wind, the flight of a rocket into space, the behavior of electricity in a power grid — all of these can be translated into differential equations. Much of our knowledge of the nature of light, sound, heat, atomic structure, as well as other phenomena, natural and artificial, derives from these equations, which used to be extremely difficult to solve. In fact, the effort to solve them led directly to the invention of the computer.

You can attack these equations in two ways: numerically, with figures representing the variables in question, or graphically, with waves or curves drawn on paper taking the place of numbers. When they have only one variable, they are easy to figure out, but their difficulty increases dramatically as the number of variables rises; the more complicated equations may take a team of engineers or scientists months to complete, and the answers may be full of errors. Beginning in 1814, when differential calculus was in its infancy, all sorts of clever little gadgets were devised to help scientists work with the equations. These strange-looking devices, which were made of cylinders, discs, and globes, and had such multisyllabic names as planimeters and linear integrators, could be used to draw the solutions to simple differential equations and other problems.

In the 1870s, the great British mathematician and physicist William Thomson, first Baron Kelvin (1824–1907), realized that these gadgets — which were all, by the way, analog devices, like slide rules — held the seeds of much more powerful machines. Lord Kelvin had an extraordinarily wide range of scientific interests; he made important contributions to almost every branch of physics and is best remembered today as the creator of the Kelvin temperature scale, which is widely used in science. In the early 1860s, his older brother, James, who was also a distinguished scientist, invented a planimeter with a so-called disc, globe, and cylinder integrator that could measure the area delineated on paper by a simple irregular curve. It occurred to Lord Kelvin, who was interested in the mathematical problems associated with tides — an important concern in an island nation like Britain — that his brother's invention could be put to other uses, and he built three special-purpose calculating machines based on it.

*William Thomson, Lord Kelvin (1824–1907)*

One was a tide gauge, which recorded the height of sea level by a curve traced on paper. The other was a tidal harmonic analyzer, which broke down complex harmonic, or repeating, waves into the simpler waves that made them up. (By analogy, a harmonic musical note is composed of simple *tones* vibrating in unison.) And the third, and most impressive of the lot, was a tide predictor that could calculate the time and height of the ebb and flood tides for any day of the year. Kelvin, who also had a talent for words, wrote that the harmonic analyzer substituted "brass for

*Kelvin's tide predictor (right), built in 1873, was the first automatic analog calculator. By mechanically combining up to ten simple waves, it drew a harmonic wave — a tide prediction — on the drums at the base of the machine. In 1914, the U.S. Coast and Geodetic Survey put a much more sophisticated tide predictor, fifteen years in the making, into operation (below right). The device could add as many as thirty-seven simple waves. A chart compiled from the machine's data is shown below. The actual tide is on the last line; the predicted one, just above.*

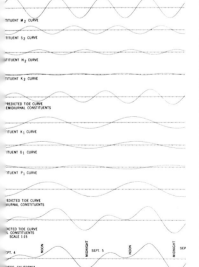

brain in the great mechanical labour of calculating the elementary constituents of the whole tidal rise and fall" — a description that also suits the tide predictor.

As a result of this work, Kelvin realized that a full-fledged "differential analyzer," capable of solving complicated differential equations graphically, was theoretically possible, and he outlined the idea in a remarkable paper published in the *Proceedings of the Royal Society* in 1876. Unfortunately, the technology of the time wasn't up to the job, and it wasn't until 1930 that a differential analyzer was built — by an engineer who claimed that he hadn't read Kelvin's paper until "a long time" after he had built his analyzer. (And we have little choice but to accept that claim, even though Kelvin's paper was quite well known among engineers and scientists.)

The inventor was Vannevar Bush (1890–1974), a no-nonsense, straight-talking engineering professor at MIT. Bush, who became famous in the 1940s as the director of America's wartime research and development efforts, was up to his ears with differential equations related to electric power networks. "I was trying to solve some of the problems of electric circuitry," he wrote in his autobiography, *Pieces of the Action,*

> such as the ones connected with failures and blackouts in power networks, and I was thoroughly stuck because I could not solve the tough equations the investigation led to. Ralph Booth [an electrical engineer] and I managed to solve one

In the mid-1920s, Vannevar Bush and his colleagues at MIT built a product integraph, a semiautomatic analog calculator that could solve fairly complicated problems in electrical theory. Bush is at the far left.

*The MIT differential analyzer wasn't easy to use. Like the product integraph, it was semiautomatic, and operators had to be stationed at the input/output tables (on the right) to keep the machine's pointers on track. The glass-covered boxes housed the integrators, the computing portion of the machine.*

problem, on the stability of a proposed transmission line, but solving it took months of making and manipulating charts and graphs. Incidentally, the study showed that the line would be unstable, and this result caused quite a commotion, for the line had been designed by the engineers of the great electrical manufacturing companies. But better ways of analyzing were certainly needed.

In 1927, Bush and his associates in MIT's Electrical Engineering Department embarked on a program to build a differential analyzer. Three years later, the first big machine was in operation. It was composed of six Thomson integrators and an equal number of electric motors, with scores of metal shafts that linked the integrators together and relayed their rotating motions, proportioned to the given variables, to an output table that displayed the results; the machine was programmed by entering the data through three so-called input tables and by rearranging the shafts and gears, a job that often took two days. The analyzer resembled a giant Erector Set — it wasn't a very elegant machine — but it worked quite well, generating solutions that were inaccurate by no more than 2 percent, about the best that could be expected from an analog calculator.

Bush's analyzer was quite influential, an impressive demonstration of the computational power of machines. Seven or eight copies of the device were built in the United States, Great Britain, and other countries, chiefly at universities, and Bush went on to build a much faster and larger electromechanical version, using vacuum tubes, in the 1940s. But he and his colleagues were barking up the wrong tree. The very nature of analog devices makes them ill-suited for accurate, versatile computing, and, although special-purpose analog calculators continued to be built, the future belonged to electronic digital computers.

*Konrad Zuse fiddling with the punched tape reader of the Z4. The tape consisted of discarded 35mm movie film.*

By the mid-1930s, in part as a result of the success of the differential analyzer, a handful of scientists and engineers in the United States, Great Britain, and Germany began to give serious thought to the mathematical potential of machines. These men worked alone or in small teams and had little or no contact with each other, although they sometimes wrote about their efforts or discussed their ideas at scientific and engineering conferences. Babbage's Analytical Engine, with its wonderfully simple but highly flexible structure of mill, store, control, and card readers, had been almost completely forgotten, except in Britain, and its underlying principles had to be rediscovered. The first man to do so was a young German engineer named Konrad Zuse.

As an engineering student at the Technical College of Berlin-Charlottenberg, in Berlin, Zuse had to master the theory of static indeterminate structures, which is based on a branch of algebra known as linear equations. Mathematically, linear equations are the flip side of differential equations; whereas the latter describe the behavior of dynamic entities, like projectiles, the former deal with the behavior of static structures, like buildings. For example, in order to provide the proper structural support for a roof, an engineer must first solve a set of simultaneous linear equations that takes into account all the relevant variables, such as the weight, strength, and elasticity of the construction materials. While these formulae are not especially intellectually profound, they were maddeningly difficult in Zuse's day; the practical limit for an individual was about six equations with six unknowns, and a doubling in the number of equations creates an eightfold boost in the quantity of calculations. Even with the help of automatic calculators, a team of engineers needed months to solve the equations related to a big roof.

Surely, thought Zuse, there must be a better way. It was 1934, and he was still in school. He hated the mathematical drudgery of his profession and didn't relish the prospect of a career spent hunched over a desk, figuring out equations, linear or otherwise. Although he wasn't much of a mathematician, he knew a lot about mechanical engineering — enough to know that another mechanical calculator, full of oily gears and axles, wasn't the answer. Fortunately, he was blessed with a good deal of insight and common sense, and his approach was fresh and original, unfettered by tradition and the opinion of experts. After carefully considering the nature of the problems of mechanical calculation, he made three conceptual decisions that put him on the right track from the beginning.

First, he decided that the only effective solution to the computational obstacles of his profession was a universal calculator, one that could solve *any* equation. Therefore, he provided his machine with a marvelously simple but highly flexible internal structure — the same structure Babbage had given the Analytical Engine. (However, Zuse didn't learn about the Englishman until 1939.) The calculator was equipped with an arithmetic unit (or central processing unit) for performing the computations; a memory for storing the numbers; a control unit for supervising the flow of numbers and instructions within the machine; a so-called program unit for reading instructions and data from punched tape; and an output unit for displaying the results.

Second, Zuse decided to use binary, rather than decimal, math — a decision that was pure inspiration and ensured his success. The irreducible economy of the binary system meant that the calculator's components could be as simple as on/off switches and that, in the final analysis, his machine was really a miniature telegraph system, with a vocabulary of zeros and ones instead of dots and dashes. Although Western mathematicians had known about binary math since Leibniz's time, Zuse was the first one to use it in a calculator; for hundreds of years, the decimal system was regarded as a God-given sine qua non until Zuse (and other inventors, unaware of Zuse's work) questioned the unquestionable. Even Babbage, who had considered using other number systems in the Analytical Engine, had come down on the side of tradition, primarily because gears were ideally suited to decimal math.

Finally, Zuse devised a simple set of operating rules to govern the machine's internal operations. Although he didn't realize it at the time, these rules were simply a restatement, in his own notation, of the basic axioms of *Boolean algebra* (or *Boolean logic*), and they enabled him to harness his machine's binary components to useful ends. Boolean algebra, named after the English mathematician George Boole (1815–64), is a system of symbols and procedural rules for performing certain operations on numbers, letters, pictures, objects — whatever. (Leibniz inaugurated the search for such a system in his *De Arte Combinatoria*.) While this form of algebra may seem forbiddingly abstract, it's really not much more complicated than ordinary arithmetic. For example, just as the appearance of a times sign ( × ) between two numbers calls for a multiplication, the appearance of a Boolean symbol between two numbers, letters, or statements, also calls for the performance of a specified operation.

There are many operations in Boolean algebra but the three most basic are called AND, OR, and NOT. They are binary in nature, able to process only two different kinds of entities, and they, along with other Boolean operations, are often called *gates*, an apt metaphor for their functions. (Although Boole's system may be applied to any group of items, we'll confine our examples to binary numbers.) AND is a gate for 1s; if both numbers trying to slip through an AND gate are 1, AND requires the passing on of a single 1 to the next gate up the road. But any other combination of digits (two 0s or a 1 and a 0) will yield a 0. OR is a less selective sieve for 1s; if either of the numbers at its gates is 1, then OR will pass on a 1. As for NOT, it acts as an inverter, transforming any 1s or 0s that come knocking on its door into their opposites (a 1 into a 0 and vice versa).

Although Boolean algebra contains other operations, AND, OR, and NOT are all you — or a machine — need to add, subtract, multiply, divide, and perform other logical processes, such as comparing numbers or symbols. Given the binary character of Boolean gates, it's a relatively easy matter to engineer a binary calculator's components into patterns that mimic AND, OR, and NOT. Of course, nothing could have been further from Boole's mind than the idea of incorporating his system into a machine; yet the invention of the computer owes almost as much to Boole, a self-taught mathematician who never went to college, as to anyone else.

*George Boole (1815–1864), the founder of mathematical logic*

*These tables illustrate the outcome of every possible operation of NOT, AND, and OR. The contemporary symbols for the operations are below.*

**NOT**

| A | Ā |
|---|---|
| 0 | 1 |
| 1 | 0 |

**AND**

| A | B | A · B |
|---|---|-------|
| 0 | 0 | 0 |
| 0 | 1 | 0 |
| 1 | 0 | 0 |
| 1 | 1 | 1 |

**OR**

| A | B | A + B |
|---|---|-------|
| 0 | 0 | 0 |
| 0 | 1 | 1 |
| 1 | 0 | 1 |
| 1 | 1 | 1 |

A ───▷o─── Ā

A ─┐
B ─┘ )── A · B

A ─┐
B ─┘ )── A + B

*In the 1880s, Allan Marquand, a logician at Princeton University, built a machine that could solve syllogisms and other simple logical problems. The photo on the left shows the back of the device and the relatively simple mechanism that ran it.*

In two epochal works, *The Mathematical Analysis of Logic — Being an Essay Towards a Calculus of Deductive Reasoning* (1847) and *An Investigation of the Laws of Thought* (1854), Boole sought to identify the procedural rules of reasoning and to establish a rigorous system of logical analysis. Before the publication of these works, formal logic was a sleepy discipline with little to show for thousands of years of efforts. Its most powerful analytical tool was the syllogism, a form of deductive reasoning that proceeds from a major to a minor premise and then to a conclusion, as in "All men are mortal; all heroes are men; therefore all heroes are mortal" — not much to crow about. One of the most important results of Boole's work was the demise of logic as a philosophical discipline and its rebirth as a vigorous branch of mathematics.

Although most logicians criticized or ignored Boole's ideas, they were absorbed by a growing number of mathematicians, who refined and amplified them, and Boole was rewarded with a professorship at Queen's College, in Ireland. (Babbage, who knew a good idea when he saw one, wrote in the margin of his copy of *The Mathematical Analysis of Logic*, "This is the work of a real thinker.") And then, in 1910, the British logicians Alfred North Whitehead and Bertrand Russell published the first installment of their three-volume *Principia Mathematica* (1910–13), which transformed Boolean algebra into a formidable intellectual system known as *symbolic logic*. We'll explore Russell and Whitehead's ideas later in the book; for the moment, though, it's important to remember that the internal operations of computers are governed by Boolean algebra, and that Zuse, in his uncanny instinct for the heart of the matter, was the first to incorporate these rules into a calculating machine.


In the spring of 1935, Zuse graduated from the Technical College and went to work for the Henschel Aircraft Company, in Berlin, as a stress analyst. He spent most of his time composing and solving linear equations. Enough was enough, and he started building his first calculator in 1936, when he was twenty-six years old. (If linear equations were used for the analysis of static structures, why was Zuse fiddling with them in an aircraft plant? At certain high speeds, aircraft wings will flap in the wind like flags in a breeze. By considering wings as static structures and pinpointing their "resonant frequency" with linear equations, engineers can design wings that will be stable enough for any wind speeds a plane is likely to encounter.)

Zuse paid for his projects out of his own pocket and constructed the first two machines in the living room of his parents' apartment, with the help of a few close friends. His father was a post office clerk and didn't have much money, but Zuse's parents possessed a good deal of indulgent understanding; their son was obviously a rather original young man. While the world around him was going insane with Nazism, Zuse quietly submerged himself in his obsession, unaware of the work of like-minded engineers and scientists in the United States and Great Britain. He completed a prototype, later named the Z1, in 1938; a large jumble of moving plates, the machine was entirely mechanical and didn't work very well, but it got him started in the right direction.

À la Jacquard and Babbage, the Z1 was controlled by punched tape. Instead of the usual gears and axles, the memory consisted of thin, slotted metal plates, the position of a pin in a slot — whether on the left or the right — representing a 0 or a 1. The memory contained more than a thousand plates, all cut by hand out of metal sheets, and stored about the same number of binary digits. It was the cleverest part of the Z1 and it operated satisfactorily, which was more than could be said of the arithmetic unit. Although the binary multiplication table is simplicity itself ($0 \times 0 = 0$ and $1 \times 1 = 1$), Zuse never managed to get his mechanical arithmetic unit to carry and borrow efficiently or to link up well with the memory.

Confident of his design, Zuse set out to build a larger and

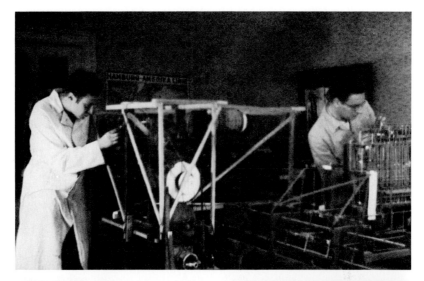

*The Z1 in the living room of Zuse's parents' apartment in Berlin. Helmut Schreyer is at left, Zuse on the right.*

more sophisticated calculator, the Z2. This machine was electromechanical. At the suggestion of Helmut Schreyer, an electrical engineer and Zuse's most imaginative collaborator, Zuse replaced the balky mechanical parts of the Z1's arithmetic unit with secondhand telephone relays. A relay is an on/off electromechanical switch. (Hollerith's tabulators and sorters used relays.) Once widely used in telephone-switching circuits, it consists of an electromagnet (a coil of wire wrapped around a spool) that closes an electrical circuit when the power is applied. The use of relays not only enabled Zuse to construct an arithmetic unit that could carry and borrow reliably, but one that operated rather fast, since relays can turn on and off hundreds of times a minute. Zuse linked the new arithmetic unit to the mechanical memory and, lo and behold, the whole thing worked, more or less.

If a calculator can be built out of relays, asked Schreyer, why not go one step further and make one out of vacuum tubes, which can switch on and off thousands of times a second? In the 1930s, tubes were used exclusively to amplify analog signals, like radio waves, and few people had thought of using them for digital applications — there weren't very many. In 1919, two English scientists invented a circuit known as flip-flop, a pair of tubes that acted as a switch; in response to a suitable signal, one of the tubes flipped on while the other flopped off. (The tubes didn't turn completely on or off but went into higher or lower states of energy; a cold tube can't be switched on quickly and the act of turning tubes on and off tended to burn them out.) However, tubes were expensive and hard to come by in Germany in the late 1930s, and Zuse, who felt more comfortable with mechanical gadgets anyway, decided to stick with relays.

In 1941, Schreyer received a doctorate for a thesis on the use of tubes as digital switches. But the advent of World War II cut Germany off from the United States and England, and his dissertation ended up gathering dust on a library shelf and had no effect on the history of computers.

In 1939, Germany invaded Poland. Zuse, who was twenty-nine, was drafted. Did the mighty German war machine embrace the promise of Zuse's calculator and, showering him with all the relays, tubes, and assistants he could use, proclaim: "Build us a computer with which Deutschland can bring the Allies to their knees?" Did Germany win the war? As Zuse recalled years later,

> In 1939, due to the perfectly private state of my workshop and due to the lack of official sponsorship, I became a soldier at the beginning of the war. The manufacturer, who assisted me [a calculator maker who partially financed Zuse's work], wrote a letter to my major requesting leave for me to complete my work on an important invention. He wrote that I was working on a machine useful for the calculations and designs in the aircraft industry. My major looked at this letter and said, "I don't understand that. The German aircraft is the best in the world. I don't see what to calculate further on." Half a year later, I was freed from military service, not for work on computers but as an engineer in the aircraft industry.

Back at Henschel, Zuse finished the Z2 in his spare time. Meanwhile, Schreyer, who had not been drafted, pursued his own calculator plans. He managed to obtain about 150 tubes from the Telefunken Company and, financed by the Aerodynamics Research Institute, a major research organization, constructed a sim-

ple machine that could convert three-digit decimal numbers into
binary numbers, and vice versa. In 1942, he submitted a proposal
for an electronic calculator to the German Army Command; the
computer would contain about 1,500 tubes and execute 10,000
operations a second. But Schreyer was turned down. Confident
that the war would be over within two or three years, the army
refused to fund any project that didn't promise to contribute immediately to the war effort.

Zuse also asked the Aerodynamics Research Institute for
help. The group wasn't interested in a *general-purpose* calculator — almost no one in Germany was — but it had an urgent computational problem that Zuse might be able to help them with.
The calculation of airplane wing flutter was tying up personnel
and other badly needed resources and delaying aircraft production. Zuse said that he could design a *special-purpose* calculator
to solve the necessary equations and asked for permission to
build a prototype; actually, he intended to devise a general-purpose machine that could handle wing flutter equations along with
other kinds of problems, and thereby prove that a general-purpose
device was the way to go. Commissioned by the institute, he established a fifteen-man company and the Z3, *the first operational
general-purpose program-controlled calculator*, was completed by
December 1941.

*Konrad Zuse, about 1982*

It was a small machine, consisting of a tape reader, an operator's console, and two cabinets packed with 2,600 relays. It had a
small memory, storing only sixty-four twenty-two-bit numbers,
but it was rather fast, multiplying two words in only three to five
seconds. In addition to the four basic operations of arithmetic, it
could find square roots and carry out other complicated tasks automatically. However, it couldn't execute conditional jumps. None
of Zuse's machines could; the idea never occurred to him. In a
typical program, the initial values were entered into the memory
by hand, an inconvenient method, and the ensuing operations
were guided by punched tape. The cost of this great experiment
in artificial computation? A mere $6,500 in materials.

By the way, the Z3 converted data into strings of twenty-
two bits, which it stored and processed as separate units. In modern terminology, these twenty-two bit strings are called *words*.
Word sizes vary from machine to machine; in many personal computers, for example, words contain sixteen bits.

Although the Z3 worked very well, the institute preferred
special-purpose machines. So Zuse built two special-purpose calculators to analyze the wing flutter of flying bombs. Installed at
Henschel, the machines were wired to carry out a fixed series of

calculations on the bombs as they came off the assembly lines, indicating how each weapon's wings should be adjusted. Despite their computational limitations, they proved to be quite efficient and the thirty women computers who had been employed to solve wing flutter equations with mechanical calculators were transferred to other jobs — a portent of the brave new world.

Henschel's flying bomb shouldn't be confused with the V-series of rocket bombs that Germany rained on Great Britain. Flying bombs were carried aloft by planes, released near their targets, and guided by radio signals from the aircraft. Fortunately, the bombs came along too late in the war to do much damage; beginning in August 1943, they were used against Allied ships in the Mediterranean and, two years later, against the Russians in the German retreat from Poland.

Encouraged by the success of the Z3, Zuse embarked on a larger version, the Z4. A faster and more powerful machine, it would process longer words — thirty-two bits as opposed to twenty-two — and possess a bigger memory — 512 thirty-two-bit numbers as compared to sixty-four. Yet by this time Berlin was coming apart at the seams. In 1944, British and American bombers were raiding the city almost daily, and Zuse's workshops were damaged repeatedly in the bombing. He was forced to move the Z4 three times; once, his building was hit as he and his workers were removing the precious Z4, and the historic Z3 was destroyed in an attack in April 1945.

In the closing months of the war, Zuse was permitted to leave Berlin. He and an assistant hauled the Z4 to Göttingen, and then, as the Allies rolled into Germany, they retreated to an underground fortification in the Harz Mountains. Their odyssey finally ended in Hopferau, a quiet village in the Bavarian Alps, where Zuse hid his cargo in the cellar of a farm building. When the Americans entered the area, army officers interrogated Zuse, inspected his machine, and concluded — correctly — that the Z4 was not a security risk. Zuse was allowed to go his way. In 1950, the Z4 was installed at a technical institute in Zurich, where it was the only mathematical calculator of any consequence in Continental Europe for several years. As for Zuse, he went on to establish a small computer company that was bought out by another firm in the early 1960s.

*The Z4 in Hopferau*

## CHAPTER 4

# The Invention of ENIAC

I explained what was to be done and pushed the button for it to be done. One of the first things I did was to add 5,000 numbers together. Seems a bit silly, but I told the press, "I am now going to add 5,000 numbers together" and pushed the button. The ENIAC added 5,000 numbers together in one second. The problem was finished before most of the reporters had looked up!

The main part of the demonstration was the trajectory. For this we chose a trajectory of a shell that took 30 seconds to go from the gun to its target. Remember that girls could compute this in three days, and the differential analyzer could do it in 30 minutes. The ENIAC calculated this 30-second trajectory in just 20 seconds, faster than the shell itself could fly!

*Arthur W. Burks, Who Invented the General-Purpose Electronic Computer?*

*Arthur Burks, a mathematician who helped design ENIAC, and an assistant set up a program on ENIAC.*

W hile Zuse, Schreyer, and friends were building their relay calculators, at least four other digital computer projects were underway in the United States, where the technological climate, not to mention political and financial conditions, was much more hospitable to experimentation. A totalitarian state like Nazi Germany may make important technical and scientific breakthroughs by marshaling men and materiel by fiat, and Zuse certainly accomplished a great deal on a shoestring budget and in the middle of a war, but the kind of sustained, concentrated development that was necessary for the invention of a large-scale electronic general-purpose digital computer depended upon the free intercourse of men, ideas, and capital.

The first of the American computing projects began in the fall of 1937, when George Stibitz, a young physicist at Bell Telephone Laboratories, then located in New York City, took a few telephone relays home "to start what I thought of as a play project." The son of a theology professor at a small college in Dayton, Ohio, Stibitz had shown an early talent for science and engineering, which led his parents to enroll him in an experimental high school that had been set up by a wealthy inventor with his own ideas about education. Stibitz attended Denison University, a small liberal arts college in Granville, Ohio, and Cornell University, where he earned a doctorate in mathematical physics.

At Bell, Stibitz was a member of a group of mathematicians who designed relay switching equipment — the same kind of on/off electromechanical switches that Zuse employed in his calculators. Bell scientists had long been aware of the similarity between the action of these humble devices and the zeros and ones of binary math, but it had never occurred to them that relays could also be used to perform symbolic logic — until the inquisitive Stibitz came along. "I had observed," Stibitz recalled thirty years later, "the similarity between the circuit paths through relays and the binary notation for numbers and had an idea I wanted to work out. . . .

*George Stibitz in 1984*

> That weekend I fastened two of the relays to a board, cut strips from a tobacco can and nailed them to the board for input; bought a dry cell and a few flashlight bulbs for output, and wired up a binary adder. I wired the relays to give the binary digits of the sum of two one-digit binary numbers, which were entered into the arithmetic unit by pressing switches made of the metal strips. The two-flashlight-bulb output lighted up to indicate a binary 1 and remained dark for binary 0.
>
>   I took my model into the labs to show to some of the boys, and we were all more amused than impressed with some visions of a binary computer industry. I have no head for history. I did not know I was picking up where Charles Babbage in England had to quit over a hundred years before. Nor did it occur to me that my work would turn out to be part of the beginning of what we now know as the computer age. So, unfortunately, there were no fireworks, no champagne.

Having built an adder, Stibitz designed more sophisticated circuits that could subtract, multiply, and divide. Although his work was quite original and, unlike most "play projects," actually resulted in the construction of something useful, Stibitz wasn't the only American who noticed the correspondence between ordinary relays, binary math, and symbolic logic.

In 1938, Claude E. Shannon, a student of Bush's at MIT, published a groundbreaking paper on the application of symbolic logic to relay circuits. Shannon had a part-time job tending the differential analyzer, which contained some relays, and Bush, who had a knack for inspiring his students and colleagues, suggested that a study of the logical organization of these circuits might make a fruitful subject for a thesis. Shannon's thesis not only helped transform circuit design from an art into a science, but its underlying message — that information can be treated like any other quantity and be subjected to the manipulation of a machine — had a profound effect on the first generation of computer pioneers. However, Stibitz had already worked out most of the circuits for a relay calculator by the time Shannon's paper appeared.

Incidentally, Shannon, whose master's thesis was one of the most influential ever written, joined Bell Labs after graduating from MIT, where he went on to do seminal work in the esoteric discipline of information theory.

A few months after Stibitz built the "kitchen adder," his boss at Bell Labs, Dr. T. C. Fry, asked him whether he could design a relay calculator for complex arithmetic. There was a group at Bell that designed noise filters and amplifying circuits for long-distance telephone lines, work that required the solution of innumerable algebraic equations with *complex numbers*. (A complex number is a mathematical expression written as the sum of two real numbers, one of which is multiplied by the square root of $-1$, as in $a + b\sqrt{-1}$.) In the late 1930s, when the Bell System was busy designing coast-to-coast phone lines, the organization employed a small team of women computers who, using ordinary desk calculators, solved the complex algebraic equations produced by the filter and amplifier design group.

Needless to say, the computational process left much to be desired and Bell Labs was willing to try another approach. So Fry introduced Stibitz to a consummate switching engineer named

*A replica of the binary adder Stibitz built on his kitchen table*

Samuel B. Williams, and Stibitz and Williams designed a "complex number calculator." Lab officials gave the go-ahead, and the Model I, as the machine came to be called, was constructed between April and October 1939 at a cost of about $20,000.

It consisted of two units: a panel containing about 400 to 450 relays, which performed the computations, and a teletype, outfitted with a special keyboard, which was used to enter mathematical problems and to record the answers. It could add two eight-digit decimal numbers in a tenth of a second and multiply two equally large numbers in about a minute. While the Model I wasn't very fast at multiplication or division — a skilled human computer with an electromechanical desk calculator could equal if not outpace it — the machine was highly reliable and very easy to use. Moreover, you didn't have to be in the same room to operate it; since the teletype was connected to the panel by cable, you could use the Model I from any point in the phone system. In September 1940, Bell Labs installed a few teletypes at Dartmouth College in Hanover, New Hampshire, for the annual meeting of the American Mathematical Society, linking them through the phone lines to the Model I in Manhattan. The machine operated flawlessly and everyone was quite impressed.

Although the Model I was a useful and impressive achievement, it wasn't a very sophisticated machine. Certainly, Zuse had accomplished much more with much less. In the first place, the Model I was not programmable, which meant, of course, that it couldn't execute conditional jumps; you typed in an equation and the machine printed out an answer. In the second, it was not a general-purpose calculator; it was permanently wired, or *hardwired*, in the jargon of electronics, to perform a given set of operations and couldn't do anything else. In the third, it did not have a memory, a central processing unit, or a clearly defined control unit. Lastly, it could be used by only one person at a time, despite its capacity for *remote*, or long-distance, computing.

Since Bell Labs wasn't in the calculator business, its interest in the Model I faded away. With the coming of World War II, however, the Labs devoted its considerable resources to the war effort, and Stibitz and Williams designed four program-controlled relay calculators for the military. Three of these machines were devoted to special chores (for instance, the Model II helped test the accuracy of a gun director), but the Model V, completed in 1946, was a general-purpose calculator in the same league as the Z4. It was, conceptually and structurally, a fairly advanced machine. Programmed by paper tape, it contained a small memory, a central processor, and a control unit. The Model V, which cost

*The calculating unit of the Model I*

$500,000 — twenty-five times the price of the Model I — provided yeoman mathematical service for more than a decade. Yet it was a technological dead letter from the moment it appeared, outmoded by the electronic digital computer.

*The Model I took its instructions from any of three modified teletypes, although it could be used by only one person at a time.*

Another well-publicized American calculator project began in 1937 at Harvard University, where Howard H. Aiken, an instructor in applied mathematics, drew up a proposal for an electromechanical calculator. Aiken's idea was to make a general-purpose calculator by modifying standard punch card tabulators and sorters and ganging them together. He first approached the Monroe Calculating Machine Company for financial backing but the firm turned him down (and, like every calculator manufacturer with the exceptions of Burroughs and the National Cash Register Company, which entered the computer business in the 1950s, eventually slipped into a commercial backwater). Then, in 1939, with the help of a Harvard business professor who had contacts at IBM, Aiken met Thomas Watson, the firm's president, and IBM agreed to back him.

Aiken's computational motivations resembled Zuse's. As a graduate student in engineering at Harvard, he had toiled over differential equations for hours on end, frustrated not by the numerical methods that were used to solve the equations but by the sheer volume of the figuring, which made the solution of certain especially complicated problems well-nigh impossible. The more Aiken pondered the nature of computation, the more he became convinced that the job could be performed by machines. Unlike most of the early computer pioneers, Aiken had heard of Babbage, and his proposal contained a brief, if rather inaccurate, summary of the Englishman's work. Aiken saw himself as Babbage's spiritual heir, yet his machine, the Automatic Sequence-Controlled Calculator (ASCC), or Harvard Mark I, had little in common with the Analytical Engine.

An ambitious, driven, blunt-spoken man, Aiken had grown up in Indianapolis, Indiana, where, interested in things electrical and mechanical, he attended a technical high school. As a boy, he was as much of an inveterate tinkerer as any of the other computer pioneers. At the University of Wisconsin at Madison, he majored in electrical engineering and worked part-time as an engineer for the local power company. Then he joined the Westinghouse Electrical Manufacturing Company; but, after more than ten years at Westinghouse, he decided to return to academia, first as a

*Howard Aiken (second from right) and the IBM engineers who designed the Mark I (from left): Francis E. Hamilton, Clair D. Lake, and Benjamin M. Durfee*

graduate student at the University of Chicago and later at Harvard. So, even though he was only an instructor when he met Watson, Aiken was a mature engineer with a lot of practical experience.

Fortunately, Watson was interested in the application of IBM equipment for scientific purposes. In 1934, he had established a computing center at Columbia University to experiment with IBM machines in astronomy, statistics, and other fields. (Rather grandiosely, the center was called the Thomas J. Watson Astronomical Computing Bureau.) Science wasn't big business in the 1930s, and most university laboratories considered themselves lucky to have a few good electromechanical calculators, let alone IBM's costly devices. Although Watson doubted that the scientific market would ever constitute an important source of revenue, he was impressed with Aiken's proposal and wanted to keep at least one of IBM's fingers in the scientific pie. Therefore, he decided to build the machine, in accordance with Aiken's general plan but under the direction of his own engineers, at an IBM plant in Endicott, New York.

Completed in January 1943, the Mark I was an impressive sight. It was eight feet tall, fifty-one feet long, and two feet thick, weighed five tons, used about 750,000 parts, and according to the

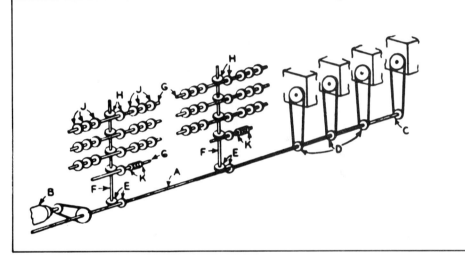

The Mark I was built at an IBM plant in New York and assembled at Harvard University (top and bottom). The machine was driven by a long metal shaft (A in the diagram) powered by a small electric motor (B). The operation of the shaft was governed by a main sequence-control mechanism (C) and three lesser ones (D). The sequence-control unit read the paper tape and turned the shafts accordingly.

Above: The Mark I, a sleek and impressive-looking piece of machinery

The sequence-control mechanism

physicist Jeremy Bernstein, sounded "like a roomful of ladies knitting." At Watson's insistence — he had a keen eye for public relations — the Mark I was encased in a shiny stainless steel and glass skin that gave the machine a snazzy sci-fi look and left a strong impression on the public, which got its first glimpse of the this new mechanical wonder in August 1944; the future was here, courtesy of IBM. To a public unaware of Zuse, the Mark I was regarded as a great achievement — the first program-controlled calculator. And in a way it was a great achievement, for IBM and Aiken had managed to give life to Babbage's dream.

But beauty is only skin deep, and like Stibitz and Williams's Model V, the Mark I was obsolete the moment it was born. It was really a giant mechanical calculator, based on the decimal system, unable to perform conditional jumps, and filled with the usual mechanical gewgaws. Still, it was quite ingenious, a clever combination of old technology and new wit. An electric motor turned a metal shaft that ran the length of the machine. When a number was entered via the paper tape input unit, a clutch coupled one of the Mark I's three thousand number wheels to the shaft for a specified time span, turning the wheel to one of ten positions. When an addition was called for, the appropriate clutch was engaged, the associated number wheels were rotated, and any carries were relayed to the next number wheel. Instead of the centralized structure that Babbage had given the Analytical Engine, the Mark I's functions were distributed all over the machine, mostly in seventy-two accumulators, packed with number wheels, that served as memories, adders, and subtractors. Other units performed multiplication and division.

Even though IBM and Aiken had driven into a technological dead end, the Mark I was a powerful computational tool. For example, it could multiply two twenty-three-digit decimal numbers in three seconds and produce the answer on punch cards.

Since it could handle basic arithmetic operations quite easily, it was particularly well suited for the calculation of mathematical tables, which became its chief occupation for most of its sixteen-year life span. By the time the Mark I appeared, however, ENIAC was nearing completion in secrecy at the University of Pennsylvania, and the Mark I, along with the three Mark-type calculators that Aiken constructed over the next eight years, had little influence on the development of computers. The Mark I had cost an enormous amount of money — $500,000, two-thirds from IBM and the remainder from the U.S. Navy, which had requisitioned it for the war — but it wasn't a very good investment. The future lay in another direction.

*A spiderweb of pulleys fed the paper tape into the sequence-control mechanism and the Mark I's other tape readers.*

The Moore School of Electrical Engineering occupies a boxy three-story brick building on the sprawling campus of the University of Pennsylvania. A former musical instrument factory, the building was taken over by the university in 1926, and it was there, in a large room on the ground floor, that ENIAC was built. Compared to most engineering schools, the Moore School was rather young, having been founded in 1923 with a bequest from a wealthy Philadelphia industrialist, Albert Fitler Moore, whose family had made a fortune manufacturing wire stays for bonnets and hoop skirts. (The Massachusetts Institute of Technology, the dean of American engineering schools, was established in 1861.) Under Dean Harold Pender, the Moore School assembled a bright and aggressive faculty — academic entrepreneurs, as one of its professors called the group — who were determined to raise the institution to the top ranks of American engineering schools.

Aside from MIT, Penn was the only university in the country with a differential analyzer. In 1934, the Moore School, convinced that such a machine was necessary for further advances in

*In the late 1940s, Aiken built a much larger and more sophisticated electromechanical calculator, the Mark II, for the Navy. But the machine, installed at the Naval Proving Ground in Dahlgren, Virginia, in September 1948 was outmoded by the invention of ENIAC and the stored-program computer.*

electrical engineering, constructed an analyzer under Vannevar Bush's direction. Unlike the MIT model, which was privately financed, Penn's machine was paid for by the government. The War Department endorsed the project (and the Civil Works Administration, one of Roosevelt's alphabet agencies, picked up the tab) on the condition that the new analyzer's plans be used to build a sister machine for the Aberdeen Proving Ground, in Maryland, which was run by the Army's Ordnance Department. The agreement, reached at a time when few military-university contracts existed, forged a link between the Moore School and the Ordnance Department that paved the way for the development of ENIAC.

When the United States entered the war, the Ordnance Department enlarged its staff at Aberdeen. In short order, the department's Ballistic Research Laboratory (BRL) trained about one hundred human computers, mostly women college graduates with an aptitude for math, to calculate ballistic firing tables, which gave gunners the necessary information to aim their weapons properly. At first, the Aberdeen computers, who used the differential analyzer and ordinary desk calculators, were sufficient for the workload. But as war production mushroomed and growing numbers of new guns left the factories, the BRL began to fall behind schedule. In an effort to catch up, it established a computing substation at the Moore School. It requisitioned the Moore School's analyzer and gave the school another contract, this one to recruit and train another hundred computers. Yet the BRL still couldn't keep up with the demand for new firing tables. Since a gun without a firing table is almost as useless as a computer without a program, the situation was quite alarming.

In order to hit a target, a gunner must aim his or her weapon in the right direction and raise the barrel to the proper angle. Many factors go into the second decision, the most important being the range and altitude of the target. Other variables, such as air temperature and wind speed, also must be taken into account. Since a gunner can't very well sit down on the battlefield and figure out the differential equations indicating the right angle of fire, the army thoughtfully provides a pamphlet — a firing table — listing all the relevant factors and showing the correct angle of fire for a given shell in a given gun. The gunner looks up the information in the table, aims the barrel, and fires away.

Before the invention of the digital electronic computer, these tables were terribly difficult to make. For only the most basic factors, altitude and range, the BRL had to calculate approximately *two to four thousand trajectories for each pair of projectile and gun.* And that was only the beginning, since a table for a typical gun like the 155-mm. Long Tom involved many other factors. In general, the BRL computed the basic factors on a differential analyzer, which could calculate a single trajectory in fifteen to thirty minutes but required one or two hours of set-up time per table. Since it wasn't practical to readjust the analyzer every time a new variable had to be calculated, the bulk of the BRL's work was relegated to human computers. (Remember, the analyzer was an analog computer, and its gears and rods had to be rearranged whenever a new equation was processed.) A skilled human computer, using an electromechanical desk calculator, took about three days to calculate a single trajectory, and the BRL as a whole

*The Moore School today*

needed a couple of months to compile a comprehensive table.

By 1943, the BRL was dangerously behind schedule. "In the specific case of sidewise firing from airplanes," wrote Professor John Grist Brainerd, the Moore School's director of war research, in a secret memo to Dean Pender, "construction of directors for guns has been held up several months because it has been a physical impossibility to supply to the manufacturers the necessary ballistic data." Under the circumstances, the BRL was willing to do almost anything to alleviate the crisis, including spending half a million dollars for the construction of a revolutionary electronic calculator at the Moore School. ENIAC was not the product of a scientist or engineer's frustration with solving equations with mechanical calculators, but of a military imperative during a national crisis.

The third American calculator project began, appropriately enough for an invention conceived in academia, with a memo. Written in August 1942 by John W. Mauchly, a thirty-five-year-old assistant professor at the Moore School, it was entitled "The Use of High Speed Vacuum Tube Devices for Calculating." A physicist turned engineer, Mauchly (Mawk-ly) proposed the construction of an "electronic calculator" or "electronic computor" (his spelling) consisting of vacuum tubes pulsing at the rate of at least 100,000 beats a second. Estimating the machine's computational speed at 1,000 multiplications a second, he explained that it would be able to compute a single trajectory in 100 seconds. Such a calculator would not only outrun the vaunted differential analyzer but, Mauchly wrote, also would be much easier to use and considerably more accurate.

Today, Mauchly's memo, which was submitted to the Ordnance Department and to the Moore School, makes for rather odd reading. Considering that it resulted in the development of the first general-purpose electronic digital program-controlled calculator, it is surprisingly poorly written and organized, and conceptually unsophisticated. The bulk of the document is devoted to a discussion of the potential speeds of electronic calculation. (Ironically, the figures Mauchly supplies — 1,000 multiplications per second, for example — turned out to be three times too high.) Yet, although he *was not* the first American to conceive of a calculator built out of tubes (we'll examine this point later in the chapter), Mauchly was one of the first to realize that an electronic calculator would be capable of tens of thousands of operations a second. While many other crucial matters, such as the device's internal structure, weren't even mentioned, it wasn't because Mauchly didn't have any ideas on the matter. Rather, it was because he wasn't thinking of a computer but of an old-fashioned calculator that happened to be made of tubes:

> As already stated, the electronic computor utilizes the principle of counting to achieve its results. It is then in every sense the electrical analogue of the mechanical adding, multiplying and dividing machines which are now manufactured for ordinary arithmetic purposes. . . . It is intended that this analogy shall be interpreted rather completely. In particular, just as the ordinary computing machine utilizes the decimal system in performing its calculations, so does the electronic device.

At the time Mauchly submitted his memo, the production of firing tables was still keeping pace with the output of new guns and an electronic calculator seemed unnecessary. As a result Mauchly's proposal was ignored. But the situation changed about half a year later, when the BRL began falling behind. In March 1943, Herman H. Goldstine, the lieutenant in charge of the BRL's computing substation at the Moore School, learned of Mauchly's ideas during a casual conversation with one of the mechanics who watched over the school's analyzer. Goldstine went to see Mauchly; Mauchly couldn't find a copy of his memo but his secretary managed to reconstruct one from her notes. Goldstine, who had been an assistant professor of mathematics at the University of Michigan before the war, immediately grasped the memo's significance and asked the Moore School to submit a thorough proposal for an electronic calculator.

In response, John Brainerd, working with Mauchly and J. Presper Eckert, Jr., a brilliant young electronics engineer who had often discussed the feasibility of an electronic calculator with Mauchly, wrote a proposal and handed it in to the BRL on 2 April 1943. Negotiations moved very quickly. Within six weeks, the Moore School and the BRL reached an oral agreement on the terms of a contract and, on 5 June, the two parties signed on the dotted line. The Moore School would receive $61,700 immediately and another $88,300 after certain technical hurdles had been passed. Brainerd was appointed project supervisor; Eckert the chief engineer; Mauchly, who continued to carry a full load of classes, the principal consultant; and Goldstine the BRL's technical liaison.

*John William Mauchly, about 1970*

A convivial but nervous man, a chain smoker who consumed two or three packs of cigarettes a day, Mauchly inherited his love of science from his father, a physicist at the Carnegie Institution in Chevy Chase, Maryland. As a boy, he often visited his father's laboratory, fiddling with the apparatus and puzzling over the lab's records. At Johns Hopkins University, Mauchly started out as an engineering major — he liked to work with his hands — but he also enjoyed the theoretical side of science and soon switched to physics, specifically molecular spectroscopy. But the field didn't quite prove to his taste; he spent most of his time working with an instrument called a mass spectroscope, identifying razor-thin spectral lines, generated by the thousands on photographic plates by heated substances, and analyzing the findings with the help of a desk calculator.

In 1932, he became an assistant professor of physics at Ursinus College, a small private school about twenty-five miles west of Philadelphia. At Ursinus, which lacked the elaborate scientific equipment of Johns Hopkins, Mauchly's interests gradually shifted from spectroscopy to statistics, to meteorology, and finally to artificial computation. In 1936, he decided to see whether the voluminous records of atmospheric observations at the Carnegie Institution could shed some light on a major meteorological debate, one that continues to this day: do sunspots influence the weather, and if so, how? With funds from the National Youth Administration, one of FDR's employment agencies, Mauchly hired a small team of students to help him sift through the institute's material.

After a while, Mauchly realized that it would take an eternity to collate the records by hand. Even if he could afford to lease a dozen punch card tabulators and sorters, the job would obviously take years. Then he got an idea — one of those astonishingly simple ideas that lay at the heart of scientific revolutions.

At about the time he began his sunspot project, physicists had succeeded in developing electronic devices that could count cosmic rays. For years, the technical stumbling block to the invention of these machines had been the lack of recorders that could keep track of hundreds of cosmic events a second; at the time, most recorders were electromechanical, unable to register more than five hundred events a minute. Since there was only so much you could do to improve the performance of the recorders, physicists attacked the problem through the back door with "scaling circuits" that cut down on the number of pulses sent to the recorders. When, say, eight events struck the sensors, the first set of circuits dispatched four electrical pulses to the second set, which sent two pulses to the third ring, which in turn issued a single pulse to the recorder.

Mauchly wondered whether these circuits could be used to make a high-speed electronic calculator of some kind. He fashioned simple versions of the circuits and, by 1940, became convinced that they could do the job. (Actually, they couldn't, but what he didn't know at the time didn't hurt him.) Unfortunately, he lacked the engineering skills and the money to proceed. Moreover, he tended to believe, along with most scientists at the time, that analog computing methods were more promising than digital ones; Bush's differential analyzer had had quite an impact on the scientific community. Accordingly, Mauchly concentrated on analog machines, building, among other things, an analog electrical system for solving certain mathematical problems (Fourier equations) and a harmonic analyzer for studying meteorological phenomena.

In December 1940, Mauchly delivered a paper on his analyzer at a meeting of the American Association for the Advancement of Science in Philadelphia. One of the scientists in the audience was a physicist by the name of John V. Atanasoff. A professor at Iowa State College, Atanasoff also had been thinking about the potential of electronic computation. In fact, he was building a small special-purpose digital electronic calculator (which he called a computer or computing machine) that could solve simultaneous linear equations (such as $x + y = 12$;

$2x - \dfrac{y}{z} = 14$). Glad to have met someone who shared his interests, Atanasoff introduced himself. He told Mauchly about his work and invited him to Ames, Iowa, to see his invention. The two men corresponded over the next few months, and in June 1941, Mauchly drove to Ames.

Mauchly spent about five days in Iowa. The day after he arrived, Atanasoff took him to his laboratory to see his calculator, which was still under construction. About as big as a large desk, the machine was covered with a sheet. Atanasoff removed the cover, pointed out the various parts of the gadget, and explained what they did. Although Mauchly spent only a short time in the lab that day — it was a Sunday — he saw the device several times that week, either in the company of Atanasoff or his assistant, Clifford Berry, a talented graduate student in electrical engineering. Mauchly and Atanasoff spent most of their time talking about electronic computing. Atanasoff also showed Mauchly a paper he had written the previous summer about the machine, an extraordinary document that was practically a step-by-step blueprint for the construction of an electronic calculator.

The paper, entitled "Computing Machine for the Solution of Large Systems of Linear Algebraic Equations," was really a grant proposal. Beginning with a discussion of the calculator's many applications, it contains an exhaustive description of the device, right down to the wiring diagrams. In brief, Atanasoff was trying to build a digital electronic calculator founded on binary math and Boolean algebra, using arithmetic units made of vacuum tubes; a memory composed of condensers (now called capacitors, which can store electrical charges); and an input and output system based on punch cards. Atanasoff's goal was a machine that could solve up to twenty-nine simultaneous linear equations at a time — which would have made it quite useful. Moreover, Atanasoff had come to realize that, with some modification, his invention could even be used to solve differential equations and, therefore, calculate firing tables, an idea that Mauchly found particularly intriguing.

Like Mauchly, Atanasoff inherited his passion for science from his father, an electrical engineer who had emigrated to the United States from Bulgaria in the late 1800s. The oldest of ten children, Atanasoff grew up in Florida, where his father worked for a phosphate mine near Lakeland. In 1913, when Atanasoff was nine, his father loaned him his slide rule and gave him a few tips on how to use it. For the most part, however, Atanasoff was left to his own devices. Guided by an instruction booklet that came with the rule and a college algebra text that belonged to his father, he learned how to use the rule to perform fairly complicated mathematical operations, including the calculation of logarithms. That

*John V. Atanasoff, in a photo taken at Iowa State University in 1981.*

rule was the beginning of his lifelong interest in artificial computation.

By the time he went to college, Atanasoff had decided to become a theoretical physicist. But the physics program at the University of Florida in Gainesville wasn't particularly good at the time, so he switched to the next best thing on the curriculum, electrical engineering. After Gainesville, he took a master's in physics from Iowa State and a doctorate from the University of Wisconsin at Madison. His thesis was on the electrical properties of helium (which isn't an electrical conductor but can, under certain circumstances, sustain an electrical field); his work was intensively mathematical, and he spent weeks toiling over equations, with only a desk calculator for help. Iowa State offered him an assistant professorship in math and physics and, at twenty-seven, Atanasoff became what he had always wanted to be, a theoretical physicist.

His interest in electronic calculation developed slowly. Over the years, Atanasoff experimented with various mechanical and theoretical methods of solving complex mathematical problems. The statistics department at Iowa State had an IBM tabulator and other calculating equipment, and Atanasoff and a colleague managed to get the machines to solve a problem in spectral analysis (Mauchly's line of work). In the course of his teaching and research, Atanasoff also did a lot of work in differential equations, solutions for which could be obtained, in a roundabout way, with linear algebraic equations. This common bit of mathe-

matical knowledge led Atanasoff, who knew a great deal about electronics, to ponder the possibility of building an electronic calculator that could solve these equations.

By 1937, he had a good idea of the kind of machine he wanted to build, and he fleshed out the details over the next two years. He had an engineer's instinct for the heart of the matter that was almost as good (or as good) as Zuse's and their overall technical approach was quite similar. In early 1939, therefore, Atanasoff was ready to proceed. On the basis of a preliminary proposal, he obtained a $650 grant from Iowa State in the summer. He hired Berry in August or September, and they managed to finish a small prototype one or two months later, a crude device that could add and subtract sixteen-digit binary numbers (the equivalents of eight-digit decimal figures). It operated well and, although it was only a test-bed, was *the first machine to calculate with vacuum tubes.*

Pleased with his work and certain of success, Atanasoff wrote a detailed grant proposal (the one he showed Mauchly) in the summer of 1940, requesting another $5,000. (He had received about $1,500 from Iowa State and other sources so far.) And it was at this point in the project, while the machine was half completed and Atanasoff was trying to raise more money, that Mauchly visited Ames. The money came through several months later, and Atanasoff and Berry completed the machine in the spring of 1942. At the time, Atanasoff called his invention simply a computing machine, but, years later, he decided to give it a catchier name — the ABC, for Atanasoff-Berry Computer.

A top view of the completed machine, showing a memory drum (center, rear); the card readers (the metal trays at left); and the control console (upper right)

The ABC was about the size of a large desk. All of its parts were mounted on a metal frame. The operator's control console, which contained numerous switches, buttons, meters, and lights, was on top. The addition and subtraction unit, which contained two hundred and ten tubes, lay under the console, with another bank of thirty tubes, which controlled the card reader and puncher, occupying the space next to the addition and subtraction unit. There was a punch card reader and puncher next to the console, within easy reach of the operator, and, behind the card units, the most interesting part of the ABC — two rotating drums that served as the memory. These drums were primitive versions of the rotating drum memories that appeared in the computers of the late 1940s and early 1950s. About twelve inches long and six inches in diameter, each drum could store thirty fifty-bit numbers (the equivalent of a fifteen-digit decimal number) in condensers set into their skins. Another thirty tubes helped maintain the charges stored in the condensers, which tended to drain away.

Except for the binary-card puncher, a rather complicated piece of equipment that created holes electrically rather than mechanically, burning them in, everything worked perfectly. The card puncher failed about once every hundred thousand times, which may not seem particularly serious — after all, it worked more than 99 percent of the time — but it prevented the ABC from solving large sets of linear equations. These equations used a veritable ocean of binary numbers, and any malfunction in the puncher meant that the numbers entering and exiting the ABC were sometimes wrong. Atanasoff and Berry tried to exorcise the

*Top: The memory drums*

*Bottom: A frontal shot of the completed machine. The operator's console is on the upper right, and the broad bank of tubes under the console is the addition-subtraction unit. The narrow bank of tubes on the left controls the card reader and puncher.*

puncher's bugs, experimenting, for example, with cards made of different materials; but they failed, and the machine could never solve more than a few simultaneous equations. Nevertheless, Atanasoff and Berry had built a working special-purpose digital electronic calculator, and their achievement was historic.

The ABC had several other shortcomings, the foremost being its lack of programmability and automaticity. Although it could carry out some operations on its own, it was controlled almost every step of the way by the operator, who stood at the console, pressing buttons, turning knobs, watching meters, and inserting and removing the punch cards. Like a car, the ABC needed a driver. In this respect, Zuse's machines were much more sophisticated — they were programmable and automatic. The ABC also lacked a central processor, the machine's arithmetic tasks being handled chiefly by thirty independent sets of tubes in the addition and subtraction units. Although this arrangement limited the ABC's flexibility, it wasn't necessarily a major drawback, because the machine was designed to solve only linear equations.

Finally, the ABC was painfully slow. Constrained by limited financial and technical resources, Atanasoff took a conservative approach to the ABC's design, combining a high-speed electronic arithmetic unit with a much slower, and quite inexpensive, set of memory drums and card readers and punchers. As a result, he couldn't capitalize on the potential speeds of a fully electronic machine — speeds that would have catapulted his invention into a transcendent technological realm — and he was forced to set the ABC's internal clock, the timer that regulated its operations, at a mere sixty pulses a second, which enabled the ABC to add two fifty-bit numbers a second. By contrast, ENIAC ran at a speed of 100,000 beats a second and could add 5,000 ten-digit decimal numbers, each containing about twenty bits, in the same amount of time.

Before leaving for Iowa, Mauchly had applied for a special six-week summer course at the University of Pennsylvania. With war on the horizon, the army was sponsoring special defense training classes at universities around the country, seeking to recruit engineers, teachers, and other people for managerial positions in the military and industry. The program, with its emphasis on electronics, was ideal for Mauchly, who had been hoping to leave Ursinus for a higher-paying job in industry; unfortunately, he lacked sufficient skill in electronics to attract any offers. He was accepted into the program and did quite well — well enough for the Moore School to offer him a job as an instructor.

Meanwhile, Mauchly continued to correspond with Atanasoff. On 30 September 1941 — about a year before he composed the ENIAC memo — he wrote his friend:

> As time goes on, I expect to get a first-hand knowledge of the operation of the differential analyzer — I have already spent a bit of time watching the process of setting up and operating the thing — and with this background I hope I can outdo the analyzer electronically.
>
> A number of different ideas have come to me anent computing circuits — some of which are more or less hybrids, combining your methods with other things, and some of which are nothing like your machine. The question in my mind is this: Is there any objection, from your point of view, to my building some sort of computer which incorporates some of the features of your machine? For the time being, of course, I shall be lucky to find time and material to do more than merely make exploratory tests of some of my different ideas, with the hope of getting something very speedy, not too costly, etc.
>
> Ultimately, a second question might come up, of course, and that is, in the event that your present design were to hold the field against all challengers, and I got the Moore School interested in having something of the sort, would the way be open for us to build an *"Atanasoff Calculator"* (à la *Bush* analyzer) here?

In reply, Atanasoff asked Mauchly to keep his work confidential until his attorney had filed a patent application. He and Iowa State had agreed to share the expense of patenting the invention and to split any profits, with a small percentage going to Berry. Atanasoff had hired a Chicago patent attorney, Richard R. Trexler, and had sent him the necessary technical information.

In another letter, Mauchly invited Atanasoff to stay with him during his next trip to the East Coast. But war broke out that December — the Japanese attacked Pearl Harbor — and Atanasoff and Berry went winging off in different directions. Berry married Atanasoff's secretary and joined an engineering firm in California that July. Two months later, Atanasoff went to work for the Naval Ordnance Laboratory in Maryland and was put in charge of an underwater mine-testing program. Incredibly, Trexler, who had not considered Atanasoff's information adequate, even though Atanasoff and Berry had showered him with material, never applied for a patent. Neither he nor Iowa State, which neglected to give him the permission to proceed, grasped the significance of

Atanasoff's work. In fact, even Atanasoff himself failed to understand the importance of his invention and, caught up in the war, eventually let the matter drop. As for the ABC? It was disassembled in 1948.

But Atanasoff's work lived on through Mauchly. As a student at the Moore School, Mauchly became friends with J. Presper Eckert, Jr., then a graduate student in charge of the student laboratories. In his early twenties, Eckert was a gifted electronics engineer, and by all accounts the Moore School's best. He was a born engineer; as a teenager at Penn Charter Academy, a prestigious private school outside Philadelphia, Eckert had built a powerful sound system with advanced features that didn't show up in commercial amplifiers until years later. He was a brash, confident, no-nonsense young man who had graduated near the top of his class at the Moore School in 1941 and who had won a two-year fellowship to study for his master's.

Mauchly spent many hours with Eckert discussing his ideas on computing — ideas that centered on the construction of a high-speed electronic calculator. Eckert, who was familiar with the differential analyzer and who was involved in several military and industrial projects, readily grasped the need for a high-speed calculator and saw no technical barrier to its construction. Mauchly also told him about Atanasoff's work, and Eckert suggested changes and improvements in Atanasoff's design, recommending, for instance, that the memory be built out of tubes instead of condensers, which would, in a large high-speed machine, require a lot of supporting equipment. As a result of these discussions and his knowledge of Atanasoff's achievements, Mauchly was inspired to write the memo that led to ENIAC.

Project PX, as the military called the classified ENIAC effort, started in June 1943. From the beginning, the group's managers and engineers were under terrific pressure. Not only were their reputations, and the reputation of the Moore School, at stake, but the BRL was falling increasingly behind the demand for firing tables. By the summer of 1944, the situation had become hopeless; the BRL was incapable of producing more than about fifteen tables a week, yet the number of tabular requests had reached forty a week. Mauchly, Eckert, and the project's other engineers (about a dozen men altogether) were keenly aware of ENIAC's importance to the war effort. Moreover, every one of them had friends or relatives in the army, and the contrast between safe, cozy Philadelphia and the front was not lost on them. They worked long, hard, and brilliantly, and emerged from their corner of the war with distinction.

The general nature of ENIAC had been determined long before the project began. As Mauchly, inspired by Atanasoff, had written in his memo, the machine was to be "in every sense the electrical analogue" of a mechanical calculator. That meant that ENIAC would be a decimal, not binary, machine. Instead of a general-purpose central processor, it would carry out arithmetic operations in various separate units — accumulators, multipliers, and the like. And instead of a separate general-purpose memory, it would store numbers in the accumulators as well as in a couple of external, or peripheral, units (a conventional punch card reader and three specially designed "function tables" that held mathematical constants in large banks of numbered switches).

Mauchly apparently borrowed several technical ideas from Atanasoff, the most important being the all-important notion of using tubes as switches. Another was the idea of synchronizing ENIAC's internal operations with an electronic timer, whose

*ENIAC was unveiled to the public at a news conference on 14 February 1946, and the men responsible for the project gathered for a group photo. Left to right: J. Presper Eckert, Jr.; John Grist Brainerd; Sam Feltman, chief engineer for ballistics, Army Ordnance; Herman H. Goldstine; John W. Mauchly; Harold Pender; Major General G. L. Barnes, chief of Army Ordnance; Colonel Paul N. Gillon, chief of the Research Branch of Army Ordnance.*

pulses acted as a drummer that kept the machine's many simultaneous operations marching in step. At the same time, however, he (and Eckert) ignored some of Atanasoff's best ideas, eschewing, for example, a careful division between the ABC's memory and arithmetic units — a division that heightened the efficiency of the ABC. Moreover, Mauchly and Eckert also ignored Atanasoff's use of binary math and Boolean logic, which made ENIAC unnecessarily complicated.

Yet Mauchly and Eckert decided to endow ENIAC with at least three critically important features missing from the ABC: high speed, programmability, and generality of purpose. Even though ENIAC's primary function was the computation of firing tables, no one knew precisely how a digital machine ought to go about doing that mathematically. Therefore, ENIAC was given the ability to solve almost all mathematical problems in accordance with a specified set of instructions. Nevertheless, ENIAC fell short of being a full-fledged computer in the modern sense of the term. Like the Analytical Engine, Zuse's calculators, the Mark I, and the ABC, ENIAC was a program-controlled calculator. But it was thousands of times faster and more powerful than any of these machines and, for these and other reasons, was clearly in a class by itself. It was a revolutionary achievement — the bridge to the invention of the modern computer.

Since ENIAC's general structure had been set by Brainerd's April 1943 proposal to the BRL, the first order of business was the

*In the early 1940s, MIT built an electronic differential analyzer that was much faster, more accurate, and easier to use than its mechanical predecessor. One of the machine's electronic units is shown at left; the output units, two paper-covered drums, are at right.*

*A bank of tubes from ENIAC (bottom) compared to a similar but more economical array from ENIAC's direct descendant, EDVAC (see Chapter 5). Much more powerful than ENIAC, EDVAC used only 3,563 tubes — about a fifth as many as ENIAC.*

design and construction of its most important component, the accumulator. At Mauchly's suggestion, Eckert studied the circuits used in cosmic ray recorders, but they turned out to be, surprisingly, too slow. Instead, Eckert devised a clever gadget based on the flip-flop circuit. He installed twenty tubes — two for each of the ten digits — in a long panel, using the first pair of tubes to represent the number 1, the second pair the number 2, and so on. When, say, a signal signifying 2 entered the panel, *one* of the tubes in the pair representing that number flipped off. (Actually, its voltage fell.) At the same time, the *other* tube in the pair flopped on, thus storing a 2 (or adding a 2). In subtraction, the process was reversed: the lighted tube was flipped off and its partner flopped on.

By June 1944 — about a year after the ENIAC project had begun — the first two accumulators were completed. Each one was about eight feet tall, two feet wide, and three feet thick, and contained ten of Eckert's twenty-tubed panels, or decade ring counters, which gave each one the capacity to add, subtract, or store a ten-digit decimal number. (One of the ten counters represented the units column, another the tens column, and so on.) Operating at 200,000 pulses a second, the accumulators were twice as fast as ENIAC's stipulated speed and they demonstrated, beyond any doubt, the feasibility of the project. Their completion was a turning point for ENIAC. Pleased with the devices, the BRL and the Moore School decided to boost the number of accumulators in ENIAC from the original four to twenty. As a result, ENIAC took longer to build, but the outcome was a considerably more powerful machine.

Eckert also gave a great deal of thought to the reliability of ENIAC's tubes. Fragile, fickle, power-hungry devices, they were

the weakest link in the machine. One faulty tube could stymie ENIAC and invalidate its calculations, and most engineers (those who knew about Project PX, anyway) believed that ENIAC, which would employ almost twenty thousand tubes, would sink on this rock. No other invention had ever contained more than a few thousand tubes; an electronic version of the differential analyzer completed at MIT in 1942 was the record holder, with some two thousand tubes. But it was an analog device, and a few malfunctioning tubes didn't necessarily jeopardize its results. Fortunately, Eckert devised a makeshift solution. He not only had ENIAC's tubes tested beforehand — an obvious measure — but ran them well below their rated voltages, which dramatically increased both their endurance and performance. Nevertheless, tube failure remained one of ENIAC's most serious shortcomings.

It took about a year to design ENIAC and a year and a half to build it. There were the usual construction delays — unobtainable parts, faulty components, errors in the design and the wiring — and the machine wasn't finished until November 1945, about three months after the Japanese surrender. It had run about 200 percent over budget. According to Goldstine, the military liaison and the officer who had brought Mauchly's idea to the attention of the BRL, the project had cost approximately $500,000, including the expense of moving the machine to Aberdeen in 1946, where it labored until 1955. But the BRL and the world as a whole unquestionably got their money's worth, for ENIAC kicked off the computer industry.

An enormous concoction of tubes and wires, ENIAC consisted of forty panels arrayed in a horseshoe pattern around the walls of a large room on the ground floor of the Moore School. It contained 17,468 tubes, and approximately 70,000 resistors,

10,000 capacitors, 1,500 relays, and 6,000 manual switches. It was eight feet high, eighty feet long, weighed thirty tons, and consumed 174,000 watts of power, about the same amount of energy generated by a 174-horsepower motor (a typical four-cylinder automobile engine produces about 75 horsepower). Large air blowers had to be installed in the room to dissipate the heat generated by the tubes, which turned out, thanks to Eckert's common-sense measures, to be far more reliable than anyone expected. Fifty tubes failed in the first month, fifteen in the fifth.

Although ENIAC was much too complicated to examine in detail here, we will outline its structure and operation. The machine's forty panels contained nine basic units. Three controlled the operations: an initiating unit started and stopped the machine; a master programmer orchestrated its overall activity; and a cycling unit generated an internal drumbeat of 100,000 pulses a second. Three performed the arithmetic: a multiplier; a divider/ square-rooter; and twenty accumulators. Another three handled

*ENIAC was laid out in the shape of a horseshoe.*

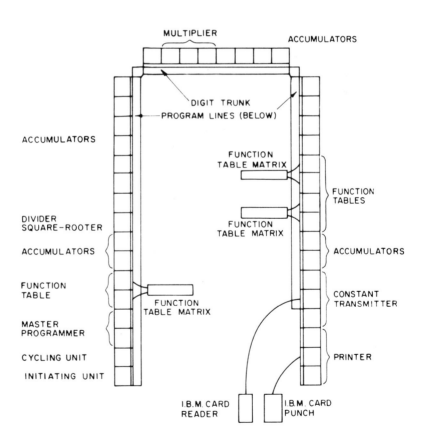

Solving a problem on ENIAC was a time-consuming and painstaking affair, involving the setting of thousands of switches and cables.

The rear of the machine

Tracking down a misplaced cable or an improperly set switch was a maddeningly difficult job, but the ENIAC team eventually developed effective troubleshooting techniques.

Opposite: A technician at the Moore School enters a number on one of ENIAC's three function tables.

the input and output: a constant transmitter transferred numbers from a modified IBM punch card reader into the machine; three function table units relayed mathematical constants from the function tables, which rested on wheels outside ENIAC, into the machine; and a printer unit linked ENIAC to an IBM card puncher.

Programming ENIAC was a one-way ticket to the madhouse. You did not sit down at a computer terminal and type in the instructions; instead, you set thousands of switches and plugged in hundreds of cables (like the cables on old telephone operator consoles) by hand, one at a time. In general, it took about two days to set up ENIAC to carry out a program. Since ENIAC was intended to calculate firing tables, no one foresaw the need for a convenient programming process; having set up the machine to compute one firing table, you only had to change a few switches and cables to process another table. However, what ENIAC lacked in programming convenience it made up for in speed: it could multiply 333 ten-digit numbers a second, or add 5,000 of them. While the differential analyzer needed fifteen to thirty minutes to compute a trajectory, ENIAC did the job in twenty seconds.

Exactly how did ENIAC work? Suppose you wanted to add two numbers, $x$ and $y$. First, you divided the problem up into sections that a machine could digest; for example, read $x$ and $y$ from a punched card, load $x$ into one accumulator, $y$ into another, and so on. Then you figured out precisely how ENIAC's many units should be linked up and coordinated to execute your instructions; unfortunately, to do that you had to know the machine almost as well as ENIAC's designers, and writing a complicated program could take months. Next you set up the machine by throwing various switches on the front of the units and by plugging in various cables between the unit's upper and lower sections; the switches carried out specific instructions while the cables arranged those instructions into the proper sequence. Then you crossed your fingers, took a deep breath, and pushed a button on the initiating unit.

That button dispatched a program pulse to the master programmer, which orchestrated the machine's overall operation. The master programmer in turn sent a pulse to the unit that ran the card reader, directing that unit to relay the contents ($x$ and $y$) of the first punch card to the constant transmitter. After that step was accomplished, the card reader control unit emitted a program pulse to one of the accumulators, which sent for $x$. The accumulator acknowledged $x$'s receipt by dispatching a pulse back to the

*Opposite: ENIAC was an enticing recruitment asset.*

# HOW MUCH IS $\sqrt[3]{2589^{16}}$?

## The Army's ENIAC can give you the answer in a fraction of a second!

Think that's a stumper? You should see *some* of the ENIAC's problems! Brain twisters that if put to paper would run off this page and feet beyond . . . addition, subtraction, multiplication, division — square root, cube root, any root. Solved by an incredibly complex system of circuits operating 18,000 electronic tubes and tipping the scales at 30 tons!

The ENIAC is symbolic of many amazing Army devices with a brilliant future for you! The new Regular Army needs men with aptitude for scientific work, and as one of the first trained in the post-war era, you stand to get in on the ground floor of important jobs

which have never before existed. You'll find that an Army career pays off.

The most attractive fields are filling quickly. Get into the swim while the getting's good! 1½, 2 and 3 year enlistments are open in the Regular Army to ambitious young men 18 to 34 (17 with parents' consent) who are otherwise qualified. If you enlist for 3 years, you may choose your own branch of the service, of those still open. Get full details at your nearest Army Recruiting Station.

**YOUR REGULAR ARMY SERVES THE NATION AND MANKIND IN WAR AND PEACE**

master programmer. Now the master programmer repeated the procedure with $y$, only $y$ was transferred to another accumulator. Next the master programmer directed the contents of the $x$-bearing accumulator to be loaded into the $y$-bearing accumulator and, after that was done, sent a signal to the punch card control unit to produce the sum $(x + y)$ on a card.

Got it? Each unit went to work as soon as it received a pulse from the master programmer or another unit and issued a pulse of its own after an operation was finished, thus triggering the next step in the program. The master programmer led the symphony, orchestrating the reading of the cards, the transfer of numbers from one unit to another, the conditional jumps, loops, and subroutines that constitute a typical program, and, finally, the punching out of the result on the cards. The need to set ENIAC up physically was its most serious drawback, and the next step in the development of computers — the one that led to the invention of the modern computer — was the construction of a machine whose wiring didn't have to be touched and whose programs could be inserted and carried out automatically.


ENIAC appeared too late for one war but just in time for another, a Cold War with a different set of military priorities. In this conflict, the demand for firing tables trailed off, replaced by an overriding necessity to perfect the atomic bomb. Even before the bombing of Hiroshima and Nagasaki in August 1945, scientists at the Los Alamos Scientific Laboratory in New Mexico had started working on a hydrogen bomb, a far more powerful and intricate weapon than the uranium- and plutonium-based ones dropped on the Japanese. At the suggestion of John von Neumann, a brilliant mathematician who served as a consultant to both the Moore School and Los Alamos and who had a profound understanding of the potential of computers, the first job given ENIAC had nothing to do with firing tables. (Von Neumann is a central figure in the history of computers and we will discuss his work in the next chapter.) Instead, it was a large and complex calculation of the feasibility of a proposed design for the H-bomb.

The calculation, a mathematical model of an H-bomb explosion, was enormous, with thousands of steps for the program and a million punch cards for the data. Since ENIAC could not store programs or remember more than twenty ten-digit numbers (one set of numbers for each accumulator), the program had to be solved in stages, an exceedingly cumbersome process. The first group of cards was fed into the machine, which punched out in-

termediate results on other cards, which were resubmitted to
ENIAC, and so on, until the mathematical model was calculated.
The program was run in November 1945 and the answers, which
were available by December, revealed several flaws in the proposed design of the bomb. "The complexity of these problems is
so great," the director of Los Alamos wrote the Moore School in
March 1946, "that it would have been impossible to arrive at any
solution without the aid of ENIAC. . . . It is clear that physics as
well as other sciences will profit greatly by the development of
such machines."

## CHAPTER 5

# The Stored-Program Computer

*Dorothy Fuldheim: Tell me, Walter, what are you going to do to report this very historic election?*

*Walter Cronkite: Well, this year [1952] we've got the same basic formula that we had before, which is, of course, straight reporting of how the returns are coming in. However, we do have a little gimmickry this year which I think is most interesting, and may turn out to be something more than gimmickry. We're using an electronic brain which a division of Remington Rand has in Philadelphia.*

*Fuldheim: What does it do?*

*Cronkite: It's going to predict the outcome of the election, hour by hour, based on returns at the same time periods on the election nights in 1944 and 1948. Scientists, whom we used to call long hairs, have been working on correlating the facts for the past two or three months. . . . Actually, we're not depending too much on this machine. It may be just a sideshow . . . and then again it may turn out to be of great value to some people.*

*— Interview on WEWS-TV, Cleveland, Ohio*

*EDVAC, ENIAC's direct descendant, was a stored-program computer. It contained a central processor and central control unit, and was based on binary math and Boolean logic. This is a photo of the machine's front panel, under construction at the Moore School in 1948 or 1949.*

Even before ENIAC's design was completed in June 1944, Eckert and Mauchly were eager to climb the next rung of the technological ladder and build a stored-program computer, one with a central processor and a memory for both data and programs. Such a machine would be a true computer, with all the characteristics now associated with the term. Herman Goldstine, who had championed ENIAC from the day it was no more than an idea in a forgotten memo, once again carried the torch — although ENIAC's construction had just begun and its success was hardly a foregone conclusion in the summer of 1944. He urged the BRL to sponsor the development of another computer, and the BRL agreed. In October, the Ordnance Department issued a $105,600 contract for the design of the Electronic Discrete Variable Computer, or EDVAC.

At first glance, the notion of storing instructions in a computer doesn't seem particularly clever, but it flies in the face of mechanical tradition. Machines have always been controlled from the outside; you turned some knobs and set some switches and the gadgets did your bidding. Even if the devices were controlled by punched tape or cards, like the Jacquard loom or the Analytical Engine, the best modus operandi seemed to be to stash the cards outside the machine and insert them when you needed them. Indeed, you couldn't very well hope to do more, since the practical shortcomings of gears and axles made it difficult if not impossible to build a large memory — although relays made the job much easier. As a result, no one, with the possible exception of Zuse, conceived of the stored program before the invention of ENIAC.

But electronic technology made large and fast memories, and therefore stored programs, possible — in fact, necessary. A high-speed calculator like ENIAC, operating at the unprecedented pace of 100,000 pulses a second, cries out for an internal memory that can store all the data and programs it needs for a given task and supply them instantly; otherwise, it has to depend on much slower external storage units, like card and tape readers, which are best employed for bulk storage. The more internal memory, the better. And there was another reason ENIAC demanded the capacity to store programs: the machine, with its thousands of cables and switches, was excruciatingly difficult to program. It would be a lot easier, for example, to feed your instructions directly into the machine.

Admitting the wisdom of storing both programs and data, a crucial question arises. Should they be kept in the same memory or stored in separate units? Since data and programs are two different things, like oil and water, shouldn't they be treated as such and given their own compartments? The answer is no — they should be lumped together. From a machine's point of view, data and programs are both symbols that are manipulated according to the same rules — the rules of Boolean algebra. As long as the two of them are encoded in such a way that the computer can always tell them apart, they can be stashed in the same memory spaces, inside and outside the computer, without any disadvantages — but with many advantages.

And what are those advantages? First, a computer's wiring doesn't have to be altered whenever a change of program is called for. In fact, there's no reason to touch the hardware. Second, a computer can modify its instructions. Third, a computer can store a library of programs, providing an easily accessible array of instructions to meet various contingencies. Operating at electronic speed, it can call up and carry out one program after another.

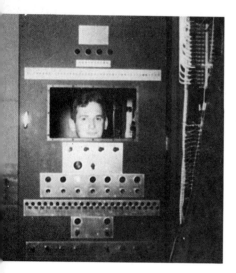

*Harry J. Gray, a graduate student at the Moore School and one of the EDVAC engineers, pauses for some fun in the oscilloscope panel, which was part of the operator's console and which he helped build. Gray is now a professor at the Moore School.*

*The innards of EDVAC's control unit. Right: Engineers John Broomall and Simon Gluck (standing) testing part of EDVAC's central control unit.*

Fourth, it can apportion its memory space between data and programs according to need, thus deploying its memory capacity to the best advantage. Some computer problems have short programs and reams of data; others have long programs and a few lines of data. And, finally, it can carry out instructions written in everyday human language (or in terms close to human language). A computer really understands only the 1s and 0s of binary math, and the first computers were programmed with binary instructions, which took a devil of a time to write. Once computers possessed sizable memories, however, they could store programs telling them how to break down ordinary words, like "run" or "stop," into binary numbers. In short, the advent of stored-program computers led to the birth of easy-to-use programming languages.

Eckert and Mauchly probably conceived of the idea of the stored program in late 1943. In the 31 December 1943 progress report on ENIAC, they make an oblique reference to the idea: "No attempt has been made to make provision for setting up a problem automatically. This is for the sake of simplicity and because it is anticipated that the ENIAC will be used primarily for problems of a type in which one setup will be used many times before another problem is placed on the machine." By late 1943, then, Eckert and Mauchly had considered some form of automatic internal programming. And in the first few months of 1944, in the course of their many discussions about EDVAC — late at night, after putting in their double shifts supervising the construction and testing of

ENIAC — they arrived at the idea of the stored program. But, until quite recently, that is not how historians described the origin of the stored program.

In the summer of 1944, a few weeks before the EDVAC contract was let, a powerful new figure stepped into the history of computers — a figure who would exercise enormous influence on both the development of computers and on the historical record of that development. John von Neumann (Noy-man) was one of the world's most talented and famous mathematicians, a dazzlingly productive and original intellect. He was a consultant to Los Alamos and the BRL and a professor at the Institute for Advanced Study in Princeton, New Jersey. Despite his connections with the BRL, he learned about ENIAC and EDVAC by accident, not through channels. One day in August, Goldstine was at the Aberdeen train station waiting for the train back to Philadelphia . . .

*J. Robert Oppenheimer (left) and John von Neumann at the October 1952 dedication of the computer built for the Institute for Advanced Study. Oppenheimer, who was head of the Los Alamos Laboratory during the war, became the institute's director in 1947.*

when along came von Neumann. Prior to that time I had never met this great mathematician, but I knew much about him of course and had heard him lecture on several occasions. It was therefore with considerable temerity that I ap-

proached this world-famous figure, introduced myself, and
started talking. Fortunately for me von Neumann was a
warm, friendly person who did his best to make people feel
relaxed in his presence. The conversation soon turned to my
work. When it became clear to von Neumann that I was concerned with the development of an electronic computer capable of 333 multiplications per second, the whole atmosphere of our conversation changed from one of relaxed good
humor to one more like the oral examination for a doctor's
degree in mathematics.

Soon thereafter the two of us went to Philadelphia so that
von Neumann could see the ENIAC. At this period the two
accumulator tests were well underway. I recall with amuse-
ment Eckert's reaction to the impending visit. He said that he
could tell whether von Neumann was really a genius by his
first question. If this was about the logical structure of the
machine, he would believe in von Neumann, otherwise not.
Of course this *was* von Neumann's first query.

Von Neumann arrived on 7 September 1944. According to
Mauchly, writing in 1979, this is what he and Eckert told him
during their briefing:

> We started with our basic ideas: there would be only *one*
> storage device (with addressable locations) for the *entire*
> EDVAC, and this would hold both data and instructions. All
> necessary arithmetic operations would be performed in just
> *one* arithmetic unit (unlike the ENIAC). Of course, there
> would be devices to handle input and output, and these
> would be subject to the control module just as the other
> modules were.

Von Neumann was fascinated by the Moore School's work.
"Like a child with a new toy," wrote Mauchly, "he could not put
it aside." Flattered by his interest, the school invited von Neumann to join the staff as a consultant. Although he had arrived
too late to influence ENIAC's design — his chief contribution to
ENIAC was the suggestion that it be used to solve the implosion
problems of Los Alamos — von Neumann came in time to participate in the development of EDVAC.

As a highly respected scientist, von Neumann lent a badly
needed air of legitimacy to the school's pioneering endeavors.
Many scientists — in particular, Bush at MIT, Aiken at Harvard,
and Stibitz at Bell Labs — regarded ENIAC as a foolish endeavor,
bound for failure, and a waste of government funds that would
have been better spent on the proven technologies of relay calculators and differential analyzers. There was a lot of bad blood between the University of Pennsylvania and its detractors. (After

visiting MIT, which built a two-thousand-tube electronic differential analyzer in 1941, Goldstine wrote: "It was, I think, a pretty sad spectacle of what the supermen at NDRC can do." NDRC, or the National Defense Research Committee, was a major source of government research funds.) But if von Neumann thought the Moore School's work was good enough to merit his attention, then perhaps there was something to it after all; at least the chiefs of the Ordnance Department probably slept better knowing that he was involved with EDVAC.

For von Neumann was one of the most respected scientists of his time. Born in Budapest, Hungary, in 1903, von Neumann had a genius's ability to perform complicated calculations in his head. At eighteen, he published his first mathematical paper; at twenty-two, he earned his doctorate in mathematics from the University of Budapest; at twenty-four, he became a *privatdozant* ("lecturer") at the University of Berlin, a rare honor for one so young. By that time he had published several papers on algebra, set theory, and quantum mechanics, the first installments of a creative output that filled six volumes by the time of his death in 1954. His most influential mathematical achievement was the invention of the theory of games; in a paper published in 1928, he showed how to find the best line of play, the one guaranteeing the smallest losses, in any game of strategy. Since a "game" in mathematics is more than a pair of dice and a brightly colored playing board, game theory has many important applications in economics, military strategy, and the social sciences.

In 1930, von Neumann emigrated to the United States, where the opportunities for academic advancement were greater than in Central Europe. (A little study of the odds of his becoming a professor in Europe as opposed to America had sent him packing.) He became a visiting lecturer at Princeton University and then, when the mighty Institute for Advanced Study (IAS) was established at Princeton in 1933, he received a permanent professorship on the IAS faculty. (Einstein also joined the institute that year.) A dapper, worldly, sophisticated man, Johnny, as his friends called him, was fluent in four languages and spoke English without an accent. He possessed an Old-World courteousness and a racy, Americanized sense of humor; he knew an endless string of jokes and anecdotes and his friends and colleagues delighted in telling him the latest ones. He had a substantial income — $10,000 a year from the IAS plus a large inheritance from his father, a successful banker — and moved easily in the highest academic and government circles, where he was a much sought-after consultant.

His keen interest in ENIAC and EDVAC was more than a mathematician's natural curiosity in calculating machines. As a consultant to Los Alamos, he played a central role in the development of the atomic bomb; he, Edward Teller, and other scientists on the Manhattan Project devised the all-important implosive lens of the first bombs. (Using conventional explosives, the lens generated a powerful spherical shock wave that imploded, or compressed, a ball of plutonium or uranium isotope to an atomically critical point, thus setting off the chain reaction.) He also showed the scientists at Los Alamos how to model an implosion mathematically and how to solve the resulting equations numerically, with the help of IBM card punchers and sorters. Los Alamos set up one of the largest punch card installations in the world, but the going was slow and von Neumann was on the lookout for faster computational methods when he met Goldstine at Aberdeen in August.

Eight months earlier, in January 1944, von Neumann had written the Office of Scientific Research and Development [OSRD], a governmental clearing house for scientific research, for information on the country's computational resources. OSRD was headed by Vannevar Bush, who knew all about ENIAC, but the agency held to the conventional wisdom about the ineluctable fallibility of tubes and didn't have much faith in the Moore School's effort. As a result, OSRD didn't tell von Neumann about ENIAC and instead referred him to Aiken at Harvard, Stibitz at Bell Labs, and Wallace Eckert — no relation to the Moore School's Eckert — at the IBM computing center at Columbia. But the Columbia operation relied on punch card tabulators, Aiken's machine was still under construction, and Stibitz's Complex Number Computer could only process imaginary numbers and was unprogrammable.

At the Moore School, von Neumann helped Eckert and Mauchly and the other EDVAC engineers refine their ideas. He was particularly influential on the subject of the machine's internal logic; that is, its organization from the point of view of the efficient processing of information. In a team effort where ideas are batted about in informal discussion, it is difficult if not impossible to pinpoint the originator of one or another notion, and von Neumann certainly contributed many good ideas. But there is no question that Eckert and Mauchly had conceived of the all-important stored program long before von Neumann joined the effort. However — and this is a very important point — Eckert and Mauchly had not gotten around to outlining a design for a stored-program computer when von Neumann appeared.

*Some of the EDVAC technicians gather before a completed section of the machine.*

In the spring of 1945, von Neumann offered to write an analysis of EDVAC's logical design, summarizing the staff's thinking and expanding and developing it according to his own lights. Eckert, Mauchly, and the rest of the EDVAC staff agreed to the idea — in fact, they welcomed it. Working mostly at Los Alamos, where the first bombs were being readied for Japan and the demand on his time was less pressing than it used to be, von Neumann roughed out a 101-page manuscript on EDVAC and mailed it to Goldstine in June. It was a preliminary report, containing numerous blank spaces for names, cross-references, and other information that von Neumann intended to insert after his colleagues on the EDVAC project had read the paper and commented on it. The final draft would give credit where credit was due, identifying the originators of the more important ideas.

Although the report was grounded in the work of others — notably Eckert and Mauchly — it was von Neumann's through and through. Not surprisingly, it was a lucid and masterful analysis of the structure and operation of a computer, full of interesting ideas and written with an overarching concern for "logical" control. In brief, von Neumann recommended the construction of a computer based on a central control unit that would orchestrate all operations; a central processor unit that would carry out all arithmetical and logical operations; and a *random-access read/write memory* (this is a contemporary term) that would store programs and data in such a way that any piece of information could be entered or retrieved directly (rather than sequentially). He also recommended the use of binary math and Boolean algebra and, furthermore, the processing of all binary words in series rather than in parallel. In other words, instead of operating on every bit in a word at the same time, as ENIAC did, EDVAC would process every bit one at a time. All things being equal, a parallel computer is faster than a serial one, but it is more difficult to build — thus the reason for von Neumann's suggestion.

Without Eckert and Mauchly's knowledge, Goldstine put a cover on von Neumann's report, listed him and him alone as the author, and distributed it under the title "First Draft of a Report on the EDVAC." Thirty-two people in and out of the Moore School were on the original mailing list and many others received copies later on. "Report on the EDVAC" was not only the first paper on the design of a general-purpose digital electronic computer, it was also a work from the hand and mind of the great von Neumann, and it had a strong impact on everyone who read it. He, not Eckert and Mauchly, was regarded as the inventor of the stored-program computer. Goldstine's actions were presumptuous but understandable, since he had chiefly wished to enhance the Moore School's reputation and let other people in on the latest thinking on computers; it probably never occurred to him that the premature distribution of "Report on the EDVAC" would spawn years of misunderstanding and jeopardize Eckert and Mauchly's patent rights to EDVAC.

As it turned out, EDVAC wasn't completed until 1952. By that time, the distinction of developing the first stored-program computer had fallen to another country — Babbage's homeland. Seeking to stimulate the development of computers, the Army Ordnance Department and the Office of Naval Research sponsored a summer course on computers at the Moore School in 1946. Twenty institutions — chiefly American companies, universities, and government agencies — sent representatives. Alone among the Allies, Great Britain was invited to participate, and the infor-

*Commercially available digital test equipment didn't exist in the late 1940s, so the EDVAC team had to make their own. The gadget shown here is a word generator, which produced a continuous stream of zeros and ones; among other things, it enabled engineers to verify the reliability of data transmission lines.*

mation it picked up there, coupled with its substantial engineering and theoretical knowledge, enabled it to jump ahead. So before we examine the first American computing projects — in particular, Eckert and Mauchly's private venture and von Neumann's effort at the Institute for Advanced Study — we'll take a look at the valiant computing developments in postwar Britain.

In 1937, a remarkable paper entitled "On Computable Numbers, with an application to the *Entscheidungsproblem*," appeared in the *Proceedings of the London Mathematical Society*. In it, the author, Alan Turing, a twenty-five-year-old Cambridge mathematician, described a *hypothetical* machine consisting of only a scanner and a tape. There is nothing special about either component; the tape is divided into boxes, like the frames of a roll of film, each of which could be marked with a symbol or be left blank, and the scanner could read, write, or erase these symbols by moving one box at a time to the left or to the right. A simple device, the Turing machine could do only three things: scan a box and

*Alan Turing was an excellent long-distance runner. Here he is coming in second in a three-mile race at Dorking, England, in December 1946. He lost by a foot, finishing in a respectable 15 minutes, 51 seconds.*

stop; erase a symbol and write a new one; and scan a box and move to the left or to the right.

What's so extraordinary about all this? Plenty. Even if the symbols on the tape were as simple as a slash (/), the Turing machine could solve *almost any* logical or mathematical problem. (But not all of them, as we shall see in a moment.) For example, suppose the tape contained two strings of five slashes separated by a blank box; by erasing a slash at the end of one of the strings and writing a slash in the blank box between them, the device could add 5 and 5. By the same token, it could subtract, multiply, and divide — or square a number, divide by three, and subtract 30 if the result exceeded 144. And that's not all. Since the slashes on the tape can just as easily stand for *instructions* as numbers, it also could perform conditional jumps, subroutines, loops, and other programming tricks, and thus could control the operation of any device. In short, Turing's imaginary creation is the Holy Grail of technology, a *universal machine*.

It is obvious to us today that the Turing machine is, in principle, a computer, with many of the same characteristics and capabilities; the tape is a general-purpose memory, storing both data and instructions, and the scanner is a central processor. Yet — and this is one of the greatest ironies in the history of computers — "Computable Numbers" wasn't about computers at all and Turing never seriously considered building his machine; even with a limited tape, it would have wasted most of its time racing to and fro over the tape, a perpetually harried messenger in search of one or another precious piece of information. However, Turing didn't dream up his mighty gadget for practical purposes. Rather, the Turing machine was conceived as a theoretical solution to a central problem in logic: the *Entscheidungsproblem*, or decision problem, which David Hilbert, the great German logician, had posed in 1928. Since we can't understand "Computable Numbers" and the Turing machine — and therefore some fundamental ideas about computers — without understanding the *Entscheidungsproblem*, we'll take a brief tour into the thickets of the theory of logic.

On the surface, logic is like a game of chess, a closed system with unambiguous rules governing every square of the board (or universe). One and one is always two; a king can move only one space at a time; the square of five is always twenty-five; a chess board consists of sixty-four squares. In *Principia Mathematica*, Whitehead and Russell attempted to fashion a universal system of logic, with a neat set of rules for every situation. It was a gallant and prodigious effort — embracing three thick volumes, and, to an admirable degree, it succeeded. The work became one of the foundations of modern logic. As time went by, however, logicians began to realize that *Principia's* eternal verities didn't perform very well in certain situations.

In an effort to clarify the situation, the German mathematician David Hilbert (1863–1943) posed three questions that framed the issues at stake. Was logic complete, in the sense that every statement, from $1 + 1 = 2$ and on up, can be proved or disproved? Was it consistent, in the sense that $1 + 1$ always equaled 2? And was it decidable, in the sense that there was a method that demonstrated the truth or falsity of every statement? In other words, was there such a thing as an unsolvable problem and a tried-and-true method of determining solvability?

These questions go to the heart of logic. And it turned out that, despite the best-laid plans of Whitehead, Russell, and other logicians, certain logical statements were indeed unsolvable, for now and forever. The culprits were self-contradictory statements such as the old Greek paradox "I am lying." At one and the same time, the speaker of "I am lying" is lying and telling the truth: if he is lying, then he is telling the truth, but if he is telling the truth how can he be lying? A classic example of an incomplete and inconsistent statement, "I am lying" doubles back on itself like a figure in an Escher print. (And so does "The following sentence is true. The preceding sentence is false.") Czech mathematician Kurt Godel provided the first convincing demonstration of the incompleteness and inconsistency of logic, drawing up a statement, in logical notation, that was the logical equivalent of "I am lying." Although Godel's work tended to show that logic was also undecidable, he did not present a proof of the *Entscheidungsproblem*.

It was Turing who, in "Computable Numbers," offered the most imaginative and, for our purposes, most influential demonstration of undecidability. (But he was not the first; Alonzo Church, a mathematician at Princeton Unversity, published a proof of undecidability a few months earlier.) With its three-part operational repertoire, a Turing machine can perform any logical operation; yet, no matter what it does, it can't judge the truth or falsity of certain paradoxical statements or predetermine their solvability. Even if the machine's operational catalog were enhanced, it still couldn't resolve these statements. Turing had come up with a litmus test of decidability — a mechanical method that showed that the only way to determine whether a statement was true or false was, obviously enough, to try to solve it. At the same time, and quite incidentally, the Turing machine also provided a cogent theoretical demonstration of the potential and limitations of a machine. On the one hand, no machine, even a computer equipped with an infinite storehouse of information and instructions, can answer every problem; on the other hand, a machine with the slimmest of operational abilities can solve a phenomenal range of problems, and this was Turing's first great contribution to our understanding of computers.

A highly theoretical paper, "Computable Numbers" had no discernible impact on the very untheoretical development of ENIAC and its predecessors. None of the early computer pioneers — Zuse, Atanasoff, Stibitz, Aiken, Eckert, or Mauchly — read Turing's paper. However, von Neumann, who had met Turing at Cambridge, where the young Englishman was a fellow at King's College, was well aware of his work, and there's an uncanny resemblance between some of the central ideas in "Report on the EDVAC" and "Computable Numbers"; for example, the infinite tape of the Turing machine is essentially a general-purpose memory for both data and programs and the Turing machine itself is really an unlimited stored-program computer. Odds are, though, that these similarities were purely coincidental. The remarkable thing is that Turing had, by intuition and through the backdoor, discovered what Eckert and Mauchly had learned through hard practice.

Turing was a very peculiar man, an unappealing mixture of boy genius and absent-minded professor. He was a gruff, gauche individual, with little concern for appearances. He usually looked as though he had just gotten out of bed, with a permanent five o'clock shadow (the sight of blood made him faint, so he rarely shaved), uncombed hair, and unkempt fingernails. He held up his pants with ties instead of belts and all his clothes looked as though they came from thrift shops or rummage sales. He had a high, stammering voice and a crowing, nervous laugh, and sometimes made odd squealing sounds when lost in thought, his mind almost visibly working away. Deadly serious about his work, he tended to ignore people who weren't his intellectual equals; needless to say, he had very few friends. Furthermore, he was a homosexual in a country that considered homosexuality a crime; in 1954, after suffering a trial for "gross indecency," Turing apparently committed suicide.

During the war, however, he was one of Britain's most im-

portant cryptanalysts. Stationed at Bletchley Park, a secret installation about fifty miles north of London, Turing supervised the
effort to decode German naval messages. German military communications depended upon an electromechanical teleprinter,
known as the Enigma, that coded and decoded messages by
means of four randomly spinning rotors; you set the printer to a
certain key, plugged in some electrical cords, typed in the message, and Enigma automatically scrambled and transmitted it. At
the other end, another Enigma, set to the same key and plug patterns, automatically decoded it. With trillions of possible permu-
tations, Enigma was a devilishly clever gadget, and the Germans
had an unquestioning faith in the inviolability of their communications. (Whenever the British inexplicably stole a beat on them,
the Germans invariably blamed it on traitors or spies but never on
Enigma.) But, in part through Turing's work, the British cracked
Enigma and read German messages throughout the war.

To decipher the thousands of messages picked up every
day, the analysts at Bletchley Park developed an electronic de-
coder called Colossus. Ten versions of Colossus were built altogether; the first was in operation by December 1943 — about two
years ahead of ENIAC. A Colossus contained about 2,400 tubes,
and consisted of four tall electronic panels and five optical
punched-tape readers; a loop of tape punched with an assortment
of messages was placed in a reader, and Colossus ran through the
tape again and again, comparing the messages with known
Enigma codes, until it came up with a match. Then it printed out
the results. Colossus was neither a calculator nor a computer, although it could perform some calculator- or computer-like operations, and it never occurred to the scientists at Bletchley Park to
make a stored-program computer. Colossus's most noteworthy fea-
ture was its speed; it could process a single tape at a rate of 5,000
characters a second, and since each machine had five processors,
it could handle a phenomenal 25,000 characters a second. (Colossus was not a Turing Machine, despite its scanners, and Turing
had little to do with its development.)

As the war drew to a close, the United States invited British scientists to see ENIAC and the Harvard Mark I. J. R. Womersley, an official of the National Physical Laboratory, Britain's biggest research agency, was the first man sent over. He arrived in
March — about half a year before ENIAC's completion. The Moore
School briefed him and gave him a copy of von Neumann's "Report on the EDVAC," which he was allowed to take back to England. A mathematician who had worked on a differential analyzer
(Britain had two analyzers, one at Manchester University and the

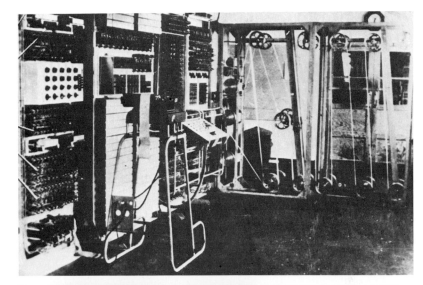

*The Colossus at Bletchley Park. The tape was read by photoelectric cells, and the data were analyzed by electronic counters.*

other at Cambridge) and had read "Computable Numbers," Womersley was quite impressed by ENIAC. Back in England, he immediately set out to organize a computing project. And within a few years, Britain, which had an abundance of technical and theoretical know-how in men like Turing and the Colossus engineers, outpaced the Americans.

The first scientist on Womersley's staff was, fittingly enough, Turing. Charged with the task of developing the machine, Turing studied von Neumann's paper and then wrote one of his own, a comprehensive plan for a large computer called ACE, or Automatic Computing Engine. (The "engine" in the name was a bow to Babbage.) ACE was an ambitious machine, with a memory of

204,800 bits and an operating speed of a million pulses a second — ten times faster than ENIAC. Turing devoted a lot of attention to ACE's programming, drawing up a roster of programs, composed in a partially numerical, partially alphabetical code, which were the first bona fide programs. But ACE became a victim of bureaucratic indecision and miscomprehension, and a drastically scaled down version, the Pilot ACE, was constructed instead. This machine was completed in May 1950, but by that time Turing, fed up by the timidity and indecision of the National Physical Laboratory, had escaped to Manchester University, where a more efficient computer project was underway.

The Manchester endeavor had been set up by Max Newman, a professor of mathematics, in mid-1946 with a large grant from the Royal Society. One of Britain's leading mathematicians, Newman was as cognizant of the possibilities of electronic computation as Turing. At Cambridge, where he had taught before the war, Newman had read "Computable Numbers" in typescript; in fact, he had been the paper's first reader. And at Bletchley Park, where most of the country's best mathematicians spent the war, Newman had been one of the originators of Colossus. He and his Manchester associates were in a perfect position to develop a computer, and they managed to build a working prototype by June 1948 (before Turing came on board). Known as the Manchester Mark I, it was *the first fully electronic stored-program computer in operation.*

The invention of an efficient and reliable form of *internal*

*The Manchester Mark I prototype, which went into operation in June 1948, consisted of six racks of electronic gear (lined up in a row, starting at left) plus several ancillary units.*

By June 1949, the Manchester Mark I had doubled in size. The round tube in the fourth rack on the left (numbered, in very small figures, 11) is a CRT, and it was used to view the contents of any of the machine's six CRT memory tubes (on the right, covered up and numbered 24, 24a, and 24b). The central processor is the third rack on the right (27–30).

memory was the most difficult task facing the Mark I's designers. There were several promising techniques, but the best was developed by F. C. Williams, the project's chief engineer. He hit upon the idea of employing ordinary cathode ray tubes (CRTs) — the same large, bottle-shaped tubes that were used in radar to display data and in TV sets to show the picture. Their operating principle was quite simple; "guns" in the bases of the tubes shot positively and negatively charged electrons at the faces of the tubes, thus storing bits in the form of charge spots, which, by the way, were quite visible to the eye. Since CRTs didn't have to be specially made, they were inexpensive. They were also small and fast and could retain a fair amount of data — 1,024 or 2,048 bits. Unfortunately, they were rather fickle, occasionally dropping a bit here and there, but they became the most prevalent internal-storage medium.

The first stored program on an electronic computer, a search for the factors of a number, ran on the Mark I on 21 June 1948. (A factor is a number that, multiplied by other numbers, yields a given product; for example, the factors of 45 are 5, 3, and 3.) The program was loaded into the machine, a jumble of racks, wires, and tubes, with three CRTs glowing in a gloomy room. As Williams described the great moment:

> When [the machine was] first built, a program was laboriously inserted and the start switch pressed. Immediately the spots on the display tube entered a mad dance. In early trials it was a dance of death leading to no useful result, and what was even worse, without yielding any clue as to what was wrong. But one day it stopped and there, shining brightly in the expected place, was the expected answer.

*The Ferranti Mark I at Manchester in 1951. Alan Turing, who developed the machine's first programming systems, leans against the operator's console. The commercial version of the machine is at right.*

Pleased by the success of the Mark I prototype, the British government, which wanted a computer for its own atomic bomb project, among other things, commissioned Ferranti Ltd., a weapons and electronics manufacturer in Manchester, to construct a computer based on the machine. Ferranti started work in 1949 and the first commercial computer, the Ferranti Mark I, was installed in Manchester's new computing center in February 1951. Aided by the British government, Ferranti went into the computer business and sold eight Mark I's in a few years. The University of Toronto, which wanted a machine to help with the design of the St. Lawrence Seaway, was Ferranti's first customer, and several Mark I's went to the British Atomic Weapons Research Establishment and to other government agencies. Soon other firms got into the act; for example, the English Electric Company built a very successful computer based on the Pilot ACE.

The third British computer of the postwar era was built at Cambridge. Known as EDSAC, for Electronic Delay Storage Automatic Computer, it was completed in June 1949 and was the first stored-program computer with any serious computational ability. (The Mark I was a prototype.) EDSAC was based unabashedly on EDVAC, and in both cases internal storage was provided by a gadget known as a mercury delay line, an idea of Eckert's. Essentially, a delay line is a thin tube, filled with mercury, that stores electronic pulses, or bits, in much the same fashion as a canyon holds an echo; generated by crystals in the tube, the pulses bounce back and forth, periodically re-energized by electronic components attached to the tube. The computer can call up the pulses at any time. Compared to CRTs, delay lines were slower, much larger, more expensive, and harder to make, but they were very reliable and could hold much more information. Delay lines were widely used until the early 1950s, when they, and CRTs, were replaced by an eminently practical form of storage known as magnetic cores.


Back in the United States, the Moore School had fallen into a nasty quarrel over patent rights. As the financial backers of ENIAC and EDVAC, the Ordnance Department wanted the right to use them, and the technology in them, without payment to the inventors. In other words, the department wanted a royalty-free license, and such a dispensation can be granted only by the rightful inventors. (And only an individual, or individuals, not an institution, can apply for a patent, although the inventor may assign his or her commercial rights to any party.) Who, then, should apply for the patents and who should receive the rights to them? As the machine's chief inventors, Eckert and Mauchly believed that they should submit the applications and that they, not the University of Pennsylvania, should get the rights and grant the necessary license to the Army. Although the Army, grateful for their work, tended to side with them, the university did not.

Unfortunately for the university, the only patent agreement it had with Eckert, Mauchly, and the rest of the ENIAC staff was a six-line notice in the school's course catalogue. That notice required the inventor to "assign his rights in the patent to the University upon payment to the patentee of his expense in securing the patent." It was hardly a watertight contract, and Eckert and Mauchly, who were planning to go into the computer business, tried to circumvent it. They hired an attorney, George A. Smith, who, splitting hairs, argued that the men were really government employees — that ENIAC and EDVAC were designed under government contract and that Eckert and Mauchly were only nominally in the university's employ. The school had merely supplied the laboratory facilities. "Under this view the University cannot properly consider itself entitled, strictly speaking, to any benefit from the developments," Smith wrote Harold Pender, dean of the Moore School, in February 1945. "To leave settlement of [patent] questions solely to the University seems hardly fair. The University would be prosecutor, judge and jury in such a case."

However jesuitical Smith's argument, the university decided to give in. The catalog notice wasn't much of a contract; the quarrel was endangering the ENIAC and EDVAC projects as well as future government contracts with the university, and Pender, who had been a successful businessman before joining the Moore

School, sympathized with Eckert and Mauchly's commercial aspirations and recommended that the university let them keep the rights. But the controversy angered many university officials, particularly John Brainerd, ENIAC's project supervisor, who regarded the pair's position as a flagrant violation of academic ethics. A university should be motivated by the pursuit of knowledge, not profit, Brainerd believed, and the proper thing would be for the school to receive the rights and to license them to all comers. Since he wasn't inclined to labor on a project that promised to enrich only Eckert and Mauchly, Brainerd resigned as the EDVAC project supervisor in early 1946.

Pender, who wished to maintain the Moore School's close relationship with the government, realized that the institution needed a clear and firm patent policy. In January 1946, he appointed Irven Travis, who had been an assistant professor at the school before the war and a contracts administrator for Naval Ordnance during it, to the new post of supervisor of research. At a few prominent universities, and at most private companies, employees had no patent rights whatsoever, and Travis, with Pender's backing, decided to establish the same policy at the Moore School. Inventors would not even be entitled to a percentage of the rights — cutting them out of any opportunity to profit from their ingenuity. Moreover, Travis also wanted to limit the faculty and staff's outside consulting.

Eckert and Mauchly refused to accept these rules and submitted their resignations on 31 March 1946. The EDVAC project,

*J. Presper Eckert, Jr., and John Mauchly at Sperry Rand in Blue Bell, Pennsylvania, in the early 1970s*

which had begun officially the previous October, slowed to a halt, and the machine wasn't finished until 1952. Meanwhile, the British jumped into the breach and the Moore School lost its leadership in computer technology to MIT and other schools; today, the only signs of its historic role in the development of the computer is a bronze plaque on a side entrance and a few dusty panels of ENIAC, stored anonymously in an out-of-the-way corridor in the basement, along with some other equipment. (Ironically, Travis himself resigned as head of research in 1947 and later became a vice president at Burroughs, where he was in charge of the establishment of a computer division.)

In the case of EDVAC, the patent fight was a three-sided affair, with the university, von Neumann, and Eckert and Mauchly in different corners. In April 1946, von Neumann submitted an official patent claim on EDVAC to the Ordnance Department, including, as evidence, a copy of his "Report on the EDVAC." Eckert and Mauchly, who had not yet filed an EDVAC patent, were incensed, and the Ordnance Department regarded von Neumann's claims as unjustified and unethical. However, according to Goldstine, von Neumann was less interested in obtaining credit for himself than in preventing Eckert and Mauchly from tying up the rights for their own corporate use. Goldstine has said that von Neumann, uninterested in personal gain, intended to place his patents in the public domain. Whatever von Neumann's intentions, the result probably pleased him. For in order to be valid a patent must be filed within a year of the act of invention; any significant prior public disclosure of the invention or of its ideas automatically invalidates the patent. Since von Neumann's "Report on the EDVAC" had been widely distributed in 1945, the Ordnance Department's attorneys ruled in April 1947 that EDVAC and the idea of the stored-program computer belonged in the public domain.

The seed planted by the Moore School took root all over the United States. Most of the twenty organizations that sent representatives to the Moore School's course on computers came from companies, universities, and government agencies that had the technical and financial resources to build their own computers — for instance, IBM, General Electric, Bell Labs, MIT, Harvard, the Institute for Advanced Study (IAS), and the National Bureau of Standards. The majority of the organizations eventually constructed their own machines, and some of them, such as IBM and General Electric, entered the computer business. By the end of

1947, six computers were under construction in America, three in academia and three in industry.

By far the most influential of the academic projects was undertaken by von Neumann at the Institute for Advanced Study. Von Neumann had no trouble rounding up the necessary financing, and the IAS, the government, and the Radio Corporation of America (RCA), which had a new research center in Princeton and wanted to get into the business of making tubes for computers, all chipped in. Meanwhile, other research institutes and universities obtained grants to build copies of the IAS computer, and at least eight duplicates were constructed in the United States and abroad, including the ILLIAC (Illinois Automatic Computer) at the University of Illinois at Urbana; the Johnniac (named for von Neumann) at the Rand Corporation in Santa Monica, California; and the marvelously named MANIAC (Mathematical Analyzer, Numerator, Integrator, and Computer) at Los Alamos.

The IAS machine embodied von Neumann's ideas on computer design, ideas first expounded in "Report on the EDVAC" and refined in another highly influential paper, "Preliminary Discussion of the Logical Design of an Electronic Computing Instrument," written in 1946 with Goldstine and Arthur Burks, a Moore School mathematician and engineer who had worked on ENIAC and EDVAC. Von Neumann's ideas on computer design had changed since EDVAC, and the IAS machine was a parallel processor, unlike EDVAC. Although each binary word raced through

*One of the earliest chess programs was written for MANIAC (below). While Paul Stein (seated) contemplates his next move, Nicholas Metropolis, who was in charge of MANIAC's construction, fiddles with the machine's paper tape reader. The first computers were no match for good chess players. The Rand Corporation's JOHNNIAC is shown on the right.*

The Institute for Advanced Study computer was retired in 1960 and put on display at the Smithsonian Institution in Washington, D.C. The protruding cylinders at the base of the machine are CRT storage tubes, each capable of holding 1,024 bits. There were twenty tubes on each side of the machine.

the machine's units in sequence, one bit after another, all the bits in each word were stored, and operated on, in parallel, as in ENIAC. Originally, von Neumann had feared that a parallel stored-program computer would be too difficult to build — hence his recommendation for a serial processor in EDVAC — but advances in computer technology had allayed his pessimism. The influence of von Neumann and the wisdom of his approach was such that the IAS machine — a stored-program, parallel processor — became the paradigm of modern computer design, and most computers built since the late 1940s have been "von Neumann" machines.

Obviously, any organization that did a great deal of work with numbers, whether in science, business, or government, could benefit from a computer. In retrospect, the proliferation of computers is easy to explain, although in the late 1940s most people — including many scientists who should have known better — were highly skeptical of the need for such machines. For example, in 1947, Aiken, a stubborn man who was then in the midst of building an electronic calculator *without* stored-program capability and who missed the technological boat in many other crucial ways, told two officials of the National Bureau of Standards (NBS), which was backing Eckert and Mauchly's commercial efforts: "There will never be enough problems, enough work for more than one or two of these computers. . . . You two fellows ought to go back and change your program entirely, stop this . . . foolishness with Eckert and Mauchly." Fortunately, the NBS ignored him.

And what was Eckert and Mauchly's "foolishness"? It was a belief in the commercial potential of computers and a proposal for an extraordinary machine known as UNIVAC, or Universal Automatic Computer. UNIVAC was not so much a computer as a computer system, a family of related machines that enabled customers to put together a data-processing system that suited their needs. There were high-speed printers, magnetic tape drives (for external memory), card-to-tape converters, tape-to-card converters, high-speed tape copiers, and other equipment. In other words, UNIVAC included everything you needed to haul your paper-laden accounting department, factory, government agency, or university into the twentieth century. And it was a truly general-purpose computer, able to process both numeric and alphabetic data. It could print bills, sort accounts, and predict elections as well as solve the kind of scientific problems that led to the invention of computers in the first place.

UNIVAC was a visionary idea, and like most visionary ideas it was brought to life only after years of agonizing labor that, on more than one occasion, nearly cast its inventors into a red sea of bankruptcy. Yet, despite the derogatory opinions of Aiken and other scientists and engineers, who tended to see nothing but greed in Eckert and Mauchly's ambitions, UNIVAC turned out to be an enormous commercial success, and it was these two men who really inaugurated the American computer industry and introduced computers into the marketplace. Most companies, particularly IBM, didn't take these machines seriously until Eckert and Mauchly had proved that there was indeed a sizable market for computers even at several hundred thousand dollars apiece. Then everyone wanted to get into the act.

Eckert and Mauchly's first problem was raising the money to develop UNIVAC. Fortunately, the government was keenly interested in fostering a domestic computer industry, and the Census Bureau was willing to foot most of the research and development cost. As the country's chief statistical agency, the Census had a compelling need for computers and a tradition of technological sponsorship dating back to Seaton and Hollerith. However, it was legally prohibited from granting research and development contracts, and its deal with Eckert and Mauchly had to be handled by the National Bureau of Standards, a sister agency at the Commerce Department that suffered from no such legal encumbrances. The NBS was glad to cooperate, and in October 1946, Eckert and Mauchly signed their first contract. They formed a partnership, the Electronic Control Company, rented office space in a building in downtown Philadelphia, and hired half a dozen engineers.

Unfortunately, there were serious problems from the start. They were so eager for that contract — the first contract is always the most important — that they were willing to accept almost any price. Although they knew it would cost at least $400,000 to develop UNIVAC, they agreed to a $300,000 *fixed-fee* contract instead of a *cost-plus-fixed-fee* agreement, which would have given them the right to pass on the unforeseen but legitimate expenses to the government. A cost-plus-fixed-fee agreement was a common deal in Washington, but Eckert and Mauchly believed, incorrectly, that such a contract gave the NBS certain patent rights, and this time they were determined to keep all the rights to themselves. Naively optimistic, they hoped to spread their development costs

*Eckert and Mauchly with the BINAC staff, 1948. Front, left to right: Eckert, Frazier Welsh, James Weiner, Bradford Sheppard, and Mauchly. Back row: Albert Auerbach, Jean Bartik, Marvin Jacoby, John Sims, Louis Wilson, Robert Shaw, and Gerald Smoliar.*

among future UNIVAC sales, yet their desperate need for capital led them to offer UNIVACS for ridiculously low prices.

Although the $300,000 fixed-fee contract was their fault, another part of the deal was not. Adhering to bureaucratic formalities, the NBS had hired a consultant to evaluate the UNIVAC proposal — and that consultant was George Stibitz of Bell Labs. Stibitz, who had frowned on the BRL's decision to finance ENIAC — he had thought the money would have been better spent on tried-and-true relay computers — was equally unenthusiastic about UNIVAC. "I find it difficult to say much about the Mauchly-Eckert proposal," he wrote the NBS in May 1946, while the UNIVAC negotiations were underway. "There are so many things undecided that I do not think a contract should be let for the whole job." He was right, of course; most things were undecided, but the ENIAC project had started the same way. Overly cautious, Stibitz recommended that the NBS give Eckert and Mauchly a three-part contract, first to conduct further studies, then to work up a detailed proposal, and finally to build the computer.

The NBS, however, decided to divide the contract into two parts, one for the development of the computer's internal and external memory, the other for the development of the processor. In October, Eckert and Mauchly received $75,000 for the construction of a mercury delay line and a magnetic tape drive. According to Eckert and Mauchly's estimate, the project was supposed to take six months, and the size of the payment was keyed to their assessment of their costs and schedule. Unfortunately, they ran into many technical problems, and the equipment wasn't finished until October 1947 — six months late. And that meant that the second part of the contract, $169,600 for the design and development of the rest of the computer, wasn't executed until June 1948. (NBS retained 15 percent of the $300,000 as an overhead fee to cover the administrative costs of the contract.)

So, between October 1946 and June 1948, Eckert and Mauchly received only $75,000 from the government. They tried to drum up other contracts, only to run into a wall of skepticism. Once again, the major obstacle was the unenthusiastic assessments of their colleagues. In 1947, the NBS asked the National Research Council, part of the National Academy of Sciences, to evaluate UNIVAC and two other government computer projects (EDVAC and a computer being built by Raytheon, the large Massachusetts electronics manufacturer). The council appointed a committee that, among others, consisted of von Neumann, Stibitz, and Aiken. These men were predisposed against Eckert and Mauchly's plans, either for technical reasons (Aiken and Stibitz) or for per-

Eckert with one of BINAC's two mercury delay line units. Each of the parallel bars housed a single tube of mercury and its associated electronic components, and each delay line unit stored 512 thirty-one-bit words.

*BINAC. The dual processors are in the background, capped with air-cooling bonnets. An input/output teletype is in the foreground, and a mercury delay line unit on the far left.*

sonal and technical reasons (von Neumann). Instead of helping Eckert and Mauchly, the committee's lukewarm report ignored most of the technical issues raised by UNIVAC, such as whether Eckert and Mauchly's decision to stick with serial processing and the decimal system was a wise one, and some government agencies shied away from UNIVAC.

Since the federal government wasn't a good bet, Mauchly, who ran the business side of the partnership, turned to private industry. The Northrop Aircraft Company, which was developing a long-range guided missile for the Air Force, was intrigued by the idea of airborne navigation by computer. It wanted a small computer to test the feasibility of the idea and, in October 1947 — about the time Eckert and Mauchly satisfied the first part of the NBS deal — it gave them a $100,000 contract for the construction of a small numeric computer called BINAC, or Binary Automatic Computer. (BINAC wasn't supposed to operate in flight; rather, it was intended to be the first step in the development of a computer that could. At the time, the thought of such a device was utterly impractical, and reliable airborne computers had to await the invention of miniature solid-state components.) Although BINAC would divert the Electronic Control Company's attention from UNIVAC, Northrop was willing to pay $80,000 up front.

Once again, Mauchly and Eckert underestimated their costs and development schedule. Completed in August 1949, BINAC was fifteen months behind schedule and $178,000 over budget — a loss that Eckert and Mauchly had to absorb. Moreover, Northrop didn't even get what it paid for. Subordinated to UNIVAC from the beginning, BINAC had failed to receive Eckert's full attention, and he and his engineers had cut corners with inferior and untested parts; according to Northrop, about 25 percent of BINAC's tubes were unsatisfactory and had to be replaced. There were many other technical problems, and BINAC — the first electronic stored-program computer in America — didn't run to Northrop's satisfaction. "BINAC seemed to operate well on sunny days," said one of the company's engineers, Florence R. Anderson, "but poorly on rainy days."

However, the machine was not without its saving graces. It was not one computer but two, with a pair of serial processors that were geared to run in tandem. If one of the processors failed, the other would kick in immediately — an essential safety net for an airplane. (Or a spacecraft; NASA's space shuttle uses five tandem computers. Many military units, government agencies, and businesses, particularly airlines and banks, also use such computers.) A fraction the size of ENIAC, each processor was a mere five feet tall, four feet long, and one foot wide, and contained 700 tubes. Each unit could perform 3,500 additions a second (compared to ENIAC's 5,000) and 1,000 multiplications a second (more than ENIAC's 333). And each processor had a sizable mercury delay line memory that could store 512 31-bit words.

*UNIVAC. The control console is on the left, the processor at the rear, and the magnetic tape units on the right.*

*Mauchly (left), Leslie Groves, and Eckert posing in front of a mercury delay line tester. Groves was Remington Rand's director of advanced research and was put in control of Eckert and Mauchly's firm after the acquisition. A former Army general, he directed the Manhattan Project during the war.*

By the summer of 1948, Eckert and Mauchly had five UNIVAC contracts worth about $1 million. The government had upped its order to two, while the Prudential Insurance Company had asked for one and the A. C. Neilsen Company, the well-known market research outfit, had requested two. Nevertheless, Eckert and Mauchly were desperately short of working capital. With only $206,000 in assets, they required at least another $500,000 in funds to meet their contractual obligations. Conventional sources of funding, like Wall Street and the banks, had little faith in their success and wouldn't touch them on reasonable terms. As a result, Eckert and Mauchly incorporated in December 1948 and began searching for outside investors.

The American Totalisator Company (AmTote) of Baltimore, Maryland, was their savior. It manufactured totalisators, or parimutuel machines, for racetracks in England and the United States, and was, in a sense, in a related business. Made of relays, AmTote's machines automatically calculated the odds for a race and displayed the payoffs to the bettors. Aside from the fancy display boards, totalisators were really special-purpose electromechanical calculators. As the world's only producer of the machines, AmTote enjoyed a highly lucrative monopoly, leasing the equipment to the racetracks for a small percentage of the take. Technologically, however, the company was in a precarious position, since its patented equipment could easily be replaced by electronic devices; one racetrack manager had already approached Eckert and Mauchly with a request to make such a machine.

Henry L. Straus, co-inventor of the totalisator and the firm's founder and vice president, decided to hedge his bets and invest in Eckert and Mauchly's firm, which had been reorganized, in an effort to attract investors, as the Eckert-Mauchly Computer Corporation. In August 1948, AmTote agreed to give the fledgling computer manufacturer $112,000 in loans and to buy 40 percent of the stock for $438,000. In return, Straus, a dynamic electrical engineer who recognized the promise of Eckert and Mauchly's work, became chairman of the company's nine-man board and received three other seats on the board. It was an excellent deal for Eckert and Mauchly, since they retained 54 percent of the stock (their employees owned the remaining six) and continued to run the enterprise.

The money kept them afloat for fourteen months. By September 1949, the corporation had 134 employees, a new office building in North Philadelphia, and six UNIVAC contracts. It

*A UNIVAC publicity shot, about 1951*

seemed on the road to success. But Straus was killed in a plane crash the following month and AmTote decided to pull out of the deal. Even if the firm had stayed on, Eckert and Mauchly would have needed much more money, and Straus's company lacked the great capital resources to support a computer manufacturer. Eckert and Mauchly renewed their search for investors and, after coming up empty-handed, finally realized that they had no choice but to sell out. Several large corporations, like Burroughs, Hughes Aircraft, and National Cash Register, were interested, but Remington Rand, the large office equipment and tabulator maker, made the first offer. Although Eckert and Mauchly stayed on, control passed to Remington Rand in February 1950.*

Remington Rand immediately moved to place the firm on sounder financial footing. In addition to injecting some badly needed capital, it sought to renegotiate the six UNIVAC contracts. Declaring that the machines simply couldn't be produced for less than $500,000 apiece, Rand's attorneys threatened to tie up the contracts in court unless Prudential, A. C. Neilson, and the NBS accepted the higher price. The government refused to yield, but Prudential and A. C. Neilsen, which had agreed to buy UNIVAC for a paltry $150,000 each, decided to cancel their contracts. Their money was returned and they eventually turned to the competition — IBM, which put a computer on the market in April 1953. In March 1951, about six years after ENIAC was completed, Eckert and Mauchly's long struggle was over and the first UNIVAC was delivered to the Census.

Since Eckert and Mauchly were most familiar with decimal-based electronic systems, UNIVAC, though a true computer, was based on decimal math. As a result, it used more tubes — 5,000 — and occupied far more space than a comparable binary machine. (The processor was fourteen and a half feet long, seven and a half feet wide, and nine feet tall — ten times larger than the IAS's binary computer.) However, it was quite fast, with an internal drumbeat of 2.25 million pulses a second and the ability to add two twelve-digit numbers in 120 microseconds or multiply them in 1,800 microseconds. The comparable addition time for ENIAC was 200 microseconds. UNIVAC's memory capacity was the most impressive thing about it. The machine could store 12,000 digits or alphabetical characters in random-access mercury delay lines and millions more in magnetic tape. And it could process ten tapes at a time, each tape storing more than a million characters.

*Opposite: A UNIVAC ad in* Fortune *magazine in 1954*

*In 1949, Mauchly became the subject of a federal "loyalty investigation." See the Appendix.

# Doubling Univac's Speed!

The famous Univac of Remington Rand has widened still further its lead over other electronic business computing systems. Univac is still the *only* completely self-checked system . . . the only one which can read, write, and compute simultaneously without extra equipment. And now, the Univac II adds to these superior features the speed of a magnetic-core memory.

The Remington Rand magnetic-core memory is more than a laboratory promise. It has been in actual customer use for over a year, passing all tests with flying colors in the first commercially available electronic computer to use core storage successfully.

The *size* of the internal memory of Univac has also been doubled, giving instantaneous access to 24,000 alphabetic or numeric characters. If needed, this capacity can be further increased to 120,000 characters.

Univac's external memory — magnetic tape — now has greater capacity, too, increasing input and output to 20,000 characters per second . . . the equivalent of reading or writing every character on this page more than 1,000 times a minute.

These new Remington Rand developments can be incorporated into any existing Univac installation to double its speed of operation and to increase its economy still further.

ELECTRONIC COMPUTER DEPARTMENT ***Remington Rand*** ROOM 2009, 315 FOURTH AVENUE, NEW YORK 10, NEW YORK
DIVISION OF SPERRY RAND CORPORATION

As the first commercial computer system in America, UNIVAC made quite an impression on the public. (And on industry too, which eventually bought forty-six of them.) At the suggestion of Remington Rand, CBS-TV used a UNIVAC to predict the outcome of the 1952 presidential election. A predictive program was written, and the election results for thousands of voting districts in 1944 and 1948, as well as state-by-state results dating back to 1924, were fed into the machine. One UNIVAC was shipped to CBS's New York studios to serve as a stage prop, and a second UNIVAC at Remington Rand in Philadelphia was assigned to perform the computations. A third machine was on call as a backup in case of technical difficulties.

At 9 P.M. Eastern Standard Time, with only 7 percent of the vote in, UNIVAC awarded 43 states and 438 electoral votes to Eisenhower and 5 states and 93 electoral votes to Stevenson. Most pollsters had forecast a close election, and the programmers, fearing that they had made a mistake, decided not to release this prediction. Instead, they reprogrammed the machine to render a more conservative judgement. This time, UNIVAC called the election a toss-up, with Eisenhower slightly ahead, and this result was broadcast at about 10 P.M. As the returns poured in, however, it was obvious that UNIVAC had been right in the first place, and the original prognostication was announced at midnight. The final election tally was 442 electoral votes for Ike, 89 for Stevenson — only a few votes off UNIVAC's prediction. "The trouble with machines," said CBS commentator Edward R. Murrow, "is people."

*Opposite: Eckert briefs CBS anchorman Walter Cronkite about Remington Rand's preparations for the 1952 presidential election. Harold Sweeney, a UNIVAC programmer, is seated at the computer console.*

## CHAPTER 6

# The Rise of IBM

Clothes don't make the man but they go a long way toward making a businessman.

Pack your todays with effort — extra effort! Your tomorrows will take care of themselves. They will also take care of you and your money.

You cannot be a success in any business without believing that it is the greatest business in the world. You have to put your heart in the business and the business in your heart.

We have different ideas, and different work, but when you come right down to it, there is just one thing we have to deal with throughout the whole organization—that is MAN.

> — *Thomas Watson, Sr., former chairman,*
> *IBM Corporation*

W ho hasn't heard of IBM? The direct descendant of Herman Hollerith's Tabulating Machine Company, it is the fifth largest industrial corporation in America and the world's biggest computer manufacturer. To a large degree — a degree that warms the hearts of its shareholders and distresses its competitors — IBM *is* the computer industry, and almost every other computer company in the world swims in its ocean. It commands about 40 percent of the international computer market, producing approximately three fourths of all medium- and large-size computers and one fourth of all personal computers. It also makes typewriters, automatic teller machines, supermarket checkout registers, subway ticket dispensers, marine navigation equipment, and dozens of other products.

IBM is very much the creation of two men, Thomas J. Watson, Sr., who ran the firm from 1914 until the early 1950s, and his eldest son, Thomas Jr., who was in charge from 1952 to 1971. The elder Watson, an autocratic executive and master salesman, built IBM into one of the strongest and most profitable companies in the country. But he was in his late seventies in the early 1950s, more interested in preserving what he had created than in forging new ground, and he had little feel for computers. Although IBM's chief competitor, Remington Rand, had bought out Eckert and Mauchly in 1950, Watson was unwilling to follow Rand's lead. At

*Thomas J. Watson (1874–1956) in his office at IBM's former headquarters in Manhattan, 1947*

that time, computers were huge, expensive machines, with seemingly little commercial potential. His son, on the other hand, belonged to the generation that had invented ENIAC, and he possessed an instinctive grasp for this new technology. With his father's grudging permission, Tom moved IBM into computers. And by 1955, three years after Tom had assumed the presidency, the company's revenues had doubled.

*Watson, about twenty years old*

Thomas Watson, Sr., was born near Painted Post, a village in upstate New York, in 1874. His father was a lumberman and farmer, and Thomas worked by his side for a few months after graduating from high school. But Watson was an ambitious young man, eager to get off the farm and make his way in the world. He took a few courses at a local business school and found a $5-a-week job as a bookkeeper in a meat market in Painted Post. Then he met a peddler who offered him a job as his assistant, at double his current wage. Bored with the meat market and tiny Painted Post, Watson accepted, and the two men hit the road, selling pianos, organs, and sewing machines. When, a few months later, the peddler went on to better things, Watson took over the route at a salary of $12 a week. He liked his work and thought he was doing well — until another salesman pointed out that he could make much more on commission.

Astonishingly enough, it had never even occurred to him that most salesmen received a percentage of their gross, and he felt like a fool, angry at his ignorance and angry at his employer for taking advantage of him. But, at the same time, he realized how, by dint of determination, hard work, and talent, he could make his fortune. If he could just get a good job as a commission agent, well then, it would be only a matter of time before he was in the money. So, in 1893, at the age of nineteen, Watson took the train to Buffalo, the nearest big city, to find a job as a salesman.

He could not have launched his career at a worse time. The country was in the midst of a depression, and Watson, who possessed the unmistakable air of a hayseed, nearly went broke before he landed a job as a sewing machine salesman. Unfortunately, he wasn't very good at it. The sales pitch that had persuaded the farmers of Painted Post fell on deaf ears in Buffalo, and Watson was soon out of work. But he found a savior of sorts in a flashy, older, and more experienced salesman named C. B. Barron, who took him under his wing. Barron, a backslapping, cigar-smoking fellow who went in for spats, silk hats, and cutaways, persuaded a local bank, the Buffalo Building & Loan Association, to let them sell its stock on commission.

Working alongside Barron, Watson learned the basic tricks of the trade, particularly the importance of making a favorable first impression. He bought a stylish new wardrobe and cultivated a friendly, cheerful demeanor. He also imitated Barron's pitches (which, given the kind of salesman Barron was, may have gone something like this: "My dear sir, the Buffalo Building & Loan Association is a Rock of Gibraltar, and it's worth its weight in gold . . . but you look like the kind of man who knows that.") Before long, Watson's efforts began to pay off. "They say money isn't everything," he remarked years later. "It isn't everything, but [it] is a great big something when you are trying to get started in the world and haven't anything."

Like most ambitious young men, Watson had his own get-rich scheme; in his case, it was going to be a chain of meat markets. Using the money he had earned with Barron and borrowing a small sum from his father, he opened a butcher shop in Buffalo and hired a few clerks to run it while he was on the road with Barron. He intended to plow most of his income into the market and open other stores as soon as his cash flow permitted. However, a few weeks after the first shop opened, Barron, true to type, absconded with most of their money. Outraged and suspicious, the bank fired Watson. Then the butcher shop failed, and Watson was right back where he had started — broke, desperate, and unable to find another job.

He finally talked his way into a position with the office of the National Cash Register Company (NCR). Once again, he was taken under the wing of an experienced salesman — this time, an honest one. John Range, the NCR district sales manager for upper New York, taught him how to sell registers the NCR way (which we'll describe in a moment), and Watson eventually became the star of the Buffalo office. In his most successful week, Watson is said to have earned $1,225; since NCR's cash registers cost between $100 and $200 and the company's sales commission was 15 percent, Watson must have sold sixty to eighty machines in six days. Whether or not the story is true, Watson turned out to be an unusually talented and dedicated salesman.

In 1899, when Watson was twenty-five, NCR rewarded him with an appointment as branch manager of the Rochester, New York, office. Staffed by mediocrities, the branch had a history of poor sales. As manager, Watson received substantial incentives to improve his staff's performance — a 35 percent cut on his own sales and a 20 percent share on his employees' transactions. With

The National Cash Register Co.

MANUFACTURERS OF CASH REGISTERS,
Adapted to Every Branch of Business.
FOR PRICE LIST & CIRCULAR ADDRESS AS ABOVE
DAYTON, OHIO.

*An early NCR newspaper advertisement*

so much money at stake, Watson resorted to some rather sneaky sales tactics. For instance, he and his men tailed the competition's salesmen, calling on their clients, criticizing the quality of their registers, and hinting darkly about the opposition's financial position. And in a few years, Watson managed to turn the office around. His success impressed NCR's executives, and they decided that he was the right man for a special job — eliminating NCR's competition from secondhand register dealers. By renovating and reselling old NCR equipment, these dealers were undercutting the company's lucrative business in new machines.

With a secret subsidy from NCR, Watson opened up a secondhand shop in Manhattan in 1903 or 1904. Watson's Cash Register & Second Hand Exchange wasn't required to produce a profit; all it had to do was ruin the opposition, and Watson apparently did a fairly good job of it. He undersold legitimate dealers, hired their salesmen, opened stores near established outlets, and otherwise bedeviled the competition. Pleased with his work, NCR authorized Watson to conduct similar charades in Philadelphia and Chicago. These operations were clearly in violation of the Sherman Antitrust Act, as Watson undoubtedly knew, but such tactics were fairly common at the time. Corporate battles were considerably dirtier matters at the turn of the century than they are today, and the federal government was much less vigilant about policing the marketplace.

John Patterson (1844–1922), NCR's philosopher-king

Having proved his mettle in the field, Watson was transferred to NCR headquarters in Dayton, Ohio, in 1907. Three years later, at the age of thirty-six, he was promoted to sales manager. He was one of a handful of executives at the top, working at the right arm of John Patterson (1844–1922), NCR's capricious czar. Patterson, who had acquired the firm in 1884 when it possessed only a handful of employees, was a taskmaster, a bully to his executives and a benevolent despot to his workers. He was also one of the most imaginative businessmen of the late nineteenth and early twentieth centuries. An executive post at NCR was a first-rate education in business, and most executives put up with Patterson's ferocious personality in return for the experience. Patterson is regarded as one of the founders of modern salesmanship, marketing, and personnel practices, and Watson carried most of his methods, in a more civilized and effective form, on to IBM.

At a time when most salesmen were cut from the same disreputable cloth as Barron, Patterson sought to fashion a sales force that was the very image of professionalism. He tended to hire a certain type of salesman — generally young, fit, white Protestant males with plenty of ambition and little or no sales experience.

"It is the men who are willing to accept information and profit by it that will get ahead in this world," he once said. "I think that better salesmen can be made of new, green men, who are willing and energetic, than can be made of men who have had some experience in their business." And he meant it; when Watson first applied for a job with NCR's Buffalo office, Range had rejected him because he had too much of the wrong kind of experience.

*One of Patterson's favorite aphorisms, emblazoned on a factory wall*

Believing that great salesmen are made, not born, Patterson established a company sales school — one of America's first — in 1894. There, NCR recruits were taught the principles of "scientific" salesmanship and company veterans were drilled in new techniques. In Patterson's opinion, NCR was really providing a service, not a product; therefore, a salesman's first job was to show customers how registers would cut down on theft by clerks and enable managers to keep close track of sales. Then he had to convince them that NCR's machines were the best. A salesman was expected to provide honest, sincere, and helpful advice, not the backslapping patter of a Barron. Patterson was fond of encapsulating his selling philosophy in catchy slogans, posted in NCR offices and factories. One of the most prevalent pieces of gospel was a single word: "THINK."

While most firms concentrated on manufacturing, slighting their salesmen with low commissions, unrestricted territories, and little promotional support, Patterson emphasized sales and marketing. His salesmen received high commissions, guaranteed territories, paid vacations, and frequent bonuses. And they were backed by extensive advertising and promotional campaigns; a pioneer in the use of direct-mail advertising, Patterson spent almost as much money on promotion as on production. Salesmen who met their annual quotas were inducted into the Century Point Club, fêted at company conventions (where liquor was forbidden and smoking frowned upon), and personally congratulated by Patterson — and their quotas were raised the following year. But they had no job security. If a salesman fell consistently short of his quota, he was fired without ceremony.

Although the salesmen were NCR's vanguard, Patterson also devoted a good deal of attention to the well-being of his factory workers. Since he believed that a company's success depends on a loyal and happy workforce — a rare point of view at the turn of the century — he made sure that NCR's wages and amenities were above average. He built safe, well-ventilated factories, and installed showers, medical facilities, lunch rooms, and gymnasiums. He was farsighted in other ways, too, establishing, for example, an Inventions Department to improve NCR equipment and

*Watson (in second seat from the aisle, first row) at the right hand of Patterson at an NCR sales convention, about 1910*

develop new products. All this — the concentration on sales, working conditions, and benefits — paid off handsomely, making NCR by far the largest register manufacturer in the country.

In 1910, the American Cash Register Company, NCR's leading competitor, sued NCR for violating the Sherman Antitrust Act. Among other things, American Cash accused NCR of trying to eliminate the secondhand trade, of filing frivolous patent-infringement suits against other firms, and of advertising phony registers in an effort to undermine the competition's business. All the charges were true, and the evidence was damning; the top ranks of American Cash were sprinkled with former NCR executives, fired on whim by Patterson, and they knew where the bodies were buried. The federal government investigated the charges, and Patterson, Watson, and twenty-eight other NCR executives were indicted and found guilty in 1913. Watson was sentenced to a year in jail and was fined $5,000. (Patterson and the other executives received similar penalities.) In 1915, a higher court ordered a retrial, but Patterson, who refused to admit any culpability, signed a consent decree on behalf of NCR and a second trial was never held.

In April 1914, a year before NCR filed its appeal, Watson was fired in one of Patterson's periodic executive shakeups. The direct cause was disagreement over sales strategy, but Watson had always had an independent streak that didn't sit well with his boss. Patterson disliked strong executives who thought for themselves, and he eventually fired most of his best men. (When Patterson said "THINK," he really meant "my way.") Fortunately, Watson had seen the writing on the wall and had started looking for a job the year before. He had an excellent reputation in the business machine industry, and even though he had been convicted of antitrust violations, it was unlikely that he would go to jail. In the eyes of most businessmen, the sentence was a badge of honor, proof of his zeal and loyalty. As a result, Watson received several job offers, including one from an interesting business machine company in Manhattan that was looking for a new president.

*Watson at the controls of a biplane at the NCR country club in Dayton, Ohio, 1911. The plane may have belonged to NCR executives.*

The Computing-Tabulating-Recording Corporation (CTR), an amalgam of four firms, was organized in 1911 by Charles Ranlett Flint, a financier who specialized in the formation of industrial consolidations. Flint was a colorful figure, an international wheeler-dealer who earned his first million selling munitions in Latin America and who was popularly known, in the catchy if exaggerated phrase of a Chicago reporter, as "the father of trusts."

Flint had a hand in the creation of more than two dozen companies. His largest and most famous merger was the United States Rubber Company, organized in 1892; and in one particularly energetic year, from 1898 to 1899, he established American Chicle, American Woolen, United States Bobbin & Shuttle, and five other firms. An indefatigable man with thick muttonchop whiskers, Flint was also an avid sportsman — a hunter, a flier, a founder of the Automobile Club of America, and the owner of one of the world's fastest yachts.

In most of Flint's mergers, a group of firms in the same industry were assembled under a single corporate umbrella, which endowed them with numerous economies of scale. But CTR was different; it was an uneasy assortment of vaguely related enterprises, much like a modern conglomerate. In addition to Hollerith's Tabulating Machine Company, based in Washington, D.C., it included the International Time Recording Company, a manufacturer of employee time clocks and other time-keeping instruments, with plants in Binghamton and Endicott, New York; Bundy Manufacturing, a much smaller time clock maker in Poughkeepsie, New York; and the Computing Scale Company of America, a Dayton, Ohio, producer of retail scales and cheese and meat slicers. Altogether, CTR had 1,200 employees and a capital value of $17.5 million.

In some ways, CTR was stronger than the sum of its parts. For instance, it enjoyed greater financial resources and borrowing power than any of its subsidiaries. At least in theory, therefore, CTR was in a better position to weather hard times, since a superior performance by one division might offset a bad showing by another. Nevertheless, the merger really didn't make much administrative or marketing sense. With distinctly different products and widely dispersed factories, CTR was a company in search of a direction. International Time, the largest division, dominated its market and was doing quite well; Tabulating Machine, the second largest, also dominated its market but was short on cash for expansion and new products and was facing competition for the first time. Meanwhile, Computing Scale, the third largest part of CTR, was getting along fairly well but the scale and slicer business didn't have a very bright future. (As for little Bundy, it was folded into International Time.)

However, Flint and his associates were considerably less interested in forging a well-integrated company than in reaping large capital gains. Although they had paid $10.5 million for the four parts of CTR, Flint and his underwriters inflated the value of the new company's stock by putting a premium on various dubious intangibles — the reputations of the firms, their positions in the market, the strength of their management, and so on. Almost overnight, the total value of CTR's stock was jacked up to $16.5 million, giving Flint and his investors a quick and clever profit of $6 million. (Another $1 million in hard assets accounted for CTR's $17.5 million capitalization.) It was all quite sneaky, but hardly illegal.

During its first decade, from 1911 to 1921, CTR was dominated by International Time. International Time's president, George Fairchild, was appointed CTR's chairman, and his chief operating officer, Frank Kondolf, became CTR's president. A congressman and newspaper publisher, Fairchild was really a figurehead for the company, and his outside interests kept him away from the firm for weeks on end. Kondolf was in charge of CTR's day-to-day affairs, but he wasn't forceful or cunning enough for Flint's taste, and the financier started looking for a replacement. Watson heard about the opening and, after meeting Flint and the CTR board, was offered the job. In May 1914, Watson stepped in as general manager, with the understanding that he would be elevated to the presidency after the favorable settlement of the NCR suit.

*Watson (center) with George Fairchild (left), CTR's chairman, and S. M. Hastings, a Flint & Company executive, on their way to Europe in 1919*

Aside from being in day-to-day control of CTR, Watson was also directly responsible for Tabulating Machine. Hollerith's outfit seemed to have the greatest growth potential, and Watson knew it. Although Tabulating Machine had only a handful of salesmen, it was swamped with orders — the market for its goods was practically limitless. At the same time, however, it suffered from several serious problems. Since it leased rather than sold its equipment, it had a steady and quite sizable annual income but a rather anemic cash flow, which inhibited its expansion. In addition, Hollerith's patents were due to expire in a few years, and Tabulating Machine was facing its first competitor.

In 1905, after Hollerith had stubbornly refused to lower his rental fees, the Census had decided to develop its own tabulating equipment. It hired a Russian-born engineer named James Powers, who managed to develop a mechanical line of punchers, sorters, and tabulators that circumvented Hollerith's patents. Much to old Hollerith's shock and outrage, the Census proceeded to make its own machines for the 1910 head count, buying only the cards from Hollerith. After the census was completed, Powers established his own company. He developed an electric card puncher that outperformed Hollerith's mechanical punchers and, even more threatening to Tabulating Machine, a tabulator that automatically printed out its results. Powers also undercut Tabulating Machine's prices, selling as well as leasing his devices.

Although Powers's outfit was much smaller and less established than Tabulating Machine, its existence forced CTR to become more competitive. Watson had no intention of switching to sales — leasing was too lucrative, once the cash-flow problem had passed — but there were several things he could do. At the very least, CTR ought to hire more salesmen and beef up production. In addition, it ought to set up a product development lab (à la NCR's Inventions Department) and get to work on a modernized line of equipment. The plan was expensive but necessary, and Watson recommended that CTR devote the lion's share of its profit to expansion, not dividends.

But Fairchild turned Watson down. A major stockholder with many friends and associates who, at his recommendation, had exchanged their stock in International Time for shares in CTR, he wanted the firm to issue regular dividends. Since none of Tabulating Machine's problems were serious enough to merit immediate attention, he believed that it would be wiser to see to the health of CTR's stock and the company's financial reputation than to devote its resources to a distant future. Moreover, he believed that CTR's future lay with International Time, his old company and the firm's largest division — and if any money was going to be spent on expansion, International Time ought to get it. Al-

*Watson (noted by arrow) and the staff of the Tabulating Machine Company, on the roof of their Manhattan office, 1916*

though Flint and the CTR board sometimes backed Watson, suspending dividends in 1914 (a year of recession) and 1915, and allowing Watson to set up a small development lab, Watson's actions were circumscribed by Fairchild and his allies during Watson's first ten years with the firm.

Watson's faith in the future of Tabulating Machine was borne out by a look at CTR's balance sheet. In 1912, the firm's first full year of operation, CTR earned $541,000 in net profit. Two thirds of that sum came from International Time. (Accounting practices have changed over the years and the figures in this paragraph have been restated in modern terms.) A year later, earnings had risen to $635,000, and once again the bulk of the figure came from International Time. But *all of the growth* between 1912 and 1913 was derived from Tabulating Machine. Then the economy fell into a slump in 1914 and CTR's profit tumbled to $490,000. Still, the earnings breakdown proved Watson's point. International Time and Computing Scale had both lost a considerable amount of business during the recession, but Tabulating Machine continued rolling merrily along, nearly oblivious to the downturn, and its profit had scarcely suffered.

*James Powers, about 1915*

The reason for its success? One quarter of its revenue was brought in by leases, and its customers — generally the accounting departments of large corporations and government agencies — were wedded to Hollerith's equipment. Once clients had installed punch card machines, changing their bookkeeping and administrative practices accordingly, they couldn't simply remove the equipment and return to the old ways. And since punch card machines tended to improve efficiency and save money in the long run, some customers even tended to lease more of them during bad times. As for the remaining *three quarters* of Tabulating Machine's revenues, they came from the sale of punch cards, which customers obviously couldn't do without and which they were contractually required to buy from CTR. In short, Tabulating Machine possessed an indispensable line of products that produced a steady stream of income in good or bad times.

When the economy picked up during World War I, CTR's overall profit began climbing again. International Time and Computing Scale found new markets for their goods in the various war industries, but Tabulating Machine outperformed both of them. By 1918, it had about 1,400 tabulators and 1,100 sorters on lease in 650 offices in industry and government — a substantial increase over 1914's rental base — and was turning out more than 110 million cards a month. Led by Tabulating Machine, CTR netted $1.6 million on $8.3 million in sales in 1917 — *more than*

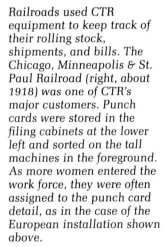

*Railroads used CTR equipment to keep track of their rolling stock, shipments, and bills. The Chicago, Minneapolis & St. Paul Railroad (right, about 1918) was one of CTR's major customers. Punch cards were stored in the filing cabinets at the lower left and sorted on the tall machines in the foreground. As more women entered the work force, they were often assigned to the punch card detail, as in the case of the European installation shown above.*

*double the sales and triple the profit of 1914.* And when, contrary to general expectations, the end of the war didn't trigger a recession, Watson undertook a major reorganization and expansion program in all three divisions. All this cost a lot of money, and CTR borrowed heavily to pay for it.

Watson's sales strategy was a page out of Patterson's book. He intended to create a well-trained and aggressive sales force in the NCR mold. His salesmen would lift the company to new heights on the strength of superior products and easy leasing terms, coupled with an efficient service organization and extensive promotional campaigns. It was a simple strategy (as the best business plans usually are); essentially, Watson was shifting emphasis from production to sales, marketing, and product development. But the scheme took a long time to put into effect, in part because of internal resistance from Fairchild and his associates. It wasn't until 1918, four years after he had joined CTR and three years after he had become president, that Watson succeeded in uniting CTR's three sales departments into a single unit. And it wasn't until 1919 that Tabulating Machine produced a printing tabulator.

Watson tended to hire the same type of salesmen as Patterson — young, tall, well-groomed, ambitious, white Protestant males. They were required to dress conservatively — the standard uniform was a dark suit, white shirt, and quiet tie — and refrain from drinking alcohol on the job, even during business lunches or at company gatherings. (Smoking was also discouraged.) Trained at a company school, Watson's recruits were taught how to approach potential clients and analyze their operations, demonstrat-

ing how the use of CTR's tabulators and sorters would boost efficiency and cut costs. Since they were selling services, not
machines, they had to learn a good deal about accounting procedures and cultivate a lasting rapport with their customers.

Watson used the same motivational techniques as Patterson: high commissions, guaranteed territories, excellent benefits,
slogans (particularly THINK), and the Hundred Percent Club for
top performers. The salesmen were the stars of the firm, and the
company's managers were drawn from their ranks. Watson even
mimicked Patterson's penchant for company sing-alongs. Every
employee received a CTR songbook filled with well-known standards adapted to company purposes, and sales conventions and
other CTR gatherings invariably opened with a hearty session of
crooning. One of the tunes was dedicated to Watson:

> Mr. Watson is the man we're working for,
> He's the leader of the CTR,
> He's the fairest, squarest man we know;
> Sincere and true.
> He has shown us how to play the game
> And how to make the dough.

*Watson delivering his "Men
— Minutes — Money"
speech at a sales convention
in Endicott, New York, 1918*

And when CTR changed its name to IBM in 1924, employees sang hymns such as this:

Our products are known
In every zone.
Our reputation sparkles like a gem.
We've fought our way through,
And new fields we're sure to conquer too,
For the ever-onward IBM.

Watson was an even more paternalistic employer than Patterson. Like his mentor, he believed that a loyal and dedicated workforce was essential to a company's success, and he spent a great deal of money on employee benefits, bracketing his workers with high salaries, paid vacations, good working conditions, company cafeterias, and, later, medical insurance, educational assistance, and country club memberships. Due in part to his distaste for Patterson's habit of firing people without justification, Watson rarely let anyone go. Instead, employees who didn't meet his exacting standards or fell out of favor were given extra training and supervision or were transferred to less demanding positions.

Watson cultivated a familial atmosphere at CTR, one that was marked by a greater degree of respect between managers and employees, and employees and their peers, than was common at the time. Although he was not as creative as Patterson, Watson was more tolerant and civilized, a much better manager of men and women, and the policies he transplanted to CTR bore greater fruit. Yet Watson was almost as much of an egomaniac and benevolent despot as Patterson. Pictures of him were posted up all over the firm, and there was a good deal of whimsy to his promotions. "When IBM was under the old man," said T. V. Learson, who served as IBM's president from 1966 to 1971, "he had a system of picking people. It was very arbitrary — sometimes it was successful, sometimes not. If he liked the cut of your jib you might move up." If not, you stayed still, slid sideways, or moved down. But at least Watson had a better eye for talent than most executives.

*The first meeting of IBM's 100 Percent Club, then called the "Go-Getters," at the company's Atlantic City, New Jersey, showroom in 1925*

Watson's ambitious expansion and reorganization plans were almost undone by the economy. As 1920 drew to a close, the country slipped into a recession — the slump that everyone had expected to arrive at the end of the war — and CTR took a drubbing. In 1920, the company realized a healthy $16 million in revenues and $1.9 million in net profit; a year later, the figures plunged to $10.6 million and $1 million respectively. Once again, it was International Time and Computing Scale that suffered the greatest reverses, while Tabulating Machine held up well. In any event, Fairchild and his associates on the board insisted on maintaining dividends, and the company doled out more than $500,000 to stockholders in 1921, leaving CTR about $200,000 in the red.

Watson had no choice but to crack down on costs. Wages were sliced by 10 percent, employees were laid off, debt was refinanced, and production of the long-awaited printing tabulator was halted. Fortunately, the economy picked up in 1922, and CTR began to recover, led by record sales at Tabulating Machine. The trip to the brink had a profound effect on Watson, who decided once and for all to concentrate on Tabulating Machine and to allow International Time and Computing Scale to wither away. He couldn't have gotten away with this a few years earlier, but he had been running the firm for almost a decade and Fairchild, who was getting on in years, was spending less time at the company. In February 1924 Watson marked the new order by changing CTR's name, which he had never liked, to the much more imposing, much more ambitious, International Business Machines Corporation. Ten months later, Fairchild died, and Watson was in full control of IBM.

The 1920s was one of the most prosperous periods in American history, and IBM flourished along with the rest of the country. The company's revenues nearly doubled, from $10.7 million dollars in 1922 to $20.3 million in 1931, while its net profit nearly quintupled, from $1.4 million to $7.4 million. To a large degree, IBM's success was linked to major economic and demographic changes. Per capita income climbed 42 percent between 1921 and 1929, when the stock market crashed and the country entered the Great Depression, while the gross national product soared an even more spectacular 48 percent. Some industries, such as automobiles and motion pictures, experienced almost exponential growth. At the same time, millions of people moved from the country to the city, hastening the development of a mass-market, white-collar economy that relied increasingly upon data-processing equipment like IBM's tabulators and sorters.

Another reason for IBM's success was the absence of effective competition. Throughout the 1920s, IBM had only one real opponent, James Powers, and his company turned out to be a paper tiger, lacking effective managers and salesmen. (During World War I, for instance, when the demand for tabulators and punch cards soared, Powers's production line broke down repeatedly. CTR happily picked up the slack.) Moreover, as a newcomer to the tabulator and sorter business, Powers lacked IBM's reputation and financial solidity (solid compared to Powers, anyway). Potential customers considering the jump to punch card machines weren't inclined to trust their fate to a beginner, and they tended to go with IBM.

But Powers's position changed in 1927, when he was bought out by the newly organized Remington Rand Corporation. Founded by the industrialist James Rand, Remington Rand was a sensibly diversified and well-financed enterprise with, it seemed at the time, a great future. In addition to tabulators, sorters, punchers, and punch cards, the company made typewriters, adding machines, office furniture, and stationery. From the moment it was born, Remington Rand was the largest business machine company in the country, far ahead of NCR, Burroughs, and IBM, the three biggest firms in the business machine industry (in that order). In its first year of business, Remington Rand's revenues were *three times* greater than IBM's (although its net profit was only slightly higher). Remington Rand seemed to possess the management, resources, and determination to give IBM and the rest of the industry a very hard time. An independent Powers was one thing; a Powers who was part of Remington Rand was another.

As for NCR, Burroughs, and Underwood Elliott Fisher, the fifth largest company in the industry, they also had the means to challenge IBM, but they were quite satisfied with their traditional markets. After Patterson's death in 1922, NCR fell into the hands of his son, a feckless executive who practically reduced the firm to bankruptcy. As if the ghost of his father were looking over his shoulder, disapproving of every effort to diversify and innovate, Patterson's heir stuck to registers and nothing but registers. Burroughs also had the skill and resources to compete with IBM, but it, too, seemed mired in the past; a conservative, unimaginative firm, it stayed chiefly with adding machines. Although more aggressive than NCR and Burroughs, Underwood Elliott Fisher wasn't interested in punch card machines; it was content to re-

*The administration building at IBM's Endicott, New York, factory, decked out in bunting for a sales convention in 1929*

main a first-rate typewriter manufacturer that dabbled in cash registers and calculators.

By the end of 1928, then, IBM was the fourth largest company in the business machine industry, with an invaluable line of products and the lion's share of a very lucrative market:

THE BUSINESS MACHINE INDUSTRY IN 1928

|  | Revenues | Net Profit |
|---|---|---|
|  | (IN MILLIONS) | |
| Remington Rand | 59.6 | 6.0 |
| National Cash Register | 49.0 | 7.8 |
| Burroughs Adding Machine | 32.1 | 8.3 |
| **IBM** | **19.7** | **5.3** |
| Underwood Elliott Fisher | 19.0 | 4.9 |

*IBM's first logo*

Ironically, Watson wasn't much more adventurous than his counterparts at NCR, Burroughs, and Underwood. After all, the world was full of potential punch card customers who had never seen an IBM salesman, and the company had its work cut out for it without branching out into cash registers, calculators, and typewriters. But Watson did make several small acquisitions that complemented IBM's product line and turned out to be powerful little engines of growth. For example, in 1922, IBM acquired Peirce Accounting Machine and, eleven years later, Electromatic Typewriter, one of the few manufacturers of electric typewriters. Electromatic Typewriter helped IBM develop a typewriterlike electric card puncher that made card punching easier and faster, but the company didn't flourish under IBM until the late 1940s and early 1950s, when electric typewriters became popular.

IBM weathered the Great Depression with astonishingly little difficulty. Once again, it was the very nature of its business that pulled it through. First, most of its revenues came from equipment leases and card sales. Second, most of its customers — large corporations and government agencies — endured the downturn with relatively little hardship. Third, most of its customers simply couldn't do without their punch card equipment. So, although earnings and revenues dipped somewhat in 1932 and 1933, they bounced back in 1934 and climbed steadily for the rest of the decade. In fact, IBM was not only immune to the worst of the depression but made an excellent profit out of it. Many New Deal agencies, such as the National Recovery Administration and the Social Security Administration, leased IBM equipment, and the federal government became IBM's largest customer, with four hundred tabulators and sorters and other IBM equipment on lease.

By 1939, IBM was the country's leading business machine manufacturer. In ten years — spanning the harshest depression in American history — its revenues *had more than doubled,* while its after-tax earnings had climbed by more than a third. Although Remington Rand's revenues were still slightly higher, IBM was the healthiest and most profitable firm in the industry, its earnings almost as large as that of the four other leading firms put together:

THE INDUSTRY IN 1939

| | Revenues (IN MILLIONS) | Net Profit |
|---|---|---|
| Remington Rand | 43.4 | 1.6 |
| **IBM** | **39.5** | **9.1** |
| NCR | 37.1 | 3.1 |
| Burroughs | 32.5 | 2.9 |
| Underwood Elliott Fisher | 24.1 | 1.9 |

It was World War II that pushed IBM firmly into the lead. In industry, government, and the military, the demand for its data-processing equipment reached unprecedented levels. Not only did the company emerge from the war with significantly higher earnings and revenues than Remington Rand, but years of high profitability had enabled it to accumulate enormous assets — nearly twice as much as the less cleverly and paternalistically managed Remington Rand ($134.1 million to $75.4 million). Remington Rand never managed to get more than 20 percent of the market for punch cards and tabulators and sorters. By 1945, IBM possessed the reputation, money, customer base, and managerial skill to enter the computer business and, if it wished, to lead it from the start.

AND IN 1945 . . .

| | Revenues (IN MILLIONS) | Net Profit |
|---|---|---|
| **IBM** | **141.7** | **10.9** |
| Remington Rand | 132.6 | 5.3 |
| National Cash Register | 68.4 | 2.2 |
| Burroughs | 37.6 | 2.3 |
| Underwood | 29.0 | 2.2 |

The Watsons in 1922, possibly on their way to Europe. Left to right: Jeannette; an unidentified woman, perhaps a governess; Jane (behind the governess); Helen; Arthur; Thomas Jr.; and Watson Sr.

Tom Watson and his wife, Jeannette, had four children, two boys and two girls. Brought up in the traditional fashion, the girls got married, settled down, and had families of their own. Thomas Jr., born in 1914, and Arthur, who came along five years later, were expected to join IBM. It was generally understood that Tom, as the oldest son, would inherit his father's mantle while Dick, as he was called by family and friends, would play a lesser role. "The company," Tom reflected years later, "is in the family uncon-scious." Tom and Dick were, in effect, IBM's youngest trainees, and Watson often took them to company conventions, where the boys fidgeted in their little suits, joined in the singing, and lis-tened politely to the speeches.

Tom entered Brown University, in Providence, Rhode Is-land, in 1933. Tall, athletic, outgoing, good-looking, he was more of a sporting playboy than a conscientious student. His grades were poor and his attendance spotty; like his father, Tom wasn't particularly interested in intellectual matters. He sowed his share of wild oats at Brown and, much to his very serious and sober father's annoyance, spent most of his time partying and drinking. He took flying lessons and, against Watson wishes, bought a small plane. Although Tom lacked ambition and direction, he was an amiable and intelligent young man, a rich man's son who, all things considered, wasn't a bad specimen of his breed.

As his graduation drew near, Tom began giving more thought to his future. Given his own head, he probably would have become a pilot, but such a decision required more independence of mind than he possessed. Chiefly out of respect for his parents' wishes, Tom joined the company after leaving Brown in 1937. (Dick joined IBM five years later, after graduating from Yale.) Naturally, Watson was overjoyed with his son's decision. As he wrote Tom in a letter that presumed more of his son than, as it turned out, the young man could give: "The thing that I am looking forward to now with so much pleasure is having you to counsel with and help me plan my future programs along various lines. I suddenly realize that now I have somebody in my life upon whom I can look with confidence."

Tom breezed through IBM's training courses — as Watson's son he could do no wrong — and was assigned to a choice territory in downtown Manhattan, where he didn't have to pound pavement for customers. Orders were sent his way merely by virtue of his kinship to the boss, and Tom made the Hundred Percent Club during his first year. And he filled his quota on the *first working day* of the following year, which left plenty of time for flying, yachting, nightclubbing, and other extracurricular activities. Fortunately, Tom was a modest young man, with few illusions about the ease of success. As he confessed in his notes for a speech to a New York business club in 1957:

> There is a reason for my success. You know it . . . I want you to know that I know it. Made unusually good choice of father so I always had a friend in the firm. . . . I have never claimed to be a great salesman . . . but I do claim to be the son of one of the greatest salesmen that ever lived. I appreciate the honor you do him today in recognizing me. The IBM Company is his monument and any sales sense that I have has come from him.

In 1940, three years after he had joined IBM, Tom was drafted. Commissioned a second lieutenant, he became a transport pilot in the Army Air Corps and spent the next five years flying generals and other VIPs between the United States and Europe. He saw a small amount of action and, like most men who have been called to war, was changed by the experience. By 1945, Tom was a lieutenant colonel and a senior pilot, a husband and a father — a mature, responsible, strong individual, accustomed to taking and giving orders. Now thirty-one years old, he was eager to return to IBM and prove himself. "Frankly I can hardly wait to begin," he wrote to his father shortly before returning to the company in January 1946. "When I think of the difference in my general outlook now as against the 1937–1940 period, I am convinced that I am now at least seventy-five percent better equipped mentally to follow in your footsteps as I intend to do."

At seventy-two the elder Watson was healthy and vigorous, and still fully in control of IBM. But he had lost his passion for change and was more interested in preserving than expanding the company. Although he had no intention of stepping aside, the time had clearly arrived for him to begin planning the succession, and he began grooming his son for the presidency. Instead of being sent back to a sales office upon his return from the war, Tom was admitted to the executive suite and appointed an assistant to Charles Kirk, a forty-three-year-old vice president and one of Watson's most trusted executives. Along with John Phillips, the firm's secretary and treasurer, Kirk, a driving and indefatigable man, supervised the company's day-to-day operations.

As Kirk's right-hand man, Tom got a crash course in managing IBM. "He had a large desk and I simply had a chair pulled up to the edge of what he did," Tom recalled. Kirk familiarized him with the company's operations, introduced him to the key executives, and briefed him on research projects, including those related to computers. Tom learned fast and his father moved him up the ladder, giving him a vice-presidency and a seat on the board in 1947. Even so, Tom was very much a junior executive, and it would be a long time before he qualified for the top post. Meanwhile, Watson retired into the background and increasingly shifted his authority to Kirk, Phillips, and Tom.

But then, in the summer of 1947, Kirk died of a heart attack, upsetting the timetable for the transition. Watson called Phillips into his office and asked him to assume most of Kirk's duties, an assignment that Phillips, a retiring man content with his position, did not relish. Two years later, Watson assumed the chairmanship, a post that he had abolished after Fairchild's death in 1921, and elevated Phillips to the presidency. Phillips's appointment was universally understood to be an interim one, a stopgap measure until young Tom was ready to take control. Finally, Tom was promoted to the executive vice-presidency. He was the third highest executive in the firm, only a step away from the throne.

In 1939, Watson Senior agreed to finance the construction of Howard Aiken's Automatic Sequence-Controlled Calculator, known as Mark I. This machine was an electromechanical program-controlled calculator composed of gears and axles, incapable of stor-

*Watson Sr. in 1944*

*The operator's console (left) and high-speed printers (right) of the electromechanical SSEC*

ing instructions or of performing conditional jumps. A costly exercise in obsolete technology, outmoded by the invention of ENIAC, the Mark I nevertheless gave IBM some valuable experience in the design and construction of large calculating machines. But IBM's relationship with Aiken came to an abrupt end after the Mark I's dedication at Harvard in August 1944; Aiken, seeking to arrogate most of the credit for the Mark I, scarcely mentioned IBM at the ceremony, and he and Watson had quite a row. ("If Aiken and my father had had revolvers they would both have been dead," Tom has said.)

Watson believed that there was little market for computers outside academia, and he had no intention of committing IBM's resources to a manufacturing effort. However, he decided to continue IBM's work in the field on a modest scale, chiefly for the public relations benefits. Despite Aiken's attempt to hog the limelight, IBM received a good deal of favorable publicity from the Mark I, and Watson, who was keenly aware of the commercial value of a good public image, considered a small computer program worth the expense. The Mark I had cost about $500,000 and had prompted a lot of good will in academia. In 1945, therefore, IBM began work on another computer, this one designed by Wallace Eckert, head of the Watson Scientific Computing Laboratory at Columbia University.

Completed in January 1948, the Selective Sequence Electronic Calculator (SSEC) was a technological hybrid, an expedient combination of old and new tricks. It contained 12,500 tubes and 21,400 electromechanical relays; the tubes carried out the arithmetic and stored a small amount of data and instructions (eight twenty-digit decimal numbers) while the relays served as a slower but larger internal memory (150 numbers). Another 20,000 numbers were stored on sixty-six reels of punched tape. When the SSEC performed an operation — say, the addition of two numbers — the necessary instructions and data were transferred from the tape to the relays to the tubes, where the instruction was executed. Although the job of transferring numbers and instructions through the hierarchy of memory consumed a lot of time, the SSEC, by virtue of the size of its memory, possessed a great deal of computational power — much more than ENIAC.

Nevertheless, it was really another decimal-based, program-controlled calculator, and it had almost no influence on computer technology. Rather than building upon ENIAC's pioneering technology, IBM had chosen a characteristically conservative approach. Some experts, chiefly at IBM, regard the SSEC as the world's first stored-program computer, but they are in the minority. True, the SSEC's instructions and data were both coded in numbers and stored in the same memories. However, the machine wasn't fully automatic; it used a series of removable plug boards to help control the transmission of numbers, meaning that a small but significant part of its programs were implemented by external wiring. The SSEC ran its first program, a calculation of the moon's position, on 27 January 1948 — six months before the fully electronic Mark I at Manchester University ran its first stored program.

The SSEC was installed in an IBM building on Madison Avenue in Manhattan, where it was visible from the street and where it attracted a great deal of attention from the public and the press. Passersby gathered in groups at the windows, watching the huge machine's blinking lights, spinning reels of punched tape, and dual printers, each spewing out data at the then phenomenal rate of 30,000 digits per minute. (The printers recorded every step of every calculation, making it easier for the programmers to pinpoint errors.) Obsolete from the start, the SSEC led a short but useful life, calculating, among other things, a table of lunar positions that was used to chart the first landing on the moon.

While the Mark I and SSEC were being built, engineers in other parts of IBM were experimenting with electronic calculators. This endeavor was a natural progression from IBM's electro-mechanical equipment, which ran on punch cards and used relays — essentially the same technology that Hollerith employed in his first tabulators and sorters. In March 1942, at IBM's main laboratory in Endicott, New York, a small team of engineers developed an electronic *cross-footing keypunch*, a sophisticated ver-

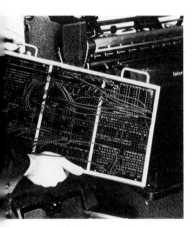

*IBM's first computers drew on the company's punch card technology. Just as some of the more sophisticated punch card machines were programmed by plug boards, so were IBM's first computers. Some of the plug boards were interchangeable, different operations requiring different plug boards.*

sion of the old-fashioned electromechanical card puncher. As the operator keyed in two numbers on a card, this gadget automatically added or subtracted the figures, punching out the result on another part of the same card. Later that year, the engineers devised an electronic multiplier that, working with prepunched cards, could multiply numbers at the modest rate of one hundred cards a minute.

Neither machine was much of a technological achievement, but the multiplier got IBM into electronics. As a former military pilot, Tom Watson was quite familiar with radar and other avionic devices — the typical B-29 had about a thousand tubes — and he had a fine appreciation for the potential of electronic technology. Although Watson Senior and other old hands at the company believed that IBM's customers would shy away from anything electronic, considering it too advanced and possibly unreliable, Watson decided to let his son test his hunch. As a result, one hundred electronic multipliers were manufactured, and the IBM 603 was put on the market in 1946 at a rental rate of $550 a month.

To everyone's surprise — including Tom's — the entire lot was snapped up. As a result, IBM decided to introduce a more sophisticated and truly useful multiplier, and the IBM 604, which had 1,400 tubes and a plug board for executing simple instructions (such as conditional branching and looping), came out in 1948. The 604 became one of IBM's most successful products. More than 5,600 of the these machines were built over the next ten years, introducing IBM's customers to electronic data processing and whetting their appetites for computers — made by tried and trusted IBM.

While Tom and the firm's other young Turks were leading the company into computers from the inside, IBM's customers were pushing it forward from the outside. In 1948, at the request of the Northrop Aircraft Company, IBM lashed a 603 electronic multiplier to an ordinary electromechanical tabulator and created — mirabile dictu! — a calculator programmed by punch cards. Other customers were interested in the machine, and IBM revved up for production. More than seven hundred card-programmed calculators, or CPCs, were built over the next few years — another electronic machine that paved the way for computers, and for IBM, entered the market. Meanwhile, the Social Security Administration, which was drowning in punch cards, also approached the company for help. IBM built a magnetic-tape processor (actually, a giant memory) that could run five tape decks, or *drives*, at once; since each ten-inch reel of tape could store the equivalent of 15,000 cards, the government got what it needed and IBM had

*Top: The cross-footing keypunch in an IBM warehouse in Endicott, New York. Middle: The 604 could store fifty decimal digits and perform arithmetic operations at a rate of 100 cards per minute. Bottom: In addition to its five tape decks, the tape processing machine contained a bank of CRTs that could store 10,000 letters or numbers and a magnetic drum that could hold another 5,000 pieces of information.*

one of the basic parts of a computer system.

By 1950, then, IBM had hundreds of computerlike products on lease and a good deal of experience making and marketing them. Still, Watson and the company's top punch card executives were reluctant to get into computers. And then, in June 1950, the Korean War broke out. In an effort to assess the computational needs of the defense establishment and to do its part for the war effort, IBM dispatched two scientists on a tour of the country's chief defense contractors, research institutes, and military branches. James Birkenstock, Tom's executive assistant, and Dr. Cuthbert C. Hurd, a mathematician who had joined IBM from the Atomic Energy Commission, visited twenty-two clients, including the National Security Agency, the Boeing Corporation, and General Electric. As Birkenstock recalled:

> It dawned on us that while all of them had different requirements they varied not that much. Probably one scientific computer wouldn't answer one hundred percent of the problems of each agency, but it would solve ninety percent of them. I was particularly anti doing anything that required giving away all our rights and data to the government and not having a solid patent position. I said to Tom, "Why not build a production lot with IBM's own money?" Tom said it was a big gamble; a three-million-dollar gamble seemed awfully big.

Birkenstock's question triggered a fierce internal debate. The product planning department — the group responsible for the commercial aspects of new products — opposed a private computer project. "Because they could not imagine classes of problems different from those treated by punched-card equipment,"

*The production version of the card-programmed calculator could process 150 cards per minute, printing out the results on the second machine from the left.*

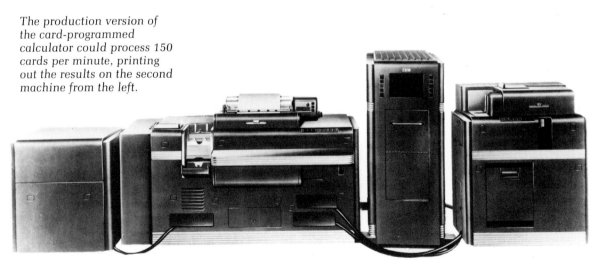

Hurd wrote years later, the planning department "told me throughout 1950 that no computer could ever be marketed at a price of more than $1,000 per month." But the Defense Calculator, as IBM's contemplated computer was at first called, would have to go for at least $8,000 a month. Other than a few government agencies and defense contractors, the planning department argued, no one, but no one, would order the machine. Therefore, the project would be a dead end, a waste of resources better spent on developing new punch card machines.

But Tom, Hurd, Birkenstock, and others saw it as a unique opportunity to get into computers. Before taking the plunge, though, Tom decided to send Hurd and an assistant on the road again, seeking firm commitments. Astonishingly, the men returned to Manhattan with thirty letters of intent. Not bad. IBM engineers got to work, and by March 1951 a detailed design was completed — showing, among other things, that the $8,000 rental rate wasn't even close to the actual production cost. The price was hiked to a forbidding $15,000 a month. Yet, even at that astro-

*An IBM computer factory in San Jose, California, in 1957. The computers under construction are the IBM 305/RAMAC (Random Access Method of Accounting and Control), which could store up to five million alphanumeric characters on fifty magnetic disks.*

*The aging Watson Sr. (seated) and Cuthbert C. Hurd with an IBM computer*

nomical fee, almost half the customers stuck with their commitments — a revealing lesson in computer economics.

In 1952, the Defense Calculator went into production at IBM's plant in Poughkeepsie. Smith Holman, the factory's general manager, told Richard Halen, the computer's production manager, to "lay out the department so it looks like a manufacturing set-up. It's the first one in the world. [Actually, Remington Rand's UNIVAC plant in Philadelphia was first.] I can't tell you how to do it. But customers will be coming to visit us, so you've got to make it look like we know how to build computers." Meanwhile, IBM, which employed only a handful of electrical engineers before it started work on the Defense Calculator, started hiring electrical engineers (EEs) in droves. Within two years the company had almost five hundred EEs on the payroll.

The first IBM 701, as the Defense Calculator was renamed, was delivered to Los Alamos in March 1953. It was a binary computer in the von Neumann style, with 4,000 tubes, a read/write electrostatic memory of 4,096 words of thirty-six bits each, and the ability to multiply two words in 456 microseconds. It was full of innovations, right down to the packaging; the machine was built in sections, and every box fit in a standard elevator and through an ordinary door. All told, IBM produced nineteen 701s — eight for aircraft companies; four for government agencies; three each for universities and large corporations, such as General Electric and General Motors; and one for itself. A data-processing company since 1890, IBM was finally in the computer business.

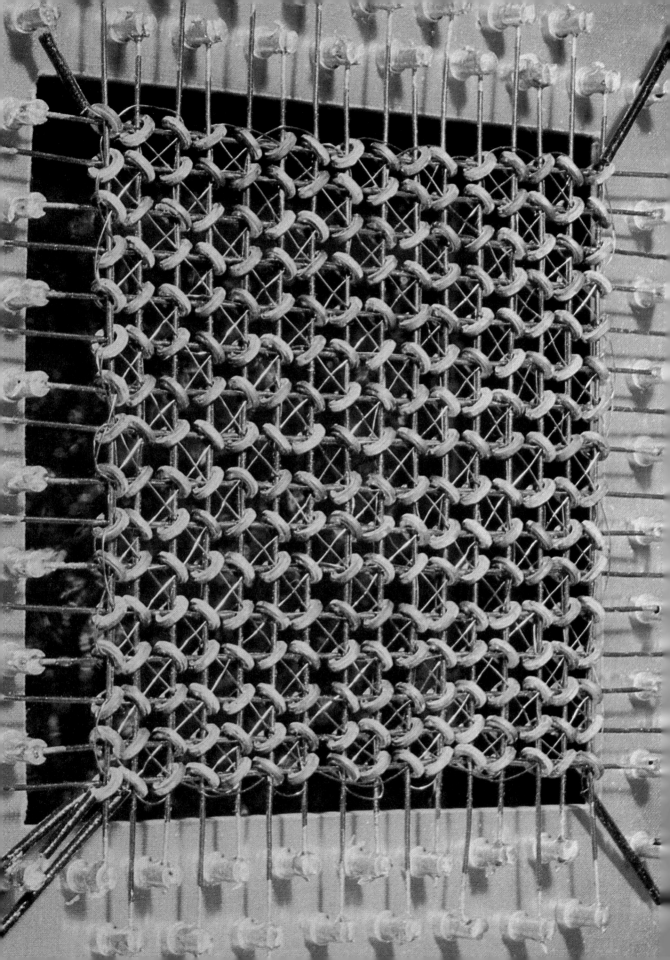

## CHAPTER 7

# The Whirlwind Project

This is not the age of pamphleteers. It is the age of engineers. The spark-gap is mightier than the pen. Democracy will not be salvaged by men who talk fluently, debate forcefully and quote aptly.
— *Lancelot Hogben*, Science for the Citizen

Is it progress if a cannibal uses knife and fork?
— *Stanislaw J. Lec*, Unkempt Thoughts

*The Whirlwind Project was the source of many important innovations in computer technology, including magnetic-core memories. This is a close-up of a magnetic-core memory plane with a storage capacity of 1,024 bits. Depending on the direction of magnetization, each ring (or magnetic core) in the picture can store a zero or a one.*

**M**ost of the computers of the late 1940s and early 1950s were sponsored by the defense establishment and put to military use. ENIAC and EDVAC were financed by the Army; von Neumann's IAS computer was underwritten largely by the Army and the Navy; the Mark I at Manchester University and the EDSAC at Cambridge were subsidized by the British military; and all but two of IBM's nineteen 701s were leased by the Navy, defense contractors, and government organizations involved in defense, such as the National Security Agency. Although many computers ended up outside the military establishment — the Census Bureau, for example, bought three UNIVACs, and the U.S. Weather Bureau acquired a 701 — the first computers were chiefly weapons of the Cold War.

These machines were not only applied to military tasks but also were designed with them in mind. ENIAC was built to calculate ballistic trajectories; EDVAC was devised to perform large scientific calculations, such as H-bomb simulations; and BINAC was intended to be a prototype of a fail-safe computer for a guided missile. In its early years, the computer industry resembled a busy little bus service. The military did most of the driving; the universities, along with a few private companies, handled the design and construction; and the passengers, those who used the computers, came from academia, defense contractors, and research institutes. There was a lot of intermingling of drivers, mechanics, and passengers, and everybody had a turn at the wheel at one time or another.

When a particular military application of computer technology (such as air traffic control) matched a commercial one, that technology entered the marketplace within a few years, whereas strictly commercial applications of computers (such as industrial process control) came along much later. Once a sizable computer industry had developed, the military's role in computer technology shrank, and private capital assumed a growing share of research and development. But that didn't happen until the early 1960s. Meanwhile, military money and necessity were the great muses of computer technology.

Take the case of Whirlwind, one of the most innovative and influential computer projects in the history of computers. Built by MIT, Whirlwind had a rather awkward childhood — it began life as an analog computer. In December 1944, the Navy's Special Devices Center asked MIT to undertake a feasibility study of a general-purpose flight trainer and stability analyzer that could be used to train pilots and to test new aerodynamic designs. At that time, flight trainers did a poor job of imitating planes in flight, and they weren't programmable, which meant that a new trainer-analyzer had to be constructed for every type of aircraft or proposed design. All this took a great deal of time and money, and the results were rather unimpressive.

MIT's Servomechanisms Laboratory assigned the study to Jay W. Forrester, a young engineer who had supervised several small projects at the lab. An extraordinarily capable, confident, though somewhat aloof man, Forrester had an engineering degree from the University of Nebraska and was working on his master's at the time. Although only twenty-six years old, he had been thinking of leaving MIT to start a company of his own, but Gordon S. Brown, the lab's director, had a keen eye for talent and was eager to keep him on. Brown called Forrester into his office, gave him a list of about a dozen projects, and invited him to take his pick. The feasibility study, which promised to be the beginning of a much larger project, caught his interest, and Forrester decided to stay on.

The trainer-analyzer had two basic parts, a cockpit and a controller. Although the cockpit promised to be a devilishly complicated piece of machinery, the real engineering hurdle was the controller. It had to be able to mimic the behavior of a wide range of aircraft, reacting to the pilot's moves, maneuvering the cockpit, driving the instrument panel, simulating wind resistance, and recording every moment of the "flight" for later analysis. The controller had to be fast and accurate; in other words, it had to be capable of *real-time* — or instantaneous — responses to human actions. And the only device that seemed suitable for the task was

an analog computer of some kind, the traditional servomechanistic solution to problems of control.

However, it would be maddeningly difficult to design an analog computer for a trainer-analyzer. An analog computer is an intrinsically inaccurate and inflexible piece of equipment; in the case of the trainer-analyzer, it would be a square peg in a round hole. Nevertheless, Forrester was optimistic — the job was not impossible — and the Special Devices Center agreed to finance a full-scale research and development effort. In the summer of 1945, therefore, MIT received an $875,000 contract for the design and construction of a trainer-analyzer. (Incidentally, the contract was granted over the sharp objections of several Navy engineers, including one officer who, well aware of the limitations of analog computers, condemned the trainer-analyzer as "a physicist's dream and an engineer's nightmare." He was right — as long as an analog computer was used.)

Forrester and his team wrestled with the controller for a few months, with little success. As chance would have it, however, in October 1945 Forrester ran into a young MIT engineer named Perry Crawford, who suggested that he look into digital computers. ENIAC was almost finished, EDVAC was under development, and the Moore School's work was stirring up a great deal of interest among engineers. Forrester took Crawford's advice, as Robert R. Everett, his second in command, wrote years later:

> Jay talked to a number of people, attended a computer conference and . . . came back and said, "We are no longer building an analog computer; we are building a digital computer."
> Things were different in those days. We didn't have a big study group, and when Jay decided to build a digital computer,

we all thought that was great. He won the support of MIT and the Special Devices Center, which was also a group of engineers, and we began to build a digital computer in late 1945 . . . . But the task was just barely possible because of [the] limited availability of test equipment and other devices and components. No technical infrastructure existed as we know it today. There were few instruments. We had to go ahead and do almost everything for the first time and when I say *we* I mean not only the Digital Computer Laboratory [which MIT established to build the computer] but everybody in the computer business.

By 1947, Forrester's team had a design for a high-speed electronic digital stored-program computer that could operate in real time. In theory, it could not only run a trainer-analyzer but perform any real-time function, such as keeping track of air traffic, monitoring a battle, or running a factory. For example, you could hook it up to a radar network, install a bank of television-like monitors, and track airplanes in a designated area. Given an appropriate method of communicating directly with the computer, you could ask questions like, "How many planes in sector four?" or, "Give intercept coordinates for target number five." Forrester and Everett had hit on a revolutionary application of computers, and they knew it.

By 1948, the project's goal, the construction of a trainer-analyzer, was jettisoned in favor of the creation of a real-time computer. Meanwhile, the Special Devices Center had closed down and the Office of Naval Research (ONR) was picking up the tab for the computer, now called Whirlwind. And it was quite a tab. Whirlwind was the largest computer project of the late 1940s and early 1950s. It had an annual budget of approximately $1 million and a staff of about 175 people, including 70 engineers and technicians.

Forrester and Everett kept tight control of the effort, and their partnership was as effective, and almost as important in the history of computers, as Eckert and Mauchly's. One engineer gave a vivid description of the pair:

> Bob Everett was relaxed, friendly, understanding — and I have never seen anyone who could go to the heart of a problem so fast! Jay was as fast, maybe faster, but he was always more formal, more remote somehow, and you weren't always sure how dumb he thought you were, or how smart. That kept us on our toes, I suppose. It was difficult to know what he was going to do next, but he was so terribly capable, it didn't matter if you couldn't follow his reasoning. He was always thinking with

seven-league boots on. It made him a pretty formidable guy to work for — partly because he and Bob always made sure you understood the problem you were working on, by finding out what you *didn't* know as well as what you did know. . . . I never resented Jay's obvious ability, but he wasn't the sort I'd call easy to work for. He definitely never was "one of the boys." He was the chief, cool, distant, and personally remote in a way that kept him in control without ever diminishing our loyalty and pride in the project.

An enormous machine consisting of a control room and eight tall banks of tubes jutting off on either side of a central corridor, Whirlwind took three years to build. Altogether, it occupied 2,500 square feet of floor space — two and a half times the size of ENIAC. Although Whirlwind contained far fewer tubes than ENIAC — 4,000 to its predecessor's 18,000 — it was spread out to make construction and maintenance easier. Since Whirlwind was designed for real-time applications, it was the fastest computer of the early 1950s, able to add two sixteen-bit words in two microseconds or multiply them in twenty microseconds. (Note the small size of Whirlwind's words, which were well suited for a real-time computer that had to run at high speed. Most computers at the time, being designed for scientific calculations, used words with at least forty bits. Whirlwind was the first sixteen-bit computer.) As for Whirlwind's internal read/write memory, it consisted of thirty-two CRTs, or electrostatic tubes, storing a total of 2,048 sixteen-bit words.

The electrostatic tubes were a constant source of headaches

The Whirlwind team built a five-digit multiplier in late 1947 as a testbed for the machine's central processor.

Workmen began erecting Whirlwind's frame in August 1948.

There were four banks of components on each side of a central corridor.

Whirlwind's operation was tested and malfunctions diagnosed at this console. By using the telephone dial on the second panel on the left, the operator could isolate a given part of the machine for testing.

Opposite: Whirlwind was composed of plug-in modules (top), which simplified construction and maintenance. Jay W. Forrester (bottom, left) and engineers Pat Youtz (middle) and Stephen Dodd examine one of Whirlwind's CRT storage tubes (the cylindrical objects at the upper right).

and Whirlwind's most serious shortcoming. Although carefully produced by hand in Whirlwind's workshops, they rarely lasted longer than a month. In brief, the faces of the tubes tended to fade, erasing their data and reducing their storage capacity. (Information was stored on the faces in the form of positively or negatively charged spots of electrons, shot from "guns" at the bottom of the tubes.) Since the tubes cost about $1,000 apiece, the Whirlwind project was spending about $32,000 a month for internal storage. Moreover, the computer was unreliable, out of order several hours a day, and unable to run programs requiring a lot of read/write memory. Whirlwind desperately needed a better form of memory.

In the spring of 1949, Forrester conceived of a solution — a solution that solved not only Whirlwind's problem but the touchy internal memory problems of all computers. "I was reading a technical journal one evening, just leafing through the advertisements in the magazine *Electrical Engineering*," he recalled in 1975,

> when I saw an advertisement for a material called Deltamax. . . . It had been developed for magnetic amplifiers. I think it was derived from a material developed in Germany in World War II. . . . When I saw this [material], I asked, "Can we use it as a computer memory? Is there some way to fit it into a three-dimensional array for information storage?" The idea immediately began to dominate my thinking, and for the next two evenings I went out after dinner and walked the streets in the dark thinking about it.

Forrester ordered some Deltamax, a metallic, magnetic material, and, without telling anyone what he had in mind, began experimenting with it. First, he flattened the stuff into thin ribbons and twisted them into small spiral rings. Next he ran a current through the rings, rapidly and repeatedly magnetizing them first in one direction (north), then in the opposite direction (south). A northerly polarity represented, say, a one; a southerly polarity, a zero. The scheme worked — the little Deltamax rings flipped from one binary state to another at the receipt of a charge and retained their states (whatever they happened to be) after the power was turned off. However, Deltamax was too slow and sensitive to physical pressures, such as touch, to serve as a practical storage element.

Confident that his notion had merit, Forrester enlisted the help of other engineers. His idea was to string up doughnutlike rings, or *cores*, of magnetic material on a grid of wires. Thus, just

as every point on a map possesses its own coordinates, so would every core on the grid. For example, a core on the third row and fourth column of the first grid would have a coordinate, or *address*, of, say, 3,4,1; likewise, a core on the third row, fourth column of the second grid would bear the address 3,4,2. By energizing the proper pair of row and column wires on a given grid, a computer could read or write a bit into a *magnetic-core memory*. If a computer used sixteen-bit words, then every bit in the word would be located at the same address on every grid.

Forrester's scheme was simple in principle, but it took a great deal of work to put into effect. A better material than Deltamax had to be found, and Forrester eventually settled on ceramic ferrite, which was much faster and hardier. And then, because Whirlwind was tied up with other important computational chores, a special computer, a smaller version of Whirlwind, had to be built to test the new memory. (The machine was constructed under the direction of Kenneth Olsen, a graduate student who, several years later, established the Digital Equipment Corporation, one of the largest computer manufacturers in the world.) The test computer worked perfectly, and a core memory was installed in Whirlwind in the summer of 1953 — four years after Forrester had dreamed up the idea. The effect on Whirlwind's performance was impressive: operating speed doubled, input data rate quadrupled, and maintenance time on the memory banks fell from four hours a day to two hours a week.

In August 1949, the Soviet Union exploded an atom bomb, and the Cold War suddenly became a much deadlier affair. The international situation was already tense; the Berlin blockade had ended only three months earlier; most of Eastern Europe was in Russian hands; China was about to fall to the communists; guerilla wars were raging in Greece and Turkey; and North Korea was making ominous threats against the southern half of the country. When, in September, the Truman administration broke the news about the Russian bomb, the disclosure provoked a wave of fear and confusion — a reaction that intensified with the equally frightful revelation that the Soviets had developed long-range bombers capable of crossing the North Pole and attacking the United States.

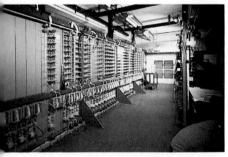

At that time, America's air defense system was a patchwork of radar stations and control centers on the East and West coasts. Left over from World War II, it was utterly inadequate to the Russian threat. When the net detected a suspicious aircraft, for exam-

Forrester holds a magnifying glass up to a magnetic-core memory plane.

Opposite, from top:

Whirlwind's control room

A CRT tester

The memory test computer

The back of the test computer

One of two magnetic-core memory banks on the test computer. Each bank stored 1,024 sixteen-bit words.

ple, the nearest Air Force base was notified and a fighter was dispatched on an interception course plotted by an air traffic controller or a navigator. As long as it wasn't confronted by many attackers, and as long as the intruders weren't flying very fast or very low, the net was satisfactory. But the polar approaches over Canada and most of the United States lay outside the surveillance system, and the country would be helpless against a massive attack, particularly by bombers sneaking in under the radar. At low altitude, ground-based radar has a very short range, and the only way (in the late 1940s) to guard against low-flying aircraft was to set up a thick battery of radar stations, which only made the job of coordinating a defense much more difficult. Planes passing from one air sector to another could easily get lost in the shuffle.

Jolted by the Soviet threat, the U.S. Air Force appointed a civilian committee — the Air Defense System Engineering Committee — to study the country's air defenses and to recommend a more effective system. In its final report, issued in October 1950, the committee called for, first, the immediate upgrading of the existing defense batteries and, second, the development of a comprehensive computerized defense network for North America. The project promised to consume billions of dollars, but the committee's recommendations reflected a national consensus to protect the United States at any cost. So, in December, the Air Force asked MIT — the inventor of Whirlwind, the world's only real-time computer — to establish a research center to design the net and supervise its construction. MIT was promised all the money it needed.

The system, which came to be known as SAGE, for Semi-Automatic Ground Environment, proceeded along several fronts. Even before the committee had released its report, Forrester's Digital Computer Laboratory was taken over by the Air Force (much to the delight of ONR, which had grown tired of footing the bills) and Whirlwind became the prototype of the SAGE computer. Forrester and his crew had to invent an entire technology. Computer monitors — televisionlike screens   were developed to display tracking aircraft and to provide a means for communicating directly with Whirlwind. And programs were written to enable Whirlwind to keep track of aircraft and to compute interception courses automatically.

On 20 April 1951, Whirlwind was put to the test. Two prop-driven planes took off into the sky above Massachusetts, one plane acting as the target, the other as the interceptor. The target plane was picked up by an early-warning radar and displayed on Whirlwind's monitor in the form of a bright spot of light, designated "T," for target. Meanwhile, the interceptor, forty miles away, was shown on the screen by a spot labeled "F," for fighter.

At the direction of the air traffic controller, Whirlwind automatically computed an interception course, and the controller steered the fighter pilot to the target by radio. Whenever the target changed course, the controller radioed new directions to the pursuing fighter. Three interceptions were tried that day, and Whirlwind brought the fighter to within 1,000 yards of the target every time. In a much more challenging test two years later, Whirlwind managed to keep tabs on forty-eight aircraft.

Meanwhile, at Lincoln Laboratory, the large research center MIT had established in Lexington, Massachusetts, to supervise the development of SAGE, scientists and military planners were trying to work out a general defense plan. In the end, they decided to divide the United States and Canada into twenty-three air sectors. All but one of the sectors were in the United States, with the twenty-third centered at North Bay, Ontario, guarding the northern approaches to the continent. Each sector would have its own direction center, a bomb-proof shelter where Air Force officers, using a real-time computer like Whirlwind, would monitor the skies and, if necessary, fight off an attack. There would also be three supreme combat centers, where the nation's overall defense would be coordinated. (Another center was installed at Lincoln Lab for ongoing research and development.)

Forrester became the chief engineer of the SAGE computers — he had come a long way since the days of the Navy's trainer-analyzer. An advanced version of Whirlwind — Whirlwind II — was built, and the SAGE computer moved a step closer to production. By the end of 1952, Lincoln Lab had started searching for a prime contractor to build the computers, and, not surprisingly, picked IBM. As the biggest data-processing firm in the country, it had the resources, the engineers, and the management to take on an enormous project like SAGE. And IBM gained much more than money from the contract; it received a front row seat on the latest and most important developments in computer technology. Magnetic-core memories appeared in commercial IBM computers (the 704, in 1955) before showing up in other companies' products, and IBM became the leading industrial expert in real-time applications.

In 1955, Whirlwind II was superseded by another prototype of SAGE, designed by MIT's Digital Computer Lab and IBM and built at IBM's Poughkeepsie, New York, factory. Despite the computer's high reliability, it was not, obviously, infallible; yet any operational failure of a SAGE computer, no matter what the reason, was unacceptable. The machines had to run twenty-four hours a day every day of the year, and a breakdown during an at-

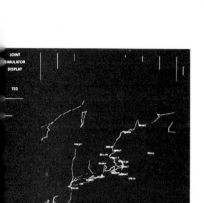

*A prototype of the SAGE system was established in 1953. As data from numerous radar stations and other sources streamed into Whirlwind, Air Force officers monitored the skies on display scopes (opposite), which presented an image of the New England sky resembling the one in the picture above.*

tack might lead to a catastrophe. Rethinking its original plans, which called for a single computer at each direction center, Lincoln Lab decided that the SAGE computer should be *duplexed*. In other words, each computer would contain two central processors, central units, and read/write memories, but share the same input, output, and bulk storage facilities. Thus, if one processor broke down, the other would kick in immediately.

In July 1958, the first SAGE center, a grim, windowless, four-story concrete blockhouse, went into operation at McGuire Air Force Base in New Jersey. Twenty-six other centers were built over the next five years. Each center contained communications equipment, air conditioners, electrical generators, sleeping quarters, and a SAGE computer. Consisting of 55,000 tubes — more than any other computer, before or since — and weighing 250 tons, a SAGE computer could run fifty monitors, or *workstations;* track as many as four hundred airplanes; store one million bits of data in internal and external memory (magnetic cores and magnetic drums); and communicate with up to one hundred radars, observation stations, and other sources of information, combining the data to produce a single, integrated picture of whatever was going on in the sky.

The SAGE computers were remarkably reliable, out of order a mere 3.77 hours a year, or 0.043 percent of the time. In large part, SAGE's reliability was the result of a clever tube-checking technique, developed for Whirlwind, that detected weak tubes before they gave out; and of a *fault-tolerant system* that, by rotating signals to redundant components, enabled the computer to work properly even when certain parts failed. Since SAGE never had to deal with a real attack, we don't know how foolproof the system actually was. (For example, an atomic blast in the atmosphere above a SAGE center probably would have damaged the computer's circuits and communications lines.)

SAGE was under almost constant development and refinement. As new weapons, such as ground-to-air missiles and surveillance satellites, appeared, they were incorporated into the system. And when advances in electronic technology led to the invention of the miniaturized solid-state components called *integrated circuits,* or *ICs* (also known as microchips), the SAGE computers were dismantled one by one. By January 1984, twenty-six years after the construction of the first SAGE center and an eon in the short history of computers, the last installation closed down. But most of SAGE's huge blockhouses are still standing, relics of the Cold War. "The buildings of the direction centers were formidable to look at," recalled Norman Taylor, a SAGE engineer:

*Opposite:*

*A SAGE computer under construction (upper right) and a completed machine (upper left). The computer, which consisted of about seventy banks of components, was built out of plug-in modules, stacked on top of each other in neat rows. The operators in a SAGE air surveillance room (bottom) communicated with the computer via light guns (lower left). When an operator aimed the gun at a spot on the screen, the computer performed a specified operation, such as intensifying an image or supplying more information.*

Bob Everett and I used to drive to Poughkeepsie and back almost every week for about three years. . . . One night we were coming home at about two o'clock in the morning and we were talking about what is important, what will be important, and where do we go from here. Bob said, "You know, Norm, you and I will be buried in some cemetery, and some guy will walk by those buildings and he'll say, 'What the hell do you suppose those guys had in mind?'"

*The SAGE center at McGuire Air Force Base*

Aside from ENIAC and von Neumann's IAS machine, which established the paradigm of the stored-program computer, Whirlwind was the source of more significant technological innovations than any other computer. As the first real-time computer, Whirlwind led the way to such computational applications as air traffic control, real-time simulations, industrial process control (in refining and manufacturing, for example), inventory control, ticket reservation systems, and bank accounting systems. It gave birth to *multiprocessing*, or the simultaneous processing of several predetermined programs by different units of the machine, and *computer networks*, or the linking of several computers and other devices into a single system. It was the first computer with magnetic-core memories and interactive monitors. And it was the first sixteen-bit computer, which paved the way for the development of the *minicomputer* in the mid-1960s (as we shall see in the next chapter).

Almost all of these innovations were incorporated in SAGE (which was, however, a thirty-two-bit computer), along with some new ones, such as back-up computers and fault-tolerant systems. But SAGE's technological significance doesn't derive from any particular technical innovation or set of innovations. Rather, it stems from a lesson. Above all, SAGE taught the American computer industry how to design and build large, interconnected, real-time data-processing systems. Through SAGE, Whirlwind's fabulous technology was transferred to the world at large, and computer systems as we know them today came into existence.

In 1954, while SAGE was under construction, IBM began work on a real-time computer seat-reservation system for American Airlines. A much smaller version of SAGE, it was known as SABRE, or Semi-Automatic Business-Related Environment. It consisted of a duplex computer — one in constant use, the other standing by in case of trouble — and 1,200 teletypes all over the country, linked via the phone lines to the airline's computing center north of New York City. The system took ten years and $300 million to develop, and wasn't in full operation until late in 1964. At that time, it was the largest commercial real-time data-processing network in the world. By the end of the decade, real-time computer systems were commonplace in industry, academia, and government.

In 1952, while the IBM 701 was under construction, Cuthbert C. Hurd, the mathematician who ran the firm's applied science department, proposed the development of a medium-sized computer that would rent for $3,000 to $4,000 a month. His department, which had representatives in IBM sales offices throughout the United States and Europe, received many requests for such a machine. IBM's Washington Federal Office, which managed the company's government accounts, estimated that it could place at least fifty computers with the military's various supply services, which were buried in paperwork. But Hurd's suggestion sparked a fierce debate at IBM. As he wrote years later:

> The opposition within IBM to this idea was even stronger than the opposition prior to the decision to build the 701. Roberts, Bury, and Rubidge [in the product planning department] continued to make statements such as, "You can never sell a machine that rents for more than $1,000 a month, except to scientists." People from the engineering and product planning departments were arguing for the development of more powerful punched-card machines. At a week-long engineering meeting at the Harriman estate, the debate continued without resolution 20 hours a day.

But the old guard couldn't have been more wrong. Determined to keep the company moving into computers, Tom Junior overruled the objections and decided to proceed. The next step was to decide how many machines to make, a question that was normally settled by agreement between several departments. Again, the old guard was uncooperative. "The market forecast procedure," wrote Hurd, "consisted of obtaining forecasts from the sales, product planning, and applied science departments. Roberts, Bury, and Rubidge said that the forecasts from sales and product planning were zero because the machine we had in mind could not be produced for $1,000 a month, and therefore no customers would buy it other than the kinds who had bought the 701."

Hurd's department, then, was the only one that was willing to make a forecast, and he called for a production run of 250 machines and a rental rate of $3,250 to $3,750 a month. (The rate depended on whether the machine contained 1,000 or 2,000 words

*There were 1,200 terminals such as this one in the SABRE system.*

of external magnetic-drum storage). In July 1953, Hurd's medium-sized machine, the IBM 650, was announced. Salesmen started taking orders, and the first 650 was delivered in December 1954.

Inexpensive, practical, reliable, the 650 turned out to be exactly what the market needed, and it was a runaway success. The 650 was the Model T of the computer industry — the first mass-produced computer. By December 1955, 120 of these machines had been installed and another 750 had been ordered. Fifteen hundred were manufactured by the time the model was phased out in 1969. The punch card side of the company was beginning to fade away.

Meanwhile, IBM also was gearing up for SAGE, the largest computer project of the decade, and continuing to turn out large computers in the style of the 701. Between 1955 and 1956 IBM introduced three new computers: the business-oriented 702, a marriage of the 701 and the tape-processing machine IBM had designed for the Social Security Administration; the 705, the 702's successor and the first commercial computer with magnetic-core memories; and the scientific 704, the 701's successor and the first computer with a bona fide computer programming language (which we'll discuss in a moment). About one hundred 704s and 705s were produced altogether. By 1956, IBM was no longer a tabulator company but the world's largest and most profitable computer manufacturer, building the machines by the hundreds.

*The IBM 650*

All the early computers — ENIAC, the IAS machine, Manchester University's Mark I, the IBM 701, and Whirlwind — were mad-

*A simplified version of an ENIAC programming diagram, showing how to wire up the machine to solve a differential equation $\left(\dfrac{dy}{dx} = y\right)$*

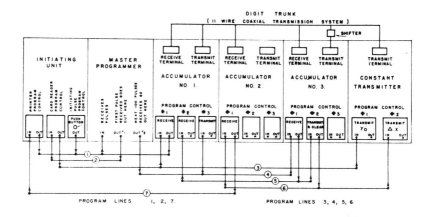

deningly difficult to program. In general, the first computers were programmed either in *machine code*, which consisted of binary numbers, or in codes known as *assembly languages*, which were composed of letters, numbers, symbols, and short words, such as "add." After being fed into the computer, assembly programs written in these languages were translated automatically into machine code by internal programs called *assemblers*, and the resulting machine code, punched out on cards or tape, was then re-entered into the computer by the operator. As computer technology advanced, *high-level programming languages* that used ordinary English phrases and mathematical expressions were developed. Because computers are only as useful as their programs, the computer industry — particularly IBM and Remington Rand — put a great deal of effort into the development of efficient and economical programming techniques.

An ENIAC program was really a wiring diagram. It showed exactly how the machine's switches and plug boards ought to be set to solve a given problem — not at all what we'd consider a program today. But ENIAC was quite unlike its stored-program descendants. For example, it possessed two kinds of circuits: numerical circuits, which relayed the electrical pulses that represented numbers, and programming circuits, which coordinated the sequences of operations that implemented a program. As a result, an ENIAC program consisted of two parts, one dealing with the numerical circuits, the other with the programming ones. Every single operation had to be provided for, and it took two or three days to set up ENIAC for a complicated problem. Programmers had to know the machine inside out, right down to the smallest circuits.

When ENIAC was built, there were no formal, standard-

ized, conceptual procedures for solving problems by computer. So
the ENIAC team set about inventing one. Herman Goldstine, the
mathematician and Army lieutenant who brought Mauchly's idea
for an electronic calculator to the attention of the Ordnance Department, thought that a pictorial representation of a computer's
operation would be the best aid to clear thinking and careful
planning. With von Neumann's help, he developed *flow charting*.
Although flow charts have since fallen out of favor as a programming tool, many programmers still use them.

By the late 1940s, ENIAC had been superseded by stored-
program computers, which meant that instead of fiddling with a
computer's wiring, you now could feed instructions directly into
the machines through punch card readers, magnetic-tape decks,
or other means. For example, the first stored program run on the
Mark I consisted of binary numbers entered via a keyboard, with
each key corresponding to a coordinate, or address, in the memory. A list of instructions for finding the highest factor of a number, it contained seventeen lines of sixteen bits each. The program
itself has been lost, but a line in it might have looked like this:
1001000010001001. The last three digits specified the operation
(addition, subtraction, and so on), while the first thirteen signified
the address either of another instruction or of a piece of data.

Although this programming method was a marked improvement over ENIAC's, it nevertheless left much to be desired.
The binary system is ideal for machines but awkward for people.
Therefore, Alan Turing, the Mark I's chief programmer, developed
an assembly language (or *symbolic language* as it was also called
at the time) that substituted letters and symbols for 0s and 1s. For
example, a "/W" ordered the Mark I to generate a random number;
a "/V," to come to a stop. The language's *instruction set*, or repertoire of commands, contained fifty items, sufficient to perform almost any operation. The system was really a mnemonic code —
and a clumsy one at that — whose symbols, entered via a teleprinter, were automatically translated into binary math by the
computer. There was nothing complicated about the translation
process; every letter and symbol was turned into a predetermined
binary number, and then executed.

By the way, the Mark I's random number generator, which
was installed at Turing's suggestion and ran off a source of electronic noise, supplied some fun and games. F. C. Williams, who
headed the Mark I project and who invented electrostatic storage
tubes, wrote a little gambling program that counted the number of
times a given digit, from 0 to 9, was produced by a run of the generator. But Williams adjusted the generator to lean toward his fa-

vorite number, and he enjoyed betting against unsuspecting visitors. The beginnings of computer crime!

UNIVAC was programmed with a simpler and more advanced language than the Mark I. In 1949, at Mauchly's suggestion, an alphanumeric instruction set was devised for BINAC and adapted, in improved form, for UNIVAC. This instruction set was called *Short Code,* and it enabled algebraic equations to be written in terms that bore a one-to-one correspondence to the original equations. For example, $a = b + c$ was represented as S0 03 S1 07 S2 in Short Code, with S0, S1, and S2 standing for a, b, and c; 03 meaning "equal to"; and 07 signifying "add." Inside UNIVAC, an *interpreter* program automatically scanned the code and executed each line one at a time. (That is, it did not produce cards or tape that had to be reentered into the machine; it carried out the program automatically.) Although Remington Rand made many extravagant claims for Short Code, you still had to supply detailed instructions for every operation.

In the early 1950s, most computers were used for scientific and engineering calculations. These calculations involved very large numbers, and the usual way of writing a number — groups of figures separated by a comma — was inconvenient. Instead, programmers used the *floating-point* system of numerical notation, which reduced big numbers to a more manageable size. (A floating-point number is a fraction multiplied by a power of two, ten, or any figure. For example, 2,500 is $.25 \times 10^4$; 250,000 is $.25 \times 10^6$; and 25,000,000 is $.25 \times 10^8$.) But the computers of the period couldn't perform floating-point operations automatically. Nor could they automatically assign memory addresses, a task known as indexing, or handle input and output. As a result, programmers had to spend a lot of time writing *subroutines,* or segments of programs, telling the machines exactly how to perform these operations. And computers spent most of their time carrying out such subroutines.

The more forward-looking programmers began tinkering with the idea of automating programming (and they're still working on it). If indexing, floating-point, and input/output operations could be performed automatically by computers, then the more creative aspects of programming — the things that only people could do — would be left to the programmers, and the machines would be freed from many time-consuming chores. Of course, all this was easier said than done. You needed an internal program that was smart enough and fast enough to translate a programmer's instructions into efficient machine code. In other words, wrote John Backus and Harlan Herrick, two IBM programmers who, as we shall see, managed to develop just such an internal program: "Can a machine translate a sufficiently rich mathematical language into a sufficiently economical program at a sufficiently low cost to make the whole affair feasible?"

In 1951, Grace Murray Hopper, a mathematician at Remington Rand, conceived of a new type of internal program that could perform floating-point operations and other tasks automatically. The program was called a *compiler*, and it was designed to scan a programmer's instructions and produce, or compile, a roster of binary instructions that carried out the user's commands. Unlike an interpreter, a compiler generated an organized program, then carried it out. Moreover, a compiler had the ability to understand ordinary words and phrases and mathematical expressions. Hopper and Remington Rand devised a compiler and associated high-level language that had some success. Although "automatic programming" helped the firm sell computers, it wasn't all that it was cracked up to be. ("Automatic programming, tried and tested since 1950, eliminates communication with the computer in special code or language," declared a UNIVAC news release in 1955.)

But Hopper was an excellent proselytizer, and her techniques spread. In 1953, two MIT scientists, J. Halcombe Laning and Niel Zierler, invented one of the first truly practical compilers and high-level languages. Developed for Whirlwind, it used ordinary words, such as "PRINT" and "STOP," as well as equations in their natural form, like a + b = c. In addition, it performed most housekeeping operations, such as floating-point, automatically. Unfortunately, the compiler was terribly inefficient. Although Laning and Zierler's language was easy to learn and use, the compiler required so much time to translate the programmer's instructions into binary numbers that Whirlwind was slowed to a crawl. "This was in the days when machine time was king," Laning recalled, "and people time was worthless." As a result, their system, though highly influential, was rarely used.

When IBM began taking orders for the scientific 704, in May 1954, they introduced it as the first of a new class of computers whose circuits could perform floating-point and indexing operations automatically. A 704 programmer wouldn't have to compose floating-point subroutines for every scientific or engineering calculation, and the computer wouldn't have to waste costly time wandering down the sticky byways of floating-point operations. At last, the two most time-consuming programming chores would be eliminated. But other programming inefficiencies now stuck out like boulders on a plain, unable to hide in the shade of floating-point and indexing subroutines. The 704 cried

*Grace Murray Hopper in 1983. One of the few women to play an important role in the history of computers, she joined the WAVES (Women Accepted for Voluntary Emergency Service) during World War II and stayed in the Naval Reserve for the remainder of her career. She became a captain in 1973.*

out for a compiler that could translate simple high-level instructions into machine codes that were just as good as those written by a programmer.

*John Backus (at left in back row) and some of the creators of FORTRAN at a computer convention in Houston, Texas, in 1982. Left to right, first row: Sheldon Best, Roy Nutt, Robert Nelson, and Richard Goldberg; second row, Lois Haibt and Irving Ziller.*

In 1953, John Backus headed a small group of programmers that was developing an assembly language for IBM's mammoth 701. Known as Speedcoding, the language was roughly similar to UNIVAC's Short Code. The Speedcoding effort had taken most of the year, and the Speedcoding interpreter and programmer's manual had gone out to 701 users in the fall. It was now time to turn to the 704, then on the drawing board. Backus sent a memo to his boss, Cuthbert Hurd, suggesting the development of a compiler and higher-level language for the 704. Hurd, who ran the applied science department, approved the idea, and the FORTRAN, or FORmula TRANslation, project was established.

It was a modest effort. At first, it consisted of Backus, an easy-going young man with a master's in mathematics from Columbia University, and Irving Ziller, another programmer. By the summer of 1954, three more programmers had joined the team, and they began running test programs on an IBM 701 in the IBM complex at 590 Madison Avenue, in Manhattan. From the beginning, the group concentrated on the compiler. "We simply made up the language [the commands that make up a user's program] as we went along," Backus recalled.

> We did not regard language design as a difficult problem, merely a simple prelude to the real problem: designing a compiler which could produce efficient [binary] programs. Of course one of our goals was to design a language which would make it possible for engineers and scientists to write programs for the 704. We also wanted to eliminate a lot of the bookkeeping and detailed, repetitive planning which hand coding [in assembly language] involved.

Backus and his team began writing the compiler in early 1955, after a year and a half of preliminary work. Although Backus had originally estimated that it would take about six months to compose this internal program, the task turned out to be far more difficult than he had imagined, and it wasn't until the summer of 1956 that the compiler was ready for troubleshooting. "The pace of debugging was intense," wrote Backus. "Often we would rent rooms in the Langdon Hotel (which disappeared long ago) on 56th Street, sleep there a little during the day and then stay up all night to get as much use of the computer . . . as possible.

It was an exciting period; when later on we began to get fragments of compiled programs out of the system, we were often astonished at the surprising transformations in the indexing operations and in the arrangement of the computation which the compiler made, changes which we would not have thought to make as programmers ourselves.

In April 1957 — about three and a half years after the project had begun — the compiler was finished. Consisting of about 25,000 lines of machine code, it was stored on magnetic tape and distributed to every 704 installation. A small, handsomely produced programming manual went along with it; only fifty-one pages long, it described the high-level language and explained what each of its thirty-two instructions, such as PUNCH, READ DRUM, and IF DIVIDE CHECK, accomplished. But FORTRAN had a difficult childhood, and there were a lot of bugs to be ironed out in the field before it was reliable. As one programmer recalled:

> Like most of the early hardware and software systems, FOR-TRAN was late in delivery, and didn't really work when it was delivered. At first people thought that it would never be done. Then when it was in field test, with many bugs, and with some of the most important parts unfinished, many thought it would never work. It gradually got to the point where a program in FORTRAN had a reasonable expectancy of compiling all the way through and maybe even of running.

*The first two pages in the FORTRAN programmer's reference manual*

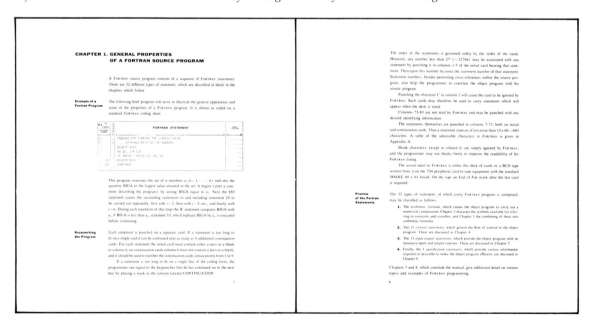

Nevertheless, FORTRAN was a landmark in the history of computing. Easy to learn and to use, it was an enormous advance over assembly languages like Short Code and Speedcoding. Now anyone with a logical mind and the desire could learn to program a computer. You didn't have to be a specialist, familiar with the inner workings of a computer and its demanding assembly language. By using FORTRAN's simple repertoire of commands, you could make a computer do your bidding, and the compiler would rapidly and automatically translate your instructions into efficient machine code. The invention of FORTRAN was one of IBM's most important technical achievements, and it certainly helped the company sell computers.

The original FORTRAN compiler ran only on the 704, but programmers went on to develop FORTRAN compilers for other IBM computers, and competing manufacturers, licensed by IBM, adapted FORTRAN to their own machines. Lo and behold, computers soon began speaking the same language — although a FORTRAN program written for one type of computer invariably had to be modified to run on another — and programmers no longer had to master a different language for every computer. Moreover, other computer languages began to appear. As a scientific and engineering language, FORTRAN wasn't well suited for business and other applications, and many languages were devised to fill the gaps, such as COBOL (COmmon Business-Oriented Language); ALGOL (ALGOrithmic Language); and one of the most popular of all, BASIC (Beginner's All-purpose Symbolic Instruction Code).

In 1955, Remington Rand merged with the Sperry Corporation, a leading producer of electronic weaponry, hydraulic equipment, and farm machinery. James Rand was sixty-nine years old in 1955 and contemplating retirement. His company, which had grown an unimpressive 75 percent between 1930 and 1946, needed a senior partner, and Sperry seemed like a good choice. Run by Harry Vickers, a self-taught hydraulic engineer and a friend of Rand's, Sperry was a healthy, prosperous, well-managed firm whose revenues had zoomed nearly 700 percent since 1946. Sperry was almost twice as big as Remington Rand, and much more vigorous. (In 1954, Sperry grossed $57 million on $441 million in revenue. Remington Rand, on the other hand, earned $27 million on $224 million in sales.) But military contracts accounted for most of Sperry's revenues, and the firm wanted to establish a broader, more stable base in the private sector, preferably in electronics.

Shortly before the merger, Remington Rand's UNIVAC had

an installed base of about thirty big computers to IBM's four. Meanwhile, UNIVAC's makers were happily scrambling to fill a substantial backlog of orders. On the basis of these facts, Vickers believed that he had acquired the country's leading computer manufacturer. But he was in for a shock. In 1954 IBM started taking orders for the 700 series of computers, then on the drawing boards and much superior to UNIVAC's machines, and UNIVAC soon slipped to second place. By 1956, IBM had seventy-six large computers in the field to UNIVAC's forty-six, and its backlog was almost three times the size of UNIVAC's. In medium-sized computers, the fastest-growing segment of the computer market, IBM seemed to be running the race alone. The company had placed seven times as many of these computers (369) as all the other manufacturers combined, and had four times as many (920) on order. Caught unprepared, UNIVAC didn't even have a medium-sized machine on the market until 1958.

What went wrong with UNIVAC? Just about everything. More of a promoter and manipulator than a manager or builder, James Rand ran a one-man show. Although his decision to get into computers was quite astute, he really regarded the UNIVAC division as a sideline; he was more interested in electric shavers, office furniture, and typewriters. UNIVAC wasn't set up right, either. It was divided into two parts, with Eckert and Mauchly's enterprise in Philadelphia, and the other arm, Engineering Research Associates (ERA), in St. Paul, Minnesota — and the two halves didn't get along with each other. In 1957, after organizational changes that put St. Paul at a disadvantage, William C. Norris, one of ERA's founders, left to form his own company, taking most of the staff with him. With masterly command of technology, Norris's venture, the Control Data Corporation, became the leading manufacturer of *supercomputers* — big, high-speed machines capable of performing tens of millions of operations a second.

Meanwhile, Remington Rand's sales force proved no match for IBM's. When a team of IBM salesmen called on a customer, they worked hard to show how the installation of an IBM computer would get the payroll out faster, keep better track of sales, boost efficiency, and save money. And they had a corps of specialists — programmers, engineers, and business experts — to assist them. When a group of UNIVAC salesmen visited a client, however, they tended to harp on technological matters — mercury delay lines, decimal versus binary computation — that went right over the heads of their customers, who were chiefly interested in the answer to one question: "What will a computer do for me?" Although UNIVAC had a team of traveling salesmen that whipped

*Introduced in 1963, Control Data's 6600 performed approximately a million operations a second. It was the most powerful computer on the market and helped make Control Data the world's biggest manufacturer of supercomputers. The round tubes on the control consoles in the center of the picture are display monitors.*

up interest in computers, Remington Rand's branch offices failed to follow through. They were more familiar with the company's traditional products, which were much easier to sell.

And if all this wasn't bad enough, UNIVAC's managers were as inept at negotiating profitable deals as Eckert and Mauchly. In 1956, in mindless repetition of Eckert and Mauchly's penchant for fixed-fee contracts, UNIVAC signed a $3 million agreement with the Atomic Energy Commission for the development and construction of a supercomputer. The Livermore Atomic Research Computer (LARC) ended up costing $20 million, and UNIVAC had to make up the difference. Although UNIVAC managed to sell a second LARC to the Navy, they didn't recoup their loss.

As long as Rand, who became Sperry's vice chairman after the merger, was in charge of UNIVAC, it was difficult to attack the division's problems. When Rand finally retired in 1959, Vickers brought in Dause L. Bibby, a former IBM vice president, to run UNIVAC. But it was too late. "At IBM," recalled a former Sperry executive, "Bibby would press a button and a thousand guys in pin-striped suits would come out and salute; when he pressed the button at UNIVAC, nothing happened. Mobilizing an effective organization takes one kind of talent; breathing life into a dead one takes another." UNIVAC lost about $250 million between 1956 and 1967, when it finally turned a minuscule profit.

IBM's lead was unassailable. By 1961, when vacuum-tube computers were giving way to a new generation of machines consisting of *transistors* (which we'll discuss in the next chapter), 71 percent of the country's $1.8 billion in computers had been built by IBM. UNIVAC was a distant second, with about 10 percent of the market, followed by Burroughs and then, more or less in a clump, Honeywell, RCA, Philco, NCR, General Electric, and Control Data. A host of smaller companies, such as Bendix and Royal McBee, fluttered at the bottom of the industry, supplying small computers. And by 1964, when transistor machines were giving way to a third generation of computers composed of integrated circuits, IBM's share of the $5.3 billion in installed computers had climbed to 76 percent. IBM had risen to the top by dint of its vision, excellence, and dedication, and the ineptitude of its competitors.

In 1964, the U.S. Patent Office finally issued Eckert and Mauchly's ENIAC patent — seventeen years after they had applied for it. The delay had been caused by technical disputes of various kinds, chiefly between Sperry Rand, which had inherited the patent rights from Remington Rand, and Bell Labs, which contended that the ENIAC patent interfered with some of its own. At long last, the disputes were settled by the Board of Patent Interferences, the patent was granted, and Sperry began notifying computer companies that they were violating the ENIAC patent. Sperry offered its competitors patent licenses at a fee of 1.5 percent of the selling price of their equipment. (IBM was excluded; it had reached a $10 million royalty agreement with Sperry in 1956.) With millions of dollars at stake, no one accepted Sperry's offer and the issue ended up in the courts.

In May 1967, Sperry sued Honeywell and the Control Data Corporation for patent violation. Meanwhile, Honeywell countersued, accusing Sperry of trying to enforce a fraudulent patent. The Honeywell–Sperry case was consolidated and assigned to the federal district court in Minneapolis (Honeywell's home city); the Sperry–Control Data suit went to a federal court in Baltimore. The cases involved two different patents. In the Control Data dispute, Sperry was seeking to enforce a 1954 patent covering Eckert and Mauchly's mercury delay line memory. The essence of this patent was the idea of regenerative memory — the notion of retaining stored information by periodically re-energizing it. In the Honeywell case, Sperry was seeking to uphold the ENIAC patent only (although the judge decided to rule on the regenerative memory patent as well).

In 1967, a Control Data attorney read about John Atanasoff

*Technicians at a Control Data factory in St. Paul, Minnesota, construct a Cyber 205 supercomputer. The machine, which cost $18 million in its most advanced version, executes 800 million operations a second. It contains 100,000 components, fifty miles of wiring, and takes six months to build. Supercomputers like the Cyber 205, which was introduced in 1981, are used for such sophisticated computational chores as airplane design and weather forecasting. A finished Cyber 205 is depicted at the lower left and right; the other pictures show the machine under construction.*

in a book on computers, and lawyers representing all sides in the cases converged on Frederick, Maryland, where Atanasoff had retired after rising to a vice president of the Aerojet General Corporation. (He had left the Navy in 1952 and established an electronics company with several colleagues. They sold the firm to Aerojet in 1956.) One of the lawyers briefed Atanasoff about the lawsuits and gave him copies of the disputed patents. Atanasoff, who had seen ENIAC and UNIVAC but had not studied Eckert and Mauchly's machines very closely, examined the documents. It seemed to him that many of Eckert and Mauchly's claims derived from his work. Angered, he agreed to help Honeywell and Control Data overturn Sperry's patents, joining their defense staffs as a paid consultant.

(A patent consists of three parts: illustrations of the device being patented; a written description of the device and its operation; and a list of claims covering only those ideas that originated with the device. In order to be valid, a patent must, among other things, be filed within a year of the creation of the invention. In addition, it cannot be preceded by a published report describing the invention in detail.)

The Honeywell–Sperry case, the first to go to trial, opened on 1 June 1971 and ended 135 days later, on 13 March 1972. Seventy-seven witnesses testified and 32,654 exhibits, including Babbage's autobiography, were filed. All told, the trial transcript filled 20,667 pages. Obviously, it's impossible to give a detailed account of the trial here, but at least two points are worth mentioning. A working model of part of Atanasoff's machine was demonstrated in court, and Sperry's attorneys glossed over the experiments Mauchly had performed in analog and digital electronics before he met Atanasoff. They did so, it seems, both because they underestimated the seriousness of Atanasoff's legal threat and because the evidence surrounding Mauchly's early work seemed too insubstantial to stand up in court.

Judge Earl Larson handed down his decision on 19 October 1973, and Sperry lost on every count. Larson invalidated the ENIAC patent on four grounds, each of which would have been sufficient to strike down Eckert and Mauchly's claims. First, that the patent had been filed more than a year after the machine had been put to use. Second, that von Neumann's "First Draft of a Report on the EDVAC" constituted prior publication. Third, that Eckert and Mauchly's attorneys had engaged in misconduct by deliberately delaying the patenting process, hoping to put off the day the patent took effect and thus increasing its financial value to Sperry Rand. And fourth, and most damaging of all, that Eckert and

Mauchly "did not themselves first invent the automatic electronic digital computer, but instead derived that subject matter from one Dr. John Vincent Atanasoff." Finally, Larson also invalidated the regenerative memory patent on the ground that it too had been derived from Atanasoff.

Larson's decision appears to be legally correct; Atanasoff's machine did embody many technical innovations that ended up in ENIAC, and it indeed does appear that Mauchly was directly influenced by Atanasoff's work. There were, however, some puzzling and contradictory aspects in Larson's decision; for example, although the judge credited Atanasoff with having invented an "automatic electronic digital computer," there was nothing automatic about the machine. ENIAC was a much better example of an automatic electronic digital computer, and one wonders exactly what Larson had in mind by the term *automatic*. Unfortunately, Sperry, which had spent about $1 million on the case, decided not to appeal, and the Honeywell and Control Data cases were dropped.

A lawsuit is one thing, historical judgment another. Atanasoff was a solitary inventor who failed to grasp the importance of his invention and didn't even bother to publicize it, let alone patent it. After leaving Iowa State in 1942 for a job with the Navy outside of Washington, D.C., he lost all interest in computers. Although he saw ENIAC after the war, he did not make any effort, even for curiosity's sake, to draw any parallels between the giant machine at the Moore School and his own, now disassembled, device. He championed his invention only after a group of lawyers invited him to join their cause. Despite Larson's rulings, it was Eckert and Mauchly's talent and industriousness that led to the development of the stored-program computer and to the birth of the computer industry. Eckert and Mauchly were stripped of their legal claim to primacy in the history of computers, but their historical position is unshakable.

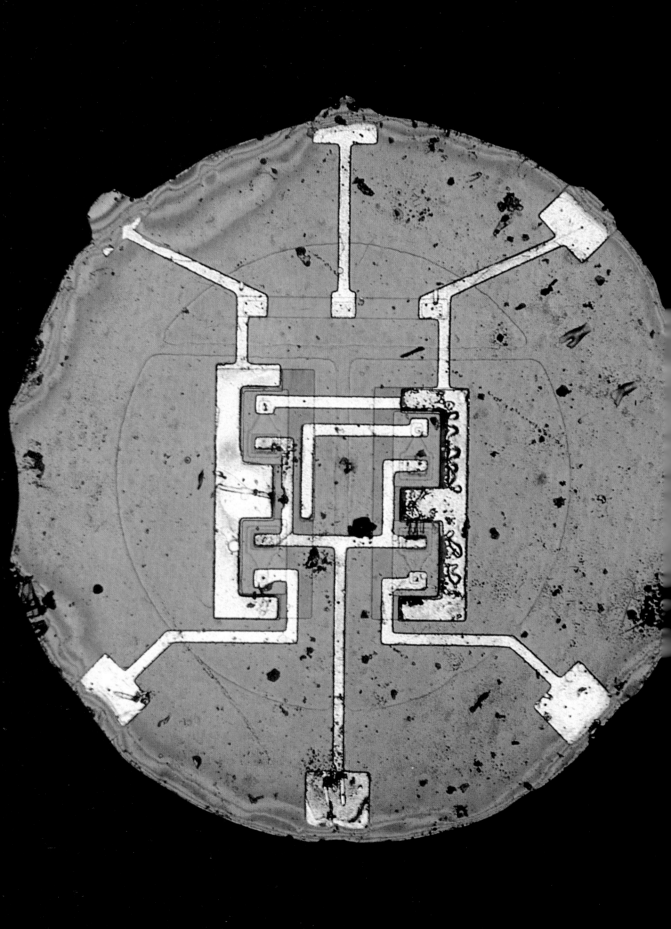

## CHAPTER 8

# The Integrated Circuit

If you take a bale of hay and tie it to the tail of a mule and then strike a match and set the bale of hay on fire, and if you then compare the energy expended shortly thereafter by the mule with the energy expended by yourself in the striking of the match, you will understand the concept of amplification.

— William Shockley, co-inventor of the transistor

O n 23 December 1947, a small team of scientists at Bell Telephone Laboratories in Murray Hill, New Jersey, created the transistor. One of the most important inventions of the twentieth century, the transistor is a solid piece of material — as solid as a rock — with the electrical properties of a vacuum tube. Like a tube, it can amplify current, detect radio waves, and serve as a switch; but, unlike its finicky and fragile counterpart, it turns on instantly, generates almost no heat, uses little power, does not burn out, costs pennies to make, is practically immune to vibration and shock, and occupies about as much space as a pencil eraser. The transistor revolutionized electronics, all the way from hearing aids to computers.

A transistor is a *semiconductor*, a class of materials whose ability to conduct electricity lies between that of insulators, like rubber, and conductors, like copper. Silicon, the chief component of sand, is the most plentiful semiconductor, followed by such exotic materials as germanium, selenium, gallium arsenide, and lead sulfide. Early radios, or crystal sets as they were called, used galena (or lead sulfide) crystals to detect the audio portions of radio waves. You simply hooked up an earphone to a galena crystal and eavesdropped on the broadcasts — quite literally. Very crude devices, crystal radios didn't use electricity and lacked the means to amplify audio signals. (You can buy a crystal radio kit at an electronics hobby shop for $5.)

In 1906, the American physicist Lee De Forest invented a device that could detect and amplify radio signals. Called the *three-electrode tube*, or *triode*, it had three basic parts: a *cathode*, which emits electrons; an *anode*, which collects electrons; and a

*An early integrated circuit, made by Fairchild Camera & Instrument Corporation in 1961 using the planar process, which produced flat, electrically insulated chips. This is a logic IC with two flip flops, or on and off switches; the four nose-cone-like blue structures in the center of the chip are transistors, and the white lines are aluminum connectors. The device is .06 inch in diameter.*

*grid,* typically a wire mesh between the cathode and plate, which acts as a valve, allowing the cathode's electrons to jump through the insulating vacuum to the anode. A fourth component, a *filament,* is also necessary; it heats up the cathode, boiling off the electrons that pass to the anode. (By the way, a tube is called a *thermionic valve* in Great Britain, *thermionic* referring to the emission of electrons by heat.) By linking an antenna to the grid, and fluctuating the grid's voltage, you could pick up radio signals. As the electrons surged from cathode to anode, the audio portion of the waves was amplified. The triode made radio a practical means of communication.

The rise of quantum mechanics gave scientists a powerful theoretical tool for the analysis of electrical phenomena, and semiconductors were given a closer look beginning in the mid-1920s. But the research didn't get very far; semiconductors are highly susceptible to contamination, which alters their electrical characteristics, and it wasn't until the early 1930s that pure silicon and germanium were available. Meanwhile, scientists in the United States and Great Britain discovered that flying objects reflected radio waves — and radar was born. At the time, however, tubes couldn't detect short waves, which were best for spotting low-flying aircraft, and physicists turned to semiconductors, hoping to turn them into effective short-wave detectors. The research was stepped up considerably when the war broke out, with universi-

*The inventors of the transistor in Washington, D.C., in 1971. Left to right: Walter Brattain, John Bardeen, and William Shockley.*

ties and industrial labs all over the United States and England participating in the effort.

For decades, scientists were baffled by the behavior of semiconductors. For example, in early 1940 a Bell Labs scientist named Russell S. Ohl fashioned a block of silicon that was divided into two different electrical regions, one containing an excess of electrons and another an excess of *holes*, or positive charges. (This was accomplished by *doping*, or chemically contaminating, the silicon with positive and negative impurities during manufacture.) Much to his astonishment, Ohl discovered that the silicon generated half a volt of electricity when a light was shined on the dividing line between the positive and negative zones, or the *pn junction*. In other words, the silicon converted light into power. Scientists had been aware of the photoelectric properties of semiconductors since the 1920s, but no semiconductor had ever produced so much electricity. Clearly, something unusual was taking place at the pn junction.

In July 1945, a month before the end of the war, Bell Labs decided to set up a larger research program on solid-state physics. The phone company used tubes and mechanical relays by the millions, but the tubes eventually burned out and the relays, being mechanical, occasionally malfunctioned — and the com-

*A replica of the original point-contact transistor (below, right), with a production version on the left. The triangular wedge of the replica is made of plastic and is covered with gold foil slit in half at the tip; one side of the wedge is the emitter, the other the collector. The wedge, about 1.25 inches per side, is pressed against a thin slab of germanium, which acts as the base. This device can amplify a signal about a hundred times.*

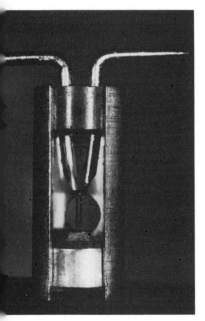

pany dreamed of replacing all these parts with uncomplaining solid-state components. As part of the research effort, Bell assigned a small group to study semiconductors. Made up mostly of theoretical physicists, the group was headed by William Shockley, a physicist with a brilliant talent for devising experiments that went to the heart of a matter. The team also included the physicists John Bardeen and Walter Brattain. Bardeen, the youngest of the three, had joined Bell only recently, and had never worked on semiconductors, but Shockley and Brattain, who had both been at the labs for years, had a long-standing interest in solid-state physics; in fact, Brattain had seen Ohl's miraculous block of silicon at work, an experience he never forgot.

The men decided to focus on silicon and germanium, the simplest semiconductors, and to try to understand the nature of the pn junction. As Brattain recalled, the group was quite close-knit:

> I cannot overemphasize the rapport of this group. We would meet together to discuss important steps almost on the moment of an afternoon. We would discuss things freely, one person's remarks suggesting an idea to another. We went to the heart of many things during the existence of this group and always when we got to the place where something had to be done, experimental or theoretical, there never was any question as to who was the appropriate man in the group to do it.

Success came fairly quickly. At the end of December 1947, after two frustrating but exhilarating years of work, Bardeen and Brattain managed to create an amplifying circuit based on a small slab of germanium with two pn junctions. "This circuit was actually spoken over," Brattain wrote in his lab notebook on December 24, the day after the first demonstration, "and by switching the device in and out, a distinct gain in speech level could be heard and seen on the scope presentation with no noticeable change in quality. . . . It was determined that the power gain was on the order of a factor of 18 or greater."

Called the *point-contact transistor*, Bardeen and Brattain's invention proved to be very difficult to manufacture. In 1951, Shockley developed an improved version, the *junction*, or *bipolar*, *transistor*, and the transistor moved from the laboratory to the factory. Both devices operate like the triode. But instead of a cathode and anode, a transistor has an *emitter* and a *collector*. And instead of a grid, it has a *base*. Unlike the parts of a triode, however, these components are intrinsic parts of the transistor — there are no glass tubes or metal grids here. Essentially, a transistor is an

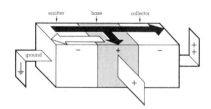

A positive charge applied to the base of a junction transistor causes electrons to rush from the emitter to the collector. Meanwhile, holes, or positive charges, travel to the ground. The voltage applied to the base determines the level of amplification, and the arrangement of pn junctions directs the flow of current.

electrical sandwich consisting of two pn junctions, one between the emitter and the base, another between the base and the collector. The emitter and the collector — the bread of the sandwich — carry a negative polarity, whereas the base — the meat of the sandwich — bears a positive charge. (In some transistors, the polarity of the components is the other way around, or positive-negative-positive.) When a voltage is applied to the base, electrons surge from the emitter across the base to the collector, amplifying the current.

Introduced to the public at a news conference in Manhattan in July 1948, the point-contact transistor attracted a modest amount of attention. In general, it was regarded as a novelty dreamed up by the phone company, and it wasn't until the early 1950s, with the advent of Shockley's junction transistor, that the importance of the device sunk in. Bell Labs was willing to license the rights to the transistor to any company in exchange for a royalty (with the exception of hearing aid manufacturers, which Bell exempted from paying royalties, as a gesture in memory of Alexander Graham Bell). In 1952, Bell Labs held a course on transistor technology for its licensees. Just as the Moore School's famous class on computers disseminated the technology of ENIAC and EDVAC, Bell Labs's symposium disseminated transistor technology to the electronics industry. Transistors first reached the public in 1953 as amplifiers in hearing aids, and transistor radios came along the following year.

Naturally, computer manufacturers were keenly interested

*The first junction transistor, a replica of which is shown at left, consisted of a mudlike slug of germanium on a wooden board. The plug was about half an inch in diameter. A production version of the transistor is shown at right, next to a vacuum tube.*

in the device. In February 1956, the scientists in MIT's Digital Computer Lab, working with IBM, started developing a transistorized computer to replace the massive vacuum-tube machines of SAGE. Although the MIT-IBM machine worked well, the 55,000-tube SAGE computers were already in production; since millions of dollars had been spent on the tube machines, the Air Force saw no reason to replace them. Meanwhile, the computer industry began designing transistorized computers for the commercial market. The first ones appeared in 1957 and 1958, introduced by UNIVAC and the Philco Corporation. Compared to their be-tubed predecessors, the new generation of computers was superior in every way — smaller, faster, more reliable and economical, and much more powerful.

*G. W. A. Dummer in 1983*

While the transistor was remaking computers, another technology, even more revolutionary, was beginning to take shape. One of the first people to point the way was an English engineer named G. W. A. Dummer. An expert in electronic reliability, Dummer worked for the Royal Radar Establishment, in Malvern, northern England, where he was in charge of a group that, among other things, developed electronic components hardy enough to withstand the effects of harsh climates. His group spent most of its time testing radar equipment, using such devices as centrifuges, refrigerators, atmospheric chambers, high-humidity tropical testing chambers, and so on. As tubes gave way to transistors and other semiconductors, radar equipment became smaller and more reliable. All things being equal, reliability and miniaturization were intertwined: the smaller the device, the fewer the parts and interconnections; the fewer the parts and interconnections, the higher the reliability.

The more Dummer considered the relation between reliability and miniaturization, the more it seemed to him that the key to the problem — how to make radar and other electronic equipment highly reliable — was miniaturization. At that time, electrical circuits consisted of various *discrete* components, each manufactured separately, packaged in its own container, and wired one at a time into a *circuit board*. Why not, Dummer asked, develop components that incorporated many transistors, capacitors (which store charges), resistors (which do just that), and other parts into the same solid, inseparable piece of material? For example, instead of inserting several transistors into a board, you'd use a single solid circuit composed of many transistors, thus cutting down on the number of components and interconnections.

Dummer's idea was beautifully simple, and other scientists and engineers in the early 1950s probably had the same thought, but Dummer seems to have been the first one to mention the idea in public. In May 1952, at a symposium on electronic components in Washington, D.C., he read a paper entitled "Electronic Components in Great Britain." An otherwise ordinary document, it contained the following, now frequently cited, glimpse of the future:

> With the advent of the transistor and the work in semiconductors generally, it seems now possible to envisage electronic equipment in a solid block with no connecting wires. The block may consist of layers of insulating, conducting, rectifying and amplifying materials, the electrical functions being connected directly by cutting out areas of the various layers.

As a general description of the modern integrated circuit (IC), Dummer's vision was astonishingly close to the mark. But the technical problems were formidable, and he had little idea of how to solve them. If many transistors were integrated into the same piece of semiconductor, how would they be isolated from each other electrically, so that the operation of one didn't short-circuit the workings of another? A current dispatched to one transistor would spread throughout the device unless an electrical or physical barrier of some kind stopped it. But what kind? And how would resistors, capacitors, and other *passive* components, then made out of nonsemiconducting materials, be fashioned out of semiconductors? (Passive parts don't amplify or otherwise change a current's power.) Finally, how would the components be wired together, so that their operation could be coordinated? If they had to be wired by hand, then a solid circuit (the term *integrated circuit* didn't come into use until the late 1950s) might be no less expensive or easier to make than discretes, and its performance no more reliable.

*A large-scale model of the solid circuit developed by Dummer and the Plessey Company. The actual circuit, which didn't work, was about 3/16ths of an inch square.*

Back in England, Dummer attempted to put his ideas into practice. He prodded the Royal Radar Establishment to award a modest research and development contract to the Plessey Company in April 1957, but nothing came of Plessey's work. "Dummer," recalled a colleague, "was preaching the gospel of integrated circuitry long before anybody, including Dummer, had the slightest idea how you could actually do this. . . . [Dummer] carried inspiration around on his back like pollen. . . . He never received the backing that his degree of inspiration would have justified." At another symposium, this time at Malvern in September 1957, Dummer and Plessey displayed a crude, inoperable model of an IC. It got a good deal of attention — from visiting Americans. But the Royal Radar Establishment was unconvinced and the contract was not renewed.

The climate on the other side of the Atlantic was much more receptive to miniaturization schemes, no matter how far-fetched. The Defense Department was spending millions of dollars on research programs to make electronic components smaller, more reliable, less expensive, and easier to build. These efforts amounted to a sizable industry and reflected the military's growing interest in electronic technology, which first became a major military concern during World War II, when all kinds of weapons contained electronic equipment; even that lumbering giant of the air, the B-29 bomber, was crammed with nearly a thousand vacuum tubes. The success of the next generation of weapons — guided missiles, H-bombs, early-warning radar, computers — obviously depended on the state of electronics technology.

Each of the military services had a favored miniaturization plan. "Project Tinkertoy" was the earliest effort, begun in secret in 1950 by the National Bureau of Standards on behalf of the Navy. Tinkertoy was dedicated not so much to miniaturization as to automation and standardization. The project's whimsical name derived from that popular wooden toy — the one with sticks and wheels that can be put together in almost any configuration — and was motivated by the same basic idea; the goal was to develop compact electronic modules, or *subassemblies*, composed of standardized discretes. If a set of modules for one project called for, say, five amplifiers, ten resistors, and twenty capacitors, the assembly line would gear up accordingly and the desired modules would be assembled automatically.

In principle, Tinkertoy was a good idea. But Tinkertoy didn't get far, at least in its first incarnation. When the project was made public in 1953, it turned out that the entire scheme had been based on tubes instead of transistors, which had been invented more than five years earlier and would have made the modules much smaller and more reliable. With one foot in the future and another firmly in the past, Tinkertoy's engineers had ignored one of the important inventions of the century. The project was cancelled in 1953, after the Navy had doled out almost $5 million in research and development funds.

Yet the need for better components remained, and Tinkertoy was resurrected four years later, this time using transistors. The project had a new sponsor, the Army Signal Corps; a new general contractor, RCA; a new name, the Micromodule Plan; and a new triad of priorities, emphasizing miniaturization as much as automation and standardization. Otherwise, the basic idea was the same. In this case, transistors, resistors, and other components were deposited on tiny, standardized ceramic wafers about the diameter of a pencil; the wafers were stacked together, linked with wires along the sides, and then plugged into circuit boards. Micromodules were much smaller and more practical than Tinkertoys, and the Army, pleased with RCA's work, spent $26 million on micromodules by 1963. Unfortunately, history repeated itself. Just as the Tinkertoy project had been done in by the invention of the transistor, the Micromodule Plan was rendered obsolete by the invention of the IC.

By the late 1950s, many physicists and electrical engineers were tinkering with the idea of miniature electronic circuits. Robert Noyce, a California physicist, was one of them. "These attempts [at miniaturization] were largely unsuccessful," Noyce wrote years later, "but they publicized the demand for miniaturization and the potential rewards for the successful development of some form of microelectronics. A large segment of the technical community was on the lookout for a solution to the problem because it was clear that a ready market awaited the successful inventor." Noyce's firm, Fairchild Semiconductor, of Mountain View, California, was one of the companies pursuing a solution. So was Texas Instruments (TI), of Dallas.

In the summer of 1958, Jack Kilby, an engineer for TI, created the first bona fide IC, a circuit known as a *phase-shift oscillator* (a device that oscillates signals at a given rate). Other ICs followed in rapid succession, and his first patent was filed on 6

*A Tinkertoy module (left) and two micromodules (right). The micromodule at the lower right has been partially assembled.*

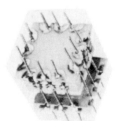

February 1959. Exactly one month later, although rumors of Kilby's work had already swept through the electronics industry, TI proudly announced the invention at a news conference at an industry convention in New York City, proclaiming "the development of a semiconductor solid circuit no larger than a match head." The trade press was full of the news. Even the popular media carried the story, and TI stock, always a high flier, rose several points. It certainly *seemed* as though TI, an aggressive, pioneering firm, had made a pivotal breakthrough.

*Jack Kilby at Texas Instruments, 1983*

A husky, soft-spoken, serious man, Kilby came to TI in May 1958, after having spent eleven years at Centralab Inc., a large radio and television parts manufacturer in Milwaukee, Wisconsin. (Centralab is a subsidiary of Globe-Union Inc., a major electrical components and equipment maker.) Kilby had grown up in Great Bend, Kansas, where his father, an electrical engineer, was president of the local power company. Like father, like son, Kilby decided to become an engineer. After being turned down by MIT — Kilby's high school grades were not outstanding — he went to the University of Illinois. Then the United States entered World War II, and Kilby joined the Army. He served with the Office of Strategic Services (the forerunner of the Central Intelligence Agency) in Burma and China, returned to college in 1945, and graduated two years later. Centralab was the only company that offered him a job, and he went to work on silk-screening techniques for printing certain simple electronic components on ceramic wafers.

Centralab was hardly a backwater. The firm had done a lot of research in miniaturization and automation, and Kilby was strongly influenced by its work. During the war, for instance, Centralab had been a subcontractor for the National Bureau of Standards in a project to develop compact and rugged ceramic circuits for proximity fuzes. (It was the Bureau of Standards that sponsored Project Tinkertoy.) After the war, when Kilby was on board, Centralab worked with the Army's Diamond Ordnance Fuze Laboratories, in Maryland, to develop ceramic circuits whose components were deposited by photolithography — a technique, pioneered by Bell Labs, that was important to the development of ICs. The company was also one of the earliest producers of transistors; along with TI and several other firms, it bought a transistor manufacturing license from Bell Labs, dispatching Kilby and a colleague to Bell's 1952 symposium on the invention.

Back at Centralab, Kilby helped set up a small transistor manufacturing line. The components were sold to hearing aid manufacturers, but the operation was only marginally profitable. By the late 1950s, the semiconductor industry was switching from germanium to silicon transistors, which offered several distinct manufacturing and operational advantages. (For example, silicon is much more resistant to heat than germanium.) But Centralab couldn't afford the substantial equipment and development costs entailed by a switch to silicon; the company was certain to fall irretrievably behind the competition if it didn't make the move. Armed with years of experience in the physics and manufacturing of transistors, Kilby decided it was time to move on. This time, he received several job offers.

He could not have found a better home than TI, an innovative, aggressive, and highly profitable firm with a knack for transforming the latest technological advances into marketable products. In 1954, in one of its best-known technical coups, TI became the first company to make silicon transistors. It did so only two years after the Bell Labs symposium, and its achievement was all the more impressive in light of the price it put on those transistors: a mere $2.50 each, five to six times less than the going rate for germanium transistors. (That figure was low enough to enable another pioneering firm, Regency, of Indianapolis, Indiana, to produce the first portable transistor radios in 1955.) Like many electronic firms, TI was deeply interested in miniaturization; the Army's Micromodule Plan had just received its initial funding and TI, always close to the military, wanted a piece of the action.

That was where Kilby fit in. He was assigned to a small research group headed by an engineer named Willis Adcock. Kilby's duties were undefined, although it was understood that he would work on miniaturization. TI was preparing to submit a micromodule proposal to the Army, and Kilby realized that he probably would be called upon to help the company's effort. But he was extremely skeptical of the Micromodule Plan — he believed that it was wiser to lay out circuits horizontally instead of vertically — and he immediately began searching for a better approach. He explained what happened next:

> At that time, radio was still a significant part of the electronics business, and I began to look at the possibility of making an IF strip [an *intermediate-frequency amplifier*, which is used widely in radios]. I proposed to do this by making all of the components in tubular form, which I think would have been an easier and preferable technique to the flat wafers of the micromodule deal. I spent a few months on this, and built a couple of models that worked. But in looking at the costs, particularly within a semiconductor company, it became apparent that the labor costs were much higher than those at Centralab, and that we really couldn't afford very much hand assembly. . . .

In those days, TI had a mass vacation policy; that is, they just shut down tight during the first few weeks of July, and anybody who had any vacation time coming took it then. Since I had just started and had no vacation time, I was left pretty much in a deserted plant; so I began to think about the lessons of the IF strip. It became clear that there were some things the semiconductor houses could do very well, and that they had some potent techniques that this IF strip did not make very good use of. I began to cast around for alternatives — and the monolithic [or solid circuit] concept really occurred to me during that two-week vacation period. I had it all written up by the time Willis got back, and I was able to show him sketches that pretty well outlined the idea — and the process sequence showing how to go about building it.

Willis Adcock, Kilby's boss, was impressed but skeptical. He doubted that it was possible to make a circuit entirely out of discrete semiconductor components, let alone integrated ones. Kilby's first challenge, then, was to build a circuit out of discretes.

The demonstration was easy enough; Kilby pulled some silicon transistors and unprocessed silicon wafers off TI's shelves, modified them, and constructed a discrete flip-flop. Making a solid circuit was a much more difficult matter, but Kilby drew on a deeper well of ingenuity and, with the help of two technicians, managed to fashion a simplified phase-shift oscillator out of a germanium wafer. This circuit was built in a hurry and was every bit as crude looking as the first transistor; Kilby was well aware of the importance of his idea and didn't want to lose the race to another company. He tested the gadget on 12 September 1959, and it worked.

Kilby constructed other solid circuits during the next few

*Two drawings from Kilby's first IC patent. Figure 6a is a flip flop; 6b, its electrical schematic.*

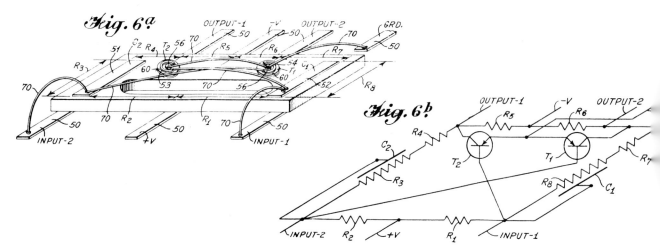

*Kilby's first IC, a phase-shift oscillator (left), next to a production version of one of TI's first Kilby-style chips. The oscillator was made out of germanium (the light blue rectangle) and contained a single junction transistor (under the large aluminum bar in the center). The small perpendicular bars are input/output terminals; the large bar on the right is a ground, and the wires are made of gold. The entire assemblage was held together with wax. The device is .062 inch long and .04 inch wide.*

months, including a flip-flop. It is the best illustration of Kilby's techniques, showing both the cleverness of his conception and the nature of its shortcomings, and it's worth a close examination. (A drawing of the circuit, reproduced from Kilby's patent, is on page 236.) In considering this IC, it's important to keep three questions in mind. How did Kilby isolate the IC's components electrically, so that the operation of one part wouldn't interfere with the workings of another? How did he manage to fashion passive devices, such as capacitors and resistors, out of a semiconductor? And how did he wire up the IC's various components? These are the same questions that Dummer and other would-be inventors of the IC had to face, and the value of their achievements rose or fell according to how well they answered them.

In brief, and without getting too technical, we can say that Kilby wired up the IC as though it were an ordinary component — that is, simply by soldering tiny wires to the various parts of the circuit. The more complicated the circuit, the more wires it had. And every one had to be affixed by hand, using tweezers and a microscope. If the wires weren't soldered on solidly and firmly, they could be dislodged by vibration and shock. (Not all electronic components go into stereos and TV sets; they are also used in missiles and tanks.) As long as the IC wasn't too small or complicated, the wiring process wasn't too difficult, but the wiring requirement of Kilby's ICs limited the potential sophistication of the devices. It would be impossible to make a Kilby-style IC containing, say, 10,000 components.

As for the second question, how to create passive devices out of a semiconductor, Kilby came up with an ingenious answer. The IC has two capacitors (the narrow raised strips on either side of the device, labeled C1 and C2) and eight resistors (intrinsic parts of the device, labeled R1 to R8). The capacitors were created by coating a section of the IC with a thin layer of silicon dioxide, an insulator, and then placing a thin strip of gold or aluminum over the oxide. The result is a very simple capacitor; when a charge is dispatched to the capacitor, it is stored safely in the gold or aluminum strip, and the silicon dioxide prevents the electricity from leaking away and interfering with the other components.

The third and last problem, how to isolate the IC's various components, was solved primarily by "shaping" the IC into L's, U's, and other configurations. "This shaping concept," Kilby wrote in his patent application, "makes it possible in a circuit to obtain the necessary isolation between components and to define the components or, stated differently, to limit the area which is utilized for a given component." Shaping was an inelegant solution to a complicated problem and, as we shall see, soon was superseded by a superior technique developed by another company. In addition to shaping, Kilby also isolated the IC's components with resistors, sprinkled liberally around the device. The resistors were merely pn junctions, which permit electricity to flow in one direction only. (If a positive current surging through a negative zone suddenly came up against a positive area, it would be repelled, and vice versa. It's an old principle: opposites attract, likes repell.) Unfortunately, pn junctions played a secondary role in Kilby's ICs.

Compared to micromodules, Kilby's ICs were a major step forward. "It is possible," Kilby declared in his patent, ". . . to

A TI publicity photo, showing the IC computer the company made for the Air Force (left) and a much larger transistorized computer (right)

achieve component densities of greater than thirty million per cubic foot as compared with five hundred thousand per cubic foot, which is the highest component density attained prior to this invention." In a vivid demonstration of the miniaturizing potential of ICs, TI built a tiny computer for the Aeronautical Systems Division of the Air Force. It contained 587 ICs, measured 6.3 cubic inches, weighed 10 ounces — and possessed the same computational power as a transistorized computer that had 8,500 components, occupied 1,000 cubic inches, and weighed 480 ounces. But the IC's chips were unreliable and difficult to make, especially compared to the elegant and eminently practical IC developed by Robert Noyce at Fairchild.

The son of a Congregationalist minister, Noyce grew up in Grinnell, Iowa, an ordinary Midwestern town with a population of 7,000 in 1948. As a physics major at Grinnell College, he was introduced to solid-state physics by Grant Gale, the school's physics professor and a friend of John Bardeen's. In the summer of 1948, Gale read a little item in the newspaper about the invention of the transistor, and he asked Bardeen to send him some samples for his students. Noyce was one of the first people in the country to experiment with a transistor, and he decided to specialize in solid-state physics at graduate school.

He went to MIT, where, much to his surprise, few people had even heard about the transistor, let alone experimented with one. There weren't any courses in solid-state physics, at MIT or any other school — and there wouldn't be until the mid-1950s. Gale was one of the few professors who knew anything about transistor electronics, and he and Noyce often compared notes. When Noyce received his Ph.D. in 1953, he headed straight for industry, where most solid-state research was being conducted. His first job was with Philco, in Philadelphia, which he chose because the company was opening a semiconductor operation and the chances for advancement seemed best there. But it turned out that Philco wasn't really interested in advanced research, and Noyce soon began to look elsewhere.

In 1955, he and a Swiss-born physicist named Jean Hoerni arrived in Mountain View, California, to go to work for Shockley Semiconductor Laboratory, a small company that William Shockley, the transistor's co-inventor, had set up in the hope of cashing in on his knowledge of solid-state physics. (Mountain View is next door to Palo Alto, Shockley's hometown and the home of Stanford University.) Shockley Semiconductor Laboratory, begun with support from Arnold Beckman of Beckman Instruments, was an unprepossessing outfit; it occupied a glorified shed on South San Antonio Road and had about fifteen employees.

Although Shockley was a brilliant research director, with an uncanny sense for the experimental jugular, he was a poor manager of people and money and held a somewhat conspiratorial view of the world. He posted a list of everyone's salaries, hoping to put an end to company secrets; he required his employees to rate one another regularly, a process that immediately degenerated into a popularity contest; and, after the lab's work ran into inexplicable delays which Shockley unaccountably blamed on sabotage, he ordered one of his employees to take a lie detector test. (The man passed.) Moreover, for all his technical brilliance, he insisted on concentrating on a device known as a *four-layer germanium diode* (a switch with a very strong off state and a correspondingly weak on state), which had only a wisp of a chance at commercial success. Noyce, Hoerni, and most of their colleagues believed that they ought to be working on silicon transistors, which had much greater commercial promise.

*Fairchild's founders in the lobby of the corporation in 1960. Left to right: Gordon Moore; Sheldon Roberts; Eugene Kleiner; Robert Noyce, who invented the planar IC; Victor Grinich; Julius Blank; Jean Hoerni, who invented the planar process; and Jay Last.*

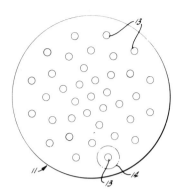

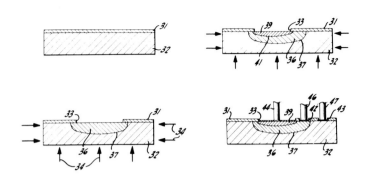

*Planar transistors were made in batches on round slices of silicon known as wafers (number 11 in these drawings from Hoerni's planar patent). First, the wafer is coated with silicon dioxide (31 in this cross section of a single transistor). Then a portion of the dioxide is etched away and a bowl-shaped region of positively charged silicon (36) is created by exposing the wafer to an impurity. Next a shallow bowl of negatively charged silicon (39) is fashioned, and the result is a junction transistor (32 is the collector; 36 is the base; and 39 is the emitter). Finally, aluminum wires are attached and all openings sealed with dioxide.*

By the summer of 1957, Noyce, Hoerni, and six other scientists and engineers at the lab had had enough. Realizing that brainpower constituted the real assets of a semiconductor firm, they decided to go into business for themselves. The Fairchild Camera & Instrument Corporation of New York agreed to finance them, and Fairchild Semiconductor was born, moving into a large garage in Palo Alto while their new two-story concrete building, near the Shockley lab, was being completed. Although Fairchild's founders had an equal say in the direction of the enterprise, Noyce's confident, relaxed manner made him the most popular member of the group, and he became the company's general manager. At that time, Fairchild and Shockley were the only semiconductor operations in the Santa Clara Valley, a sunny region of fruit farms about fifty miles south of San Francisco, now popularly known as Silicon Valley. A few large companies, such as IBM and General Electric, had divisions there, along with Hewlett-Packard, Raytheon Associates, and other homegrown outfits established by former Stanford students. The university encouraged graduates to set up companies in the area, offering them inexpensive, long-term leases on Stanford land.

Unlike Shockley's outfit, Fairchild Semiconductor concentrated on silicon transistors. In the late 1950s, the state of the art in transistors was the *silicon mesa transistor* (which had been invented by Bell Labs and which Jack Kilby had used in his ICs). It consisted of a tiny round plateau, or *mesa*, set above a surrounding base of silicon; a semicircular ring on top of the mesa served as the emitter, the transistor's controlling component, with the surrounding plane acting as the collector. Mesa transistors, which were made through photolithography, etching, and diffusion (chemically doping the semiconductor with impurities), seemed to have a great deal of promise; but a significant drawback soon appeared. Since the mesas protruded from the wafers, the transistors were subject to contamination of all kinds, and the connecting wires tended to slip. You sometimes could short-circuit a mesa transistor merely by tapping on its container.

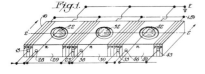

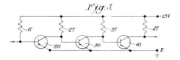

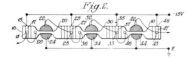

Three illustrations from Lehovec's IC patent. The thin diagonal slices in figure 1, labeled with small p's and n's, are pn junctions; the three circles, labeled 22, 32, and 42, are transistors. Figure 2 is a cross section and figure 3 an electrical schematic.

In late 1958 and early 1959, Jean Hoerni came up with a brilliant solution to the mesa's problems. He diffused the mesa into the wafer; in other words, he chemically embedded the transistor's various parts into a piece of silicon. (See the illustration on page 241.) The result was a completely flat transistor, one without any protruding parts. Then he coated the gadget with a thin layer of silicon dioxide, which insulated, or protected, the transistor much as rubber insulates wire. However, he coated the device in such a way that certain spots were left uncovered, creating convenient contact points for the wires. Although the wires jutted out, just as they did on the mesa transistor, Hoerni's device was much better protected from contamination and slipped wires, and it was, therefore, much more reliable. Hoerni's *planar process* was a great technical breakthrough, and it led directly to the invention of a commercially feasible IC.

By early 1959, only one other piece was missing from the IC puzzle, and it was supplied by the Sprague Electric Company in North Adams, Massachusetts. The company's research director, Kurt Lehovec, a Czech-born physicist who had immigrated to the United States after World War II, had been working on better ways to make *alloy junction transistors* (an advanced form of the transistor Shockley had invented). Lehovec devised an improved manufacturing process and that success inspired him to ponder the problem of how to build an IC — of how to isolate the components electrically. His solution was similar to one of Kilby's: pn junctions, which allow electricity to flow in one direction only.

"The idea was shamelessly simple," said Lehovec, now an engineering professor at the University of Southern California, "and I realized that it was important to file a patent on it immediately." He had heard about Kilby's work — and he had surmised that the Texan's devices didn't incorporate pn junctions. (They did, but Kilby had made poor use of them.) Lehovec designed an IC whose components were separated by pn junctions, and filed a patent application on 22 April 1959, six weeks after TI had gone public with Kilby's invention. Lehovec's IC wasn't much better than Kilby's, but he had hit upon the best way to isolate the components.

Meanwhile, Noyce also was thinking about how to make an IC. In January 1959 — about a year after Hoerni had developed the planar process and about four months after Kilby had fashioned his first solid circuit — Noyce made his first notes on the subject in his lab journal. Six months later, he succeeded in developing an IC based on Hoerni's planar process and Lehovec's pn junctions. As he recalled years later:

When this [the planar process] was accomplished, we had a silicon surface covered with one of the best insulators known to man, so you could etch holes through to make contact with the underlying silicon. Obviously, then, you had a whole bunch of transistors embedded in an insulating surface, and the next thing was that, instead of cutting them apart physically, you cut them apart electrically, added the other components you needed for circuits, and finally the interconnection wiring.

There were several techniques, but the main one was, basically, to build back-to-back diodes [or pn junctions] into the silicon between any two transistors so that no current could flow between the two in either direction. The other element you needed was a resistor, and it was relatively simple to make a diode-isolated piece of silicon that acts as a resistor. You now had resistors and transistors, and could start building logic circuits, which you could interconnect by evaporating metal on top of the insulating layer. [That was one of Noyce's key innovations. By evaporating the connections onto the chip through a mask, he kept the IC flat.] So it was a progressive buildup of bits and pieces of the technology to make the entire thing possible.

It was a question of having these rather vague concepts of insulators, of isolation, of interconnection, and the photoengraving for the patterns, so that you drew on your bag of tricks to combine these elements to make the integrated circuit. There was no huge flashbulb flashing, but it was almost as if you sat down as a semiconductor physicist and asked, "How can I do this job?" There is no doubt in my mind that if the invention hadn't arisen at Fairchild, it would have arisen elsewhere in the very near future. It was an idea whose time had come, where the technology had developed to the point where it was viable.

*Three diagrams from Noyce's historic IC patent. Made by the planar process, Noyce's device was the breakthrough that made the commercial manufacture of ICs practical and economical. Figure 3 is a frontal view of the chip, which contains two junction transistors (the semicircular components on the left and right, numbered 16 and 17; and 23, 24, and 25) and two diodes (19 and 26), which direct the flow of current.*

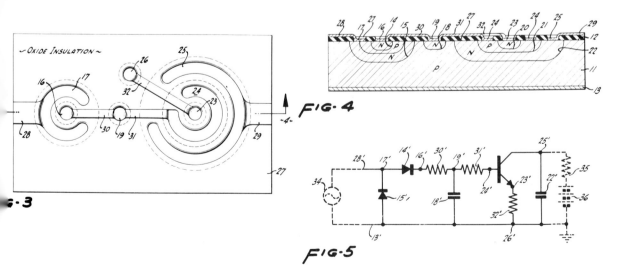

Noyce's IC was an elegant little device. Based on the planar process, it had no protruding parts. Instead of vertical contact wires, it used horizontal ones, snaking around the face of the chip. And instead of isolating components by shaping the chip, it used pn junctions. Above all, it lent itself to mass production and almost unlimited refinement. Noyce's IC was the right approach.

Commercial development of the IC followed rapidly, with all companies concerned freely licensing their patents. In 1961, Fairchild and TI (using the planar process) introduced their first chips; TI's offering, for example, consisted of six logic ICs that performed Boolean operations such as OR and NOR (or NOT OR). (An OR gate accepts two inputs; if either of them is 1, the output is also 1. A NOR gate is an OR gate followed by a NOT gate, otherwise known as an *inverter*; a NOR gate converts a 1 or a 0 into its opposite value. By stringing gates together in clever ways, engineers endow computers with the power to make decisions.)

*A chip consists of many different layers of components, and each level must be laid out separately. First, a layout of each layer is reproduced on a glass plate known as an optical reticle, which is about ten times the size of the finished IC. Then, by using a procedure known as "step and repeat," these reticular images are reduced photographically and reproduced hundreds of times on master masks, which in turn are used to make working masks for the factory. In the making of some chips, the reticles and masks are dispensed with and the devices are produced by electron-beam machines.*

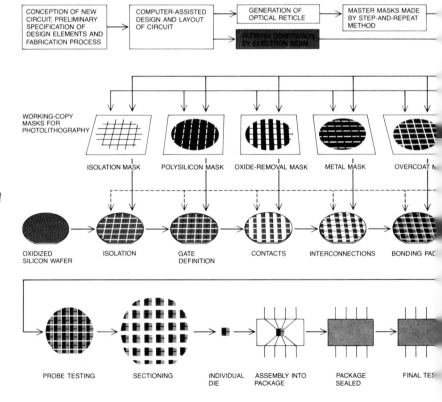

The first ICs, or electronic *chips*, were very expensive, and it wasn't until the mid-1960s that the prices descended to reasonable levels. For example, TI's chips cost $50 to $65 apiece in lots of a thousand or more, approximately double that in small quantities. Only the government could afford to buy them in bulk, and the first ICs went to defense contractors and NASA. After the space agency picked Fairchild to supply the ICs for the Gemini capsule's on-board computers, the company's sales shot up. In ten years (between 1957 and 1967), Fairchild's revenues rose from a few thousand dollars to $130 million, and the number of employees grew from the original eight to 12,000.

Of course, the computer industry also was keenly interested in the IC, which promised to bring about an exponential increase in the power and efficiency of their equipment. But the advent of the IC also presented an enormous challenge. The transition from the first to the second generation of computers — from tubes to transistors — had taken place only a few years earlier. It had cost millions of dollars to redesign the machines to accommodate transistors; just as you couldn't pull out a tube and install a transistor in its place, you couldn't remove a transistor and insert an IC. You had to redesign the circuits from the floor up. The one exception was the read/write memory, which enjoys a more or less autonomous existence within the computer; as long as the memory met the appropriate operational requirements, you could replace magnetic cores with ICs with relative ease.

"There was a lot of work on semiconductor memory at IBM," recalled an engineer at the company's Advanced Computing Systems Division in San Jose, California (not far from Fairchild), "and a small group inside the company saying that integrated circuits were the wave of the future . . .

but I wasn't one of them at the time. I became a believer later. There were projections saying it would take all the sand in the world to supply enough semiconductor memory in order to satisfy IBM's needs so many years out. IBM later became the first computer company to make the commitment to build memories with integrated circuits, but as for building *logic* circuits with ICs, there were simply too many unknowns. It was just too great a risk to commit the total corporation to integrated circuits for computer logic. In hindsight, you could say it was a bad decision, considering that the semiconductor companies soon got rather heavily into the computer people's business. But at the time it was very justifiable. The selling point with the IC was low cost [though not at first], and IBM didn't necessarily have to have the lowest cost. IBM sold on the basis of service and performance.

Opposite: Scenes from the making of a chip. From top to bottom, far left: an engineer checks a wall-sized layout of an IC; a technician inspects a photomask, an enlargement of a reticle that makes the search for defects easier; two working masks; a fresh silicon wafer. Center: wafers on a conveyor belt; a technician operates an oxidation furnace, where wafers are covered with silicon dioxide; a technician places wafers on the orbs of a centrifuge, where wafers are coated with aluminum; workers inspect finished ICs in a plant in Malaysia. Right: a chip being placed on an automatic tester; an array of IC packages; an engineer with an IC-studded circuit board; and an ant meets a memory chip.

Right: A chip on an automatic tester, whose needlelike electronic probes put each IC through a battery of tests. Defective chips are marked and discarded.

*The logic circuits of the first System/360 computers were composed of discrete components printed on tiny ceramic blocks (below). By the end of the 1960s, these blocks were replaced by ICs (bottom). The round balls are terminals, used to link the devices to other components. Both devices are about half an inch on a side.*

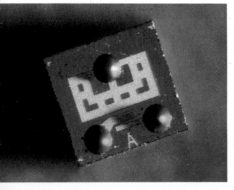

IBM, however, was caught in a bind. At about the same time the IC was making its debut, the company took a hard look at its burgeoning product line. It was turning out too many incompatible machines. A program written for one computer, even in FORTRAN, generally wouldn't run automatically on another IBM computer, and this diversity put an unnecessary strain on the company's resources. Nor was it possible to mix any of the peripheral equipment, such as magnetic-tape decks and high-speed printers. After a great deal of internal debate, the company decided to construct a comprehensive family of computers, with an array of compatible processors and software packages that would suit almost any application and budget. This meant that a small business could lease a small processor, secure in the knowledge that it could upgrade to a large processor without having to buy new peripherals and software. It also meant that a big company — for instance, a multinational bank — could buy dozens of compatible computers, machines that ran the same programs and used the same peripheral equipment.

The plan was sound, but had numerous drawbacks. First, it would render IBM's existing computers and software obsolete. Second, it would lead other companies to introduce equipment and software that was compatible with the system, thus cutting into IBM's sales. Third, it would require an enormous effort to carry out, costing billions of dollars and tying up IBM's resources for years. If it failed — if the company couldn't pull the operation off in a timely and profitable fashion — IBM might lose its dominance of the computer industry. Fourth, it caught IBM between two technological generations — transistors, on their way out, and ICs, on their way in. It seemed unwise to base the entire project on ICs, which were insufficiently proved, yet it wouldn't do to use transistors. The alternative was to compromise with small ceramic modules that would incorporate several discrete components into the same unit.

Despite the problems, IBM decided to go ahead. The effort to build the System/360, as the line of computers was called, cost at least $5 billion over four years — $500 million for research and development and $4.5 billion for a new plant and equipment. "It was roughly as though General Motors had decided to scrap its existing makes and models and offer in their place one new line of cars, covering the entire spectrum of demand, with a radically redesigned engine and exotic fuel," wrote *Fortune* magazine in September 1966. It was the largest private venture to date. IBM emerged from the ordeal with five new factories; 33 percent more employees (190,000 altogether); a components-manufacturing op-

A 1964 advertisement for the IBM 360 in Fortune magazine, showing some of the system's many units

eration that was bigger than the entire semiconductor industry; and a truly international capacity for designing and making computers.

With six processors and forty peripheral devices, the System/360 was introduced on 7 April 1964. (The system later was expanded to nine processors and more than seventy peripherals.) It was the first family of computers, and it was an enormous success, attracting orders at the rate of almost 1,000 a month and reshaping the entire computer industry. Some customers, eager to get their hands on a 360, bought places on IBM's lengthening waiting list from other firms, and a sizable *plug-compatible* industry arose, consisting of companies that made peripherals for the 360. Other firms, using a longer depreciation schedule than IBM, leased 360s from IBM and offered them to customers at lower rates. And several computer manufacturers, particularly RCA and

General Electric, were sent into a spin and eventually withdrew from the business.

Meanwhile, IC computers started appearing in the mid-1960s. Burroughs incorporated chips into parts of two medium-sized computers introduced in 1966 (the B2500 and B3500); two years later, Control Data and NCR brought out computers composed entirely of ICs (the CDC 7600 and the Century Series, respectively). But it wasn't until 1969 that ICs started showing up in IBM computers, and then only in the memories of the larger units of the 360 system. In the early 1970s, IBM replaced the 360 with the System/370, composed entirely of ICs. In general, the IC computers were hundreds of times more powerful and more reliable than their transistorized predecessors. They used less electricity, took up less space, and provided much more computational power for the purchase price.

At first, the IC's impact on computers was limited. Although the number of transistors that semiconductor engineers managed to cram onto a chip doubled almost every year, the progression didn't snowball until the early 1970s. The first 256-bit *random-access memory*, or *RAM* (a chip that serves as read/write

*IBM chairman Thomas Watson, Jr., left, and president Thomas Vincent Learson, with an IBM 360*

memory, like a magnetic core), was introduced in 1968, and the first 1,024-bit, or *1K*, RAM, came along several months later. (The memory capacity of ICs is measured in powers of 2, 1K being $2^{10}$.) The 1K RAM was an important breakthrough; all of a sudden, it was possible to replace a significant amount of magnetic cores with a tiny IC, and magnetic-core memory, the mainstay of computers since the mid-1950s, started to disappear. And then, in 1971, a Silicon Valley engineer asked a pivotal question: Why not put a central processor on a chip? Why not indeed. The result was the *microprocessor* and, a few years later, the ultimate democratization of computer technology, the personal computer.

## CHAPTER 9

# The Personal Computer

No one saw [them] . . . coming. No one, that is, in my field, writing science fictions. Oh, a few novels were written about these Big Brains, a few *New Yorker* cartoons were drawn showing those immense electric craniums that needed whole warehouses to THINK in. But no one in all of future writing foresaw those big brutes dieted down to fingernail earplug size so you could shove *Moby Dick* in one ear and pull Job and Ecclesiastes out the other.

> — *Ray Bradbury,* "Three Bright Mice; and *More*, on the Run!"

Small Is Beautiful.

The history of computers would have been quite different if Atanasoff had publicized his electronic calculating machine. Not only would he have been recognized as one of the inventors of the computer, but we might have had small and inexpensive computers from the very beginning. That's not what happened, of course. It was ENIAC, not Atanasoff's ABC, that set the pattern, and most of the computers of the 1950s and 1960s were built in ENIAC's giant mold. Only the largest institutions — universities, corporations, research institutes, and government agencies — could afford them. If the medium is the message, then these machines reflected the darker side of our institutions. Big and costly, they were the very symbols of entrenched and centralized power — arrogant, haughty, impersonal, inefficient, and inaccessible.

One of the most annoying problems, from the user's point of view, was the computer's inaccessibility. "For the first two decades of the existence of the high-speed computer," wrote John Kemeny, the mathematician and co-author of the BASIC programming language,

*Apple II computers roll off a production line at Carrollton, Texas*

machines were so scarce and so expensive that man approached the computer the way an ancient Greek approached an oracle. . . . A man submitted his request . . . and then waited patiently until it was convenient for the machine to work out the problem. Only specially selected acolytes were allowed to have direct communications with the computer. In the original mode of using computers, known as batch processing,

hundreds of computer requests were collected by the staff of a
computation center and then fed to the machine in a batch.

Actually, batch processing didn't come into being until the
mid-1950s, five to seven years after the invention of ENIAC. In the
first computing centers — those housing ENIAC, EDSAC, the
Manchester University Mark I, the IAS machine, UNIVAC, and so
on — users generally ran their own programs. The fraternity of
users was small enough to give everyone (everyone, that is, with a
bona fide reason to employ the machines) direct access to the
oracles.

But when multimillion-dollar computing centers opened
up in universities, corporations, institutes, and government agencies all over the world, another approach was necessary. You
couldn't let just anyone push the buttons and flip the switches;
the flow of material into and out of the machines had to be combined and processed in efficient batches. Consequently, computers were sequestered in air-conditioned, glassed-in rooms, and
a corps of professional computer operators arose to service them.

Therefore, if you, the user, wanted to appeal to the oracle,
the first thing you had to do was record your program on punch
cards, using any of the punch card machines at the computing
center. Then you handed the deck of cards to an operator — usually found sitting at a desk behind a window — and picked up
your printout later in the day or, if the computer was busy or had
broken down, in the week. Because most programs contained several errors, ranging from a misplaced comma to a chain of ineffec-
tive commands, your first printout was usually an abbreviated
one, containing such cryptic messages as "syntax error in line 3."
Perhaps you had used an inappropriate instruction. Or perhaps
you had misplaced a parenthesis. (If you couldn't spot the mistake, the operators, busy with their own work, weren't likely to
help you.) So you would type up a new card for line 3, resubmit
the pack, and return for the second printout. This time, there was
an error in line 20 . . .

The situation got worse as more people started using computers. Scientists and engineers began experimenting with computers that could serve many people simultaneously. However,
the technical problems were formidable. With one central processor and control unit, a von Neumann computer can execute only
one task at a time. (In an effort to break this computational bottleneck, researchers are experimenting with computers that are
equipped with multiple processors and control units. But "non–
von Neumann" computers are difficult to program and progress

has been slow.) How, then, could you get a computer to run a scientific program for one user, analyze a financial plan for another, and play a game of chess with a third?

The solution, developed at MIT in the late 1950s and early 1960s, was a brilliant idea called time-sharing. It took advantage of a computer's forte, speed. A time-sharing system consists of a computer linked to any number of *terminals* (a teletype or a monitor with a keyboard), each of which services a user. As each user fiddles with his or her own terminal, playing chess, running a scientific program, analyzing a financial plan — whatever — the computer switches from one terminal to another at a very high clip, executing a small portion of each user's program at every step. Since the machine can perform a single operation in a few millionths of a second, the users — slow-moving humans that they are — are none the wiser, and the computer seems to be giving everyone its undivided attention. Actually, it is being as single-minded as ever.

A time-sharing computer isn't the same thing as a *multiprocessing* computer, and the distinction is important. Although Whirlwind could support many terminals and perform many tasks at the same time, it couldn't run *different programs* simultaneously. It could carry out only certain predetermined tasks — such as tracking aircraft and plotting interception courses — that had been accounted for by the machine's internal programs. However, time-sharing computers are, like Whirlwind, real-time systems, capable of responding instantaneously to the actions of a human or a machine.

The advent of time-sharing computers led to the establishment of commercial time-sharing services. The customers — say, a high school or an engineering firm — would hook up its terminals to a time-sharing computer via the phone lines and buy "time" on the machine, paying for access by the minute. By the late 1960s, time-sharing was the fastest growing segment of the computer industry. It also seemed to be the wave of the future. There was a good deal of talk, by people who should have known better, of the inevitability of "information utilities" — vast centralized data banks that would be a cross between the library and the phone company. However, *mainframes*, or big computers, are expensive to buy and maintain, and although time-sharing services are still an important part of the computer business, they lost ground to another technological innovation, the *minicomputer*.

In 1957, three engineers established the Digital Equipment Corporation in an old brick wool mill in Maynard, Massachusetts, a suburb of Boston. Kenneth H. Olsen, a tall, soft-spoken man, was the leader of the group. He had grown up in Stratford, Connecticut, a machine-tool manufacturing center, and had studied electrical engineering at MIT. In 1950, at the age of twenty-four, Olsen joined Forrester's Digital Computer Lab at MIT as a research assistant. A first-rate engineer, he was in charge of the effort to build a memory-test computer (really a small-scale version of Whirlwind) for the first magnetic-core memories. Working nights and weekends, Olsen and his staff built the machine in only nine months, winning a case of Scotch for their trouble.

When the SAGE computers went into production at IBM's Poughkeepsie factory, the Digital Computer Lab sent Olsen and a few other engineers to keep an eye on the project. Norman Taylor, Olsen's boss, recalled:

> When IBM started to build this monster I told Olsen to keep control over it; we were concerned about the reliability of their circuitry. Ken lived in Poughkeepsie for two and a half years, in the bowels of IBM. There was this whole new world called production that he didn't know anything about, but he was a bona fide engineer; if something didn't work he'd take his coat off and redo it himself. He could do anything. The inefficiencies of a large operation like IBM's were appalling to Olsen. One piece of equipment had to be done over more than once. We wondered why they didn't use their own computer to keep track of parts. One day Olsen said to me, "Norm, I can beat these guys at their own game." The next job I gave him was a transistorized research computer. He was the manager, not the designer, and he built a strong team spirit. He'd learned a lot from IBM, from watching the way large companies operate.

*The PDP-1 (below, left) and the PDP-8 (right), open to reveal part of its interior*

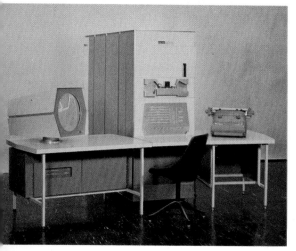

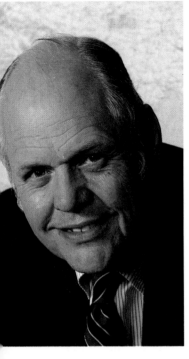

*Kenneth H. Olsen in 1981*

Eager to go into business for themselves, Olsen and his younger brother, Stan, and a colleague, Harlan E. Anderson, put up several thousand dollars of their own money and raised $70,000 from a Boston venture capital firm, American Research and Development Corporation (ARD). ARD exacted an arm and a leg for its support — about 60 percent of Digital's stock. Although Olsen wanted to make computers from the beginning, ARD recommended a more conservative approach, and Digital's first product was a set of electronic modules for computer test equipment. Three years after its founding, the company introduced its first computer, the Programmed Data Processor model 1, or PDP-1, a small machine that sold for about $120,000 — a good deal less than the going price of comparable computers.

The PDP-1 was the first embodiment of Olsen's unconventional ideas about computers, cultivated during his years at MIT. Most computational problems, such as calculating a payroll or monitoring a scientific experiment, are relatively small and straightforward, and you don't require a mainframe to perform them. Olsen realized that many computer users would be better off with a small, rugged, inexpensive real-time machine — one that didn't have to be housed in a computing center and pampered by a staff of trained operators, one that would be easy to program and available precisely when and where it was needed. Despite the need for small computers, Olsen was one of the few engineers to recognize it; most computer manufacturers, especially IBM and Sperry Rand, concentrated on big computers, which were both profitable and prestigious. Moreover, most people thought that time-sharing systems were the most efficient and economical way to deploy computers.

But all that changed in 1963 when Digital introduced the PDP-8, the first successful *minicomputer*. About the size of an ordinary refrigerator, the PDP-8, which was made out of transistors and magnetic cores, cost only $18,000. Compared to a mainframe, it was a very limited device. It ran only one program at a time, processed data in twelve-bit words (in contrast to the much faster and more powerful mainframes, whose words were at least thirty-two bits long), and contained only 4K words of memory. Yet it cost a fraction of the price of a mainframe, which meant, first, that customers who had only dreamed of owning their own computers now could afford one; and, second, that customers who had relied strictly on big computers could shift many computational chores to Digital's small and efficient minicomputers.

Scientists ordered PDP-8s for their laboratories; engineers got them for their offices; the Navy installed them on submarines.

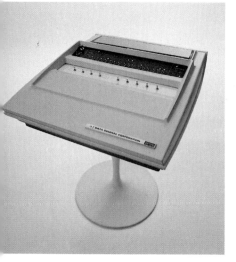

In refineries, PDP-8s controlled the flow of chemicals; in factories, they operated the machine tools; in warehouses, they kept track of inventory; in computing centers, they ran programs that didn't require the power of a mainframe; in banks, they kept track of accounts. The notion of the information utility gave way to *distributed processing*. For example, a bank would install a minicomputer in each of its branches; the machines handled the branches' transactions during the day and sent records of their operations to the bank's central computer at closing time. The applications were endless. And with every drop in the PDP 8's price, a new class of users — people who had never thought they would be able to afford a computer — appeared.

Meanwhile, Digital prospered, its sales rising ninefold between 1965 and 1970, its profits almost twentyfold. When the company went public in 1966, ARD's initial $70,000 investment was worth $228.6 million. Under the circumstances, Olsen's most difficult job was keeping a tight rein on the company's growth. Fortunately, he proved to be a superb manager. He funneled Digital's profits back into the company, shunned acquisitions and mergers, and didn't even bother to build a new company headquarters; the firm is still run out of the old wool mill in Maynard. Although Digital is now the largest private employer in Massachusetts, Olsen and his executives stuck to their work and stayed out of community affairs. "This may sound trivial," he said in 1968, "but it's important. There are all kinds of pressures on senior people in organizations to do things peripheral to their business. . . . After a while, these demands can take up approximately 300 percent of your time. It's somewhat unfair of society to expect people running a business responsible for thousands of jobs to also solve these other problems."

*In 1969, the Data General Corporation, of Westborough, Massachusetts, introduced the Nova minicomputer. It cost $8,000 and was one of the least expensive and most successful of the early minis. Data General was founded in 1968 by four engineers, three of whom had worked for Digital.*

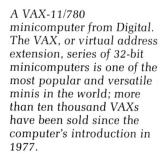

*A VAX-11/780 minicomputer from Digital. The VAX, or virtual address extension, series of 32-bit minicomputers is one of the most popular and versatile minis in the world; more than ten thousand VAXs have been sold since the computer's introduction in 1977.*

On the heels of Digital's success, dozens of companies entered the minicomputer business. By one count, at least seventy-five firms were making minicomputers by 1971. Although the established computer makers — IBM, Sperry Rand, Burroughs, and so on — possessed the skill and capital to get into minicomputers, they suffered from a tunnel vision that prevented them both from recognizing the existence of major new markets for their products and, once having seen the market, from moving quickly into it. (As we shall see, the affliction wasn't confined to the established firms; even Digital had it.) As a result, IBM and the other major computer firms didn't get into minicomputers until the 1970s. Meanwhile, Digital became one of the largest computer companies in the world, with 78,000 employees and $4.3 billion in sales in 1983.

In 1959, two years after Digital was founded, Fairchild Camera & Instrument bought out Fairchild Semiconductor, giving Robert Noyce, Jean Hoerni, and the six other founders $250,000 in corporation stock. Although the founders stayed on, they soon became dissatisfied with their positions. They were prospering but they weren't getting rich, and the firm was no longer theirs but Fairchild's — and Fairchild's formal, structured management methods didn't mesh with Silicon Valley's casual, free-form California style. In 1961, Hoerni and three other founders resigned and established Amelco (later Teledyne Semiconductor). Other, lower-level executives followed suit, and IC firms began to crop up all over Silicon Valley, bearing such high-tech neologisms as Signetics, Intersil, Advanced Micro Devices, and Qualidyne. All told, about fifty IC companies have their roots in Fairchild.

Even Noyce, Fairchild's general manager, resigned. He and Gordon Moore, a mild-mannered physicist who was one of Fairchild's founders, established Intel (an acronym that stands for integrated electronics) in 1968. Such was Noyce and Moore's reputation that the pair didn't even have to write a business plan to attract investors; they simply said that they intended to specialize in memory chips, the most promising segment of the IC market, and the money flowed in. Noyce and Moore put up $250,000 each, and Arthur Rock, the venture capitalist who had introduced Noyce, Moore, and their fellow Shockley expatriates to Fairchild Camera & Instrument, raised $2.5 million. Intel moved into a small building in Santa Clara, not far from Fairchild, and patiently and confidently devoted its first two years to the development of more sophisticated memories.

At that time, the most advanced RAMs held sixty-four bits. That wasn't sufficient to supplant magnetic cores, which were inexpensive and reliable. In 1970, Fairchild, now Noyce and Moore's competitor, introduced a 256-bit RAM, and the switch from cores to ICs gathered momentum. By the end of the year, Intel had leaped ahead with the creation of a 1K RAM. For the first time, an IC could hold a truly significant amount of information — 1,024 bits on a chip that measured a mere 0.113 by 0.139 inches. Magnetic cores could store only a few bits in the same amount of space. Orders poured into the company. In 1971, Intel had $9 million in sales and about five hundred employees; three years later, revenues had almost tripled, while the workforce had doubled. But that was only the beginning, for, in November 1971, Intel introduced a revolutionary new chip, the *microprocessor.*

The first electronic calculator was introduced in 1963 by a British firm called the Bell Punch Company. Made out of discrete transistors, it was about the size of a cash register. Four years later, Texas Instruments came out with a slightly smaller IC calculator, and other companies followed suit. These gadgets were composed of logic ICs and two types of memory chips: RAMs, for storing numbers entered by the user and calculated by the machine; and *read-only memories (ROMs)*, for holding the device's internal operating instructions, such as the procedure for finding square roots. (RAM is like a scratchpad, ROM like a reference book.) Although the first IC calculators were quite limited and cost hundreds of dollars, they led to the development of cheap pocket versions in the early 1970s — and the slide rule, that utilitarian holdover from the early seventeenth century, became extinct.

In the summer of 1969, Busicom, a now-defunct Japanese calculator manufacturer, asked Intel to develop a set of chips for a new line of programmable electronic calculators. (The IC's extraordinary capabilities were leading to a blurring of the line between calculators and computers.) Busicom's engineers had worked up a preliminary design that called for twelve logic and memory chips, with three to five thousand transistors each. By varying the ROMs, Busicom planned to offer calculators with different capabilities and options. One model, for example, contained a built-in printer. The company's plans were quite ambitious; at the time, most calculators contained six chips of six hundred to a thousand transistors each. But Intel had recently developed a technique for making two-thousand-transistor chips, and Busicom hoped that the firm could make even more sophisticated ICs.

*Silicon Valley in 1981, looking south toward San Jose. Interstate 101 stretches through the valley, surrounded on both sides by electronic and computer companies.*

Intel assigned the Busicom job to Marcian E. Hoff, a thirty-two-year-old engineer with a B.S. in engineering from Rensselaer Polytechnic Institute in Troy, New York, and a doctorate from Stanford. A natural engineer, with the thoughtful manner of a professor and the caution of a corporate executive, Hoff — Ted to his friends — had a knack for spotting new solutions to technical problems. "When my washing machine breaks," said one of Hoff's colleagues and admirers, "I call the Sears repairman. When a clever person's machine breaks, he goes down to Sears, buys a new part, and installs it himself. But if Ted's machine breaks, he analyzes the problem, redesigns the faulty part, casts it in his own crucible, polishes it on his lathe, and installs it himself — and the machine works better than ever."

*Marcian E. Hoff, Jr., in 1981*

Hoff studied Busicom's design and concluded that it was much too complicated to be cost effective. Each calculator in the line needed one set of logic chips to perform basic mathematical functions and another to control the printers and other peripheral devices. (A logic chip can only carry out a fixed series of operations, determined by the pattern of its logic gates. A logic chip that has been designed to control a printer usually can't do anything else.) Even though some of the calculator's functions would be controlled by ROM, which sent instructions to the logic chips and, therefore, enabled some of them to do slightly different tasks, the bulk of the operations would be performed by the logic ICs. Although Intel could have produced chips of the required complexity, the productive yield — the number of working chips — would have been prohibitively low.

Busicom was looking forward and backward at the same time. The first logic chips, produced in the early 1960s, contained only a handful of components. As the state of IC technology advanced, the devices became more complex and powerful, but they also became more difficult and expensive to design. Since a different set of logic chips was required for every device, the chips destined for one gadget couldn't be used in another. The IC companies developed various techniques to streamline the design process — using computers to help lay out the chips, for example — but the results were disappointing. An engineering bottleneck was developing; unless a simpler way of designing the chips was perfected, the IC industry wouldn't be able to keep up with the burgeoning demand for its components, no matter how many engineers it employed.

Fortunately, Hoff came up with a solution. Why not, he suggested, develop a general-purpose logic chip, one that could, like the central processor of a computer, perform any logical task?

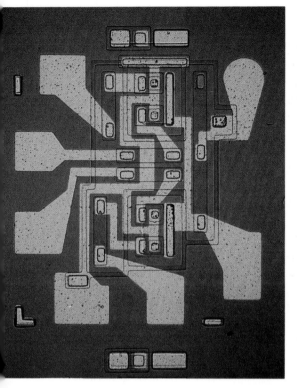

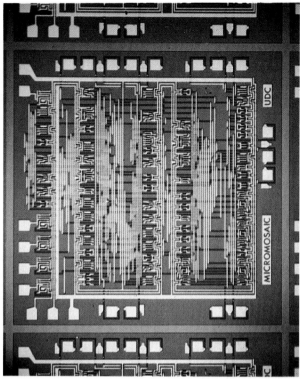

*Two early logic chips. The one on the left, made by Fairchild in 1963, was a simple device with four flip flops. The one on the right, made by Fairchild in 1967, was more sophisticated. Its transistors (the dark horizontal lines) could be hooked up in almost any pattern of logic gates by changing the arrangement of aluminum interconnections (the vertical beige lines) during manufacture. Thus the chip could be customized to meet the needs of many different users. The chip on the left is .048 inch long and .038 inch wide; the chip on the right, which contains about 150 logic gates, is .15 inch square.*

Like a conventional central processor, the microprocessor would be programmable, taking its instructions from RAM and ROM. So if a customer (like Busicom) wanted to make a calculator, it would write a calculator program, and Intel would insert that program into ROM. Each calculator would need one microprocessor and one programmed ROM, along with several other chips (depending on the complexity of the device). Similarly, if another customer came along with plans for a digital clock, it would devise a clock program, and Intel would produce the requisite ROMs. This meant that Intel wouldn't have to work up a new set of logic chips for every customer; the burden of design would be shifted to the customer and transformed into the much less costly and time-consuming matter of programming.

It was a brilliant idea. Instead of twelve chips, Busicom's calculators now needed only four — a microprocessor, a ROM, a RAM, and an input/output IC to relay signals between the microprocessor and the outside world. Not only did Hoff's invention cut down the number of chips and, therefore, the number of interconnections (thereby increasing the calculators' reliability), it also resulted in a much more flexible and powerful family of calculators. Literally a programmable processor on a chip, a microprocessor expands a device's capabilities at the same time as it cuts its manufacturing costs. In other words, it's one of those rare innovations that gives more for less. Busicom accepted Hoff's scheme, and the first microprocessor, designated the 4004, rolled off Intel's production line in late 1970.

The 4004 wasn't a very potent computational tool. With 2,250 transistors, it could process only four bits of data at a time and carry out about 60,000 operations a second. It wasn't powerful enough to serve as the central processor of a minicomputer, but it was quite adequate for a calculator and other relatively simple electronic devices, like taximeters or cash registers. The other three chips in the set were also limited. The ROM, which contained the inner program that governed the calculator, stored 2K bits of data, and the RAM, which provided temporary storage, held a mere 320 bits. Nevertheless, the four chips constituted a bona fide computer that, mounted on a small circuit board, occupied about as much space as a pocketbook.

Because Intel had developed the 4004 under contract for Busicom, the Japanese company had an exclusive right to the chip and Intel couldn't offer it on the open market. But in the summer of 1971, Busicom asked Intel to cut its prices — the calculator business had become quite competitive — and, in exchange for the price reduction, Intel won the right to market the

*Intel's first advertisement for the 4004 microprocessor appeared in the 15 November 1971 issue of Electronic News.*

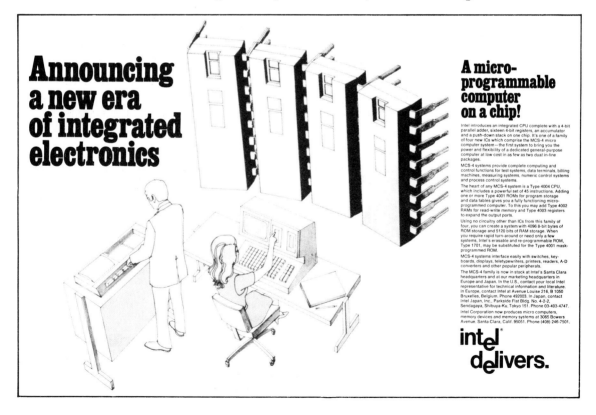

4004. Even so, the company hesitated. No one had fully grasped the enormous utility of Hoff's invention, and Intel assumed that the chip would be used chiefly in calculators and minicomputers. About 20,000 minicomputers were sold in 1971; at best, the 4004 (and other, more sophisticated microprocessors Intel was considering developing) would wind up in 10 percent of these machines — a prospect that wasn't very interesting to a small semiconductor company bent on becoming a big one.

Although Intel didn't realize it at first, the company was sitting on the device that would become the universal motor of electronics, a miniature analytical engine that could take the place of gears and axles and other forms of mechanical control. It could be placed inexpensively and unobtrusively in all sorts of devices — a washing machine, a gas pump, a butcher's scale, a jukebox, a typewriter, a doorbell, a thermostat, even, if there was a reason, a rock. Almost any machine that manipulated information or controlled a process could benefit from a microprocessor. Fortunately, Intel did have an inkling, just an inkling, of the microprocessor's potential. The company decided to take a chance, and the 4004 and its related chips were introduced to the public in November 1971.

Not surprisingly, the 4004 sold slowly at first, but orders picked up as engineers gained a clearer understanding of the chip's near-magical electronic properties. Meanwhile, Intel went to work on more sophisticated versions. In April 1972, it introduced the first eight-bit microprocessor, the 8008, which was powerful enough to run a minicomputer (and, as we shall see, at least one inventor used it for just that purpose). The 8008 had many technical drawbacks, however, and it was superseded two years later by a much more efficient and powerful microprocessor, the now-legendary 8080. The 8080 made dozens of new products possible — including the personal computer. For several years, Intel was the only microprocessor maker in the world, and its sales soared. By the end of 1983, Intel was one of the largest IC companies in the country, with 21,500 employees and $1.1 billion in sales.

By the early 1970s, ICs were sophisticated and inexpensive enough to make a small and inexpensive personal computer possible. Many computer companies, especially Digital and the larger minicomputer makers, could have developed one. Technically, the task wasn't complicated, either with logic chips or microprocessors. Yet there is a big difference between the ability to make a

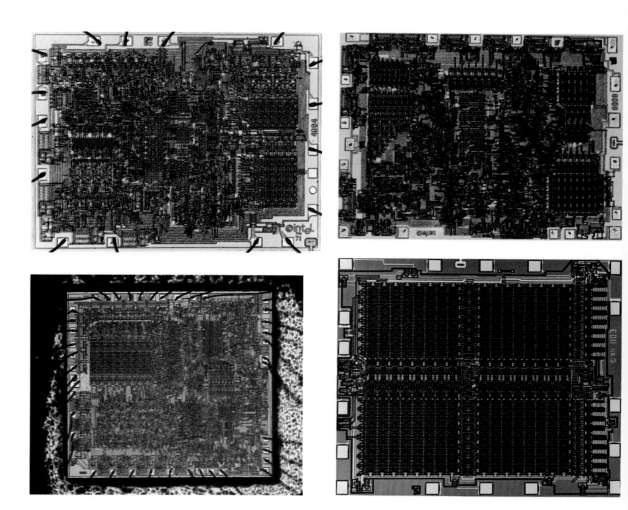

*Four historic chips, all from Intel. From left to right, top: the 4004, developed in 1970, was the first microprocessor; the 8008, introduced in 1972, was the first eight-bit microprocessor. Bottom: the 8080, which came along in 1974, was the first microprocessor powerful enough to run a minicomputer; and the 1103, introduced in 1970, was the first 1K RAM. These chips are about a tenth of an inch wide and two tenths of an inch long.*

machine and the realization that a market for it exists. The computer companies couldn't imagine why anyone — any ordinary person, that is — would want a computer. You don't need a computer to balance your checkbook or write letters. A calculator is good enough for the former and a typewriter for the latter. And if, for some reason, you did need a computer, you'd be much better off renting a terminal and joining a time-sharing system.

At least two firms dabbled with the idea of making a personal computer in the early 1970s. One of them was the Hewlett-Packard Company, of Palo Alto, California, and we'll return to this lost opportunity later in the chapter. The other was Ken Olsen's Digital, where an engineer named David Ahl headed a small effort to market minicomputers to schools. In all probability, other companies also toyed with the notion of making a personal, or home, computer. (The terms *home computer* and *personal computer* mean more or less the same thing, a small machine designed for an individual's use.) The arrival of the personal computer was not a triumph of engineering skill but of marketing acumen or — to use a word that does greater justice to the determination of some of the people behind the personal computer industry — vision.

A tall, curly-haired fellow, David Ahl had joined Digital in 1969 as a market researcher. In addition to an engineering degree, Ahl had an M.B.A. and an M.A. in educational psychology. In 1970, he set up an educational products group at Digital, selling packaged computer systems that included both hardware and software to high schools and colleges. Ahl's little group did quite well; in 1973, it had about $20 million in sales and about half of the educational computer market for minicomputers, with Hewlett-Packard close behind.

Most of Digital's sales were made to other computer manufacturers or to large institutions, corporate and educational, that had the financial and technical resources to operate their own computers. Very few individuals bought minicomputers, both because they were beyond most people's budgets and because you had to know a good deal about computers in order to run them. However, every once in a while Ahl's group received an order from an individual — usually a consulting engineer — for one of its machines. Ahl began wondering whether a market for a simple personal computer existed.

In 1973, Ahl moved to the research and development group, where he helped prepare marketing materials for certain products and investigated new business opportunities. Among other things, the research and development group was working on a small business computer, and Ahl suggested that there just might be a market for the thing in schools and homes. His boss, an energetic engineer named Richard Clayton, was intrigued by the idea. While Ahl explored the marketing side of his suggestion, a small team of engineers developed two prototypes.

One was a computer terminal containing a circuit board filled with logic and memory chips. (In other words, it did not use a microprocessor.) It was a scaled-down PDP-8, a limited version of Digital's popular minicomputer. (The device resembled the Radio Shack TRS-80 personal computer, developed several years later.) The other prototype was a much more daring effort. It was a portable computer, about the size of a thick attaché case, that contained a monitor, a keyboard, and a *floppy disk drive* (a small piece of equipment that stores information on a recordlike piece of magnetized Mylar). Floppy disk drives, now a standard part of computers, were new at the time, and the research and development group never managed to get the disk drive on the pro-

*David Ahl in his office in Morris Plains, New Jersey, 1984*

totype to work reliably. But the first machine, the one that was
made out of a terminal, operated quite well.

In May 1974, Ahl went before Digital's operations committee, chaired by Olsen, with a marketing plan for the computers.
Ahl intended to sell both machines to schools for about $5,000
apiece, not including peripherals, and to anyone else who wanted
one. He had contacted the Heath Company, a maker of hobbyist
kits, and the firm had expressed interest in offering the computer
in the form of a kit. He had even gotten in touch with Abercrom-
bie & Fitch and Hammacher Schlemmer, two well-known retailers
of unusual and costly items. Both companies were attracted by
the idea of a home computer, but the people Ahl had talked to
knew next to nothing about computers and weren't quite sure
what he was getting at. In any event, Ahl asked the operations
committee for permission to perfect the prototypes and see if he
could dig up some orders.

The committee was split. About half of the members came
from the engineering side of the firm; dedicated tinkerers themselves, they had a weakness for interesting new gadgets and were
gung-ho about Ahl's proposal. But the other half of the committee
came from the sales department, and they were much more hard-
nosed. Why would a school buy such a limited machine when a
time-sharing minicomputer was much more cost effective? An inexpensive minicomputer could handle many students at the same
time; Ahl's machine could serve only one, and it hardly seemed
likely that a school would order a couple dozen of them. Likewise, the salesmen didn't see a market for the gadget in the home;
again, what would you do with it? These were very good questions, and Ahl didn't have convincing answers. Olsen — a fallible
human being, just like the rest of us — ended the debate by coming down on the side of the salesmen, and Ahl's project was scut-
tled. Disappointed, Ahl left Digital a few months later. Today, he
owns a successful personal computer magazine called *Creative
Computing.*

Given the computer industry's early indifference to personal computers, the task of developing such a machine fell to those people
who dreamed of owning their own computers — electronic hobbyists. One of those hobbyists was a graduate student named Jonathan A. Titus, who was studying for a doctorate in chemistry at
Virginia Polytechnic Institute, in Blacksburg. The son of an attorney, Titus grew up in Huntington, New York, a comfortable mid-
dle-class suburb on Long Island's north shore. After taking a B.S.

in chemistry at Worcester Polytechnic Institute in Worcester, Massachusetts, he went on to Rensselaer Polytechnic Institute (Hoff's alma mater), where he picked up a master's. Along the way, he became deeply interested in scientific instrumentation. Titus knew a great deal about electronics — he loved to tinker with gadgets in his spare time — and he, for one, was fully aware of the microprocessor's significance.

When Intel introduced the eight-bit 8008, Titus studied the chip's specifications. Realizing that it was powerful enough to run a minicomputer, he ordered an 8008 from Intel — the chips cost $120 apiece — and received a free applications manual, full of circuit diagrams, along with it. Using the diagrams as his jumping-off point, he went to work and had a computer prototype ready by the fall of 1973. Although he had built the gadget for his own enjoyment, Titus wanted to share his design with other hobbyists; the idea of establishing a computer company didn't even occur to him. So he wrote a couple of letters to *Popular Electronics* and *Radio-Electronics*, two well-known hobbyist magazines, asking whether they would be interested in running a how-to-build-it article on the Mark-8, as he called his invention. *Popular Electronics* turned him down, considering the Mark-8 more of an educational project than a truly useful computer, but *Radio-Electronics* was intrigued, and Larry Steckler, one of the magazine's editors, flew down to Blacksburg to examine the Mark-8.

The machine was about the size of a large breadbox. It consisted of six circuit boards, one of which held the 8008 and related chips, another the RAM chips, and so on. At the very least, it required a memory of eight 256-bit RAMs (in other words, 256 bytes or words), but the memory could be expanded up to 16K by adding more RAM memory boards. There wasn't any ROM — Titus would have had to pay Intel thousands of dollars to make ROMs for the Mark-8 — which meant that every instruction had to be entered by the user and that the programs were lost when the machine was shut off. (RAMs retain their data only as long as the power is on.) And those programs had to be entered one bit at a time by flipping a set of toggle switches on the face of the machine — a painstaking and error-prone procedure. The results were displayed on a panel of lights next to the switches.

Titus's piece ran in the July 1974 issue of *Radio-Electronics*. Although the article was the magazine's cover story, it appeared without any hoopla. The cover featured a picture of the machine and, above it, a sober, unimaginative headline: "Build the Mark-8, Your Personal Minicomputer." There were six other headlines on the page, all competing for the reader's attention.

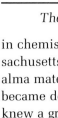

*Jonathan Titus in Blacksburg, Virginia, 1984*

*The July 1974 cover of Radio-Electronics*

The article itself was quite technical, but, being only four pages long, it didn't supply enough information to actually build the machine. That was intentional; if you wanted more details, you could send away for a forty-eight-page instruction manual, written by Titus and published by *Radio-Electronics*, for $5.50. You could also buy the circuit boards, in an arrangement worked out by Titus, for $47.50 from Techniques, Inc., a small firm in Englewood, New Jersey. (Titus earned royalties for every booklet and set of boards sold.) As for the components, you had to buy them from Intel and other companies. Altogether, the Mark-8 cost about $250 to build — in addition to a lot of time and trouble.

Titus's invention struck a vibrant chord among *Radio-Electronics*'s readers. About ten thousand people bought the instruction booklet and about a fourth as many sent away for the boards. Unfortunately, there's no way of knowing how many Mark-8's were actually built; probably one to two thousand. At least two Mark-8 computer clubs sprung up — one in Lompoc, California, another in Denver, Colorado — each with its own chatty and informative newsletter. Not satisfied with the basic machine, some of the more determined and talented hobbyists went on to build their own paper-tape readers and other peripherals, which made the chores of entering programs and recording results considerably easier. Although it's inappropriate to call Titus the inventor of the personal computer — the machine had many parents, including Intel — the Mark-8 was the first seed in a grassroots movement to make computers available to everyone.

In January 1975, six months after the Mark-8's introduction, *Popular Electronics* published the first installment of a two-part article on a much more sophisticated computer, the Altair 8800. The Altair was the first — the very first — full-fledged personal computer on the market, and it launched the personal computer industry. It was based on Intel's 8080 microprocessor, the successor to the weak 8008, and it had been designed by a small electronics-hobby-kit company called Micro Instrumentation and Telemetry Systems (MITS), of Albuquerque, New Mexico. The Altair was, surprisingly, astonishingly inexpensive. Fully assembled, it cost $650; in a kit, containing all the necessary parts and instructions, it was priced at only $395. Thousands of orders poured into MITS in the months following the *Popular Electronics* articles — a deluge that no one, least of all MITS, had expected.

MITS was founded in 1969 by four men, including Edward Roberts, an electronics engineer, Air Force captain, and the com-

*Edward Roberts in his study in Glenwood, Georgia, 1984.*

pany's driving force. Twenty-eight years old at the time, Roberts was a research engineer in the laser division of the Air Force Weapons Lab at Albuquerque's Kirtland Air Force Base. (Two of his partners were also engineers and captains at the lab; the third was a civilian.) A big, burly man with a dry, matter-of-fact manner, Roberts had been born in Miami, Florida, where his father had owned an appliance shop. After attending college for several years, Roberts joined the Air Force and ended up as an electronics teacher at Lackland Air Force Base, in San Antonio, Texas. With financial aid from the Air Force, he returned to school and received a B.S. in electrical engineering from Oklahoma State University, in Stillwater.

For the first two years of MITS's existence, Roberts and his partners were in the Air Force, and the company was a shoestring, part-time operation based in Roberts's garage in the northeast section of Albuquerque. Its first product was a telemetry kit for model rockets. But the world wasn't overflowing with model rocket devotees, and the kit, not surprisingly, did poorly. The company's next product, a gadget that could send and receive voices via infrared light, was more ambitious. Forrest Mims III, one of the company's cofounders and an aspiring writer, wrote an article on the "Opticom," as the device was called, for *Popular Electronics*. Despite the publicity — the magazine's monthly circulation was approximately 350,000, about 130,000 more than *Radio-Electronics* — this kit also failed to catch on. Discouraged, Mims and the other partners decided to pull out of the company, and Roberts, who was determined to make a go of it, bought them out for $100 apiece.

Once on his own, Roberts decided to get into electronic calculator kits. It proved to be a smart move. MITS was one of the first companies to put a calculator kit on the market — a $169 model that rivaled many assembled, and much more expensive, calculators — and the company filled ten to fifteen thousand orders between 1972 and 1974. By 1973, MITS occupied two large rooms in a shopping center in northeast Albuquerque and employed about twenty-five people, most of whom packaged the kits and filled orders. The company also went public that year, issuing $500,000 worth of stock on the over-the-counter market. However, the calculator business wasn't very profitable — the competition was murderous — and MITS made little money. (The stock hovered between 50¢ and 75¢ a share.) And when, also in 1974, the semiconductor manufacturers entered the calculator business, the bottom fell out of the market, and MITS could no longer compete. Fully assembled calculators suddenly were selling for much less than the company's kits.

Roberts decided to go for broke with an unprecedented product — a computer kit. He had always been interested in digital electronics and had always wanted to build a minicomputer. He studied the 8080's specifications and decided that, unlike the 8008, this chip possessed enough power to run a sophisticated small computer. He discussed his idea with *Popular Electronics,* and the magazine's editorial director, Arthur Salsberg, and technical editor, Leslie Solomon, encouraged him. They had been searching for a good computer project since early that year. But they had certain requirements; the machine had to be more than a toy — more than a gadget with flashing lights — and it had to sell for under $400. And so, in 1974, Roberts and his engineers, in a desperate effort to keep the company afloat, started building the Altair.

The Altair was designed by Roberts and two engineers, William Yates, a former Air Force officer with a degree in aeronautical engineering, and Jim Bybee, another ex–Air Force officer and electronics engineer. Roberts sketched out the general plan and Yates, a quiet, serious man with a knack for electronics, laid out the circuit boards, planning the pathways for each electrical signal. At the start of the project Roberts made a very clever decision: he made sure that the Altair would be easy to expand. A typical minicomputer contained slots for the installation of additional circuit boards, whether for memory or other functions; these slots not only enabled users to enlarge the capacity of their machines, but gave the computer manufacturer a lucrative aftermarket. (It was also an open invitation to other companies to offer boards of their own.) The Altair, beginning a trend that succeeding personal computer manufacturers followed, contained sixteen slots for extra boards.

While Roberts, Yates, and Bybee were building the computer, MITS was about $300,000 in debt and running out of money. Hard pressed, Roberts applied for a $65,000 loan. Half comprehendingly, the Fidelity National loan officer listened to his plans: MITS intended to market a computer kit through ads in electronic hobbyist magazines, offering the gadget, unassembled, for less than $400. MITS also intended to sell peripheral products, such as memory boards, paper-tape readers, and so on, but not at first. At the moment, Roberts said, there was no other product like the Altair and he expected to sell at least eight hundred machines a year. Although the loan officer had his doubts about the eight hundred figure — two hundred seemed to be a more realistic estimate — he granted the loan. The bank wanted to keep MITS, and thereby its chances of repaying its debts, alive.

In the summer of 1974, Roberts put the one and only Altair in a crate and shipped it to New York for Salsberg and Solomon's evaluation. However, the package, sent via Railway Express, didn't arrive at the appointed time. Assuring the editors that the machine was on its way — that it probably had been delayed somewhere along the line — Roberts flew to New York to deliver his articles and to demonstrate the Altair. Yet the computer still wasn't there when he reached New York; it had been lost in transit, and MITS couldn't possibly assemble another machine in time for the magazine's deadline. (The package turned up a year later.) Instead, *Popular Electronics* decided to fake it. Yates and Bybee assembled the outer shell of an Altair, placed some flashing lights on the front, and shipped it to New York, where *Popular Electronics* photographed it for the front cover. No one was the wiser.

Unlike *Radio-Electronics*, which had been subdued in its treatment of the Mark-8, *Popular Electronics* proclaimed the arrival of the "home computer" with appropriate fanfare. The Altair was prominently featured on the cover of its January 1975 issue, and Salsberg, writing in the editor's column, announced:

> For many years, we've been reading and hearing about how computers will one day be a household item. Therefore, we're especially proud to present in this issue the first *commercial type* of minicomputer project ever published that's priced within reach of many households — the *Altair 8800*, with an under-$400 complete kit cost, including cabinet.
>
> To give you some insight into our editorial goal for this momentous project, we were determined *not* to present a digital

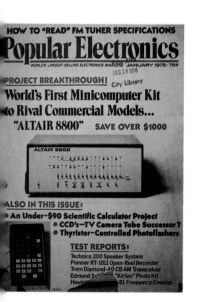

*The January 1975 cover of* Popular Electronics

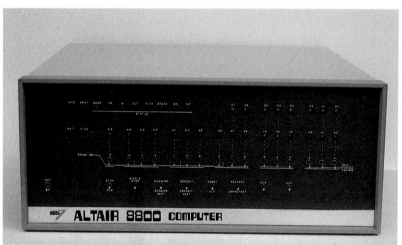

*A MITS advertisement (left) and the Altair (right).*

computer demonstrator with blinking LED's [light-emitting diodes] that would simply be fun to build and watch, but suffer from limited usefulness. . . . What we wanted for our readers was a state-of-the-art minicomputer whose capabilities would match those of currently available units at a mere fraction of the cost.

After turning down three computer project proposals that did not meet these requirements, the breakthrough was made possible with the availability of the Intel 8080 . . . the highest-performance, single-chip processor available at this time. As a result, the *Altair 8800* offers up to 65,000 words [containing eight bits each] of memory, 256 inputs and outputs simultaneously, buss line expansion [for additional boards], subroutines that are enormously deep, and fast cycle time, among other desirable characteristics. Peripheral equipment such as a "smart" CRT terminal is expected to be available, too, to make up a within-pocketbook-reach sophisticated minicomputer system.

Although MITS's ads promised delivery within sixty days, the firm was swamped with orders, and it didn't manage to fill the bulk of them until the summer. Even so, most of the promised optional equipment, such as printers, paper-tape readers, memory boards, and terminals, wasn't available until the end of the year. Nor did MITS have any prepackaged software; if you wanted to get the Altair to do something — anything — you had to write a program in machine code and enter it, bit by bit, via the toggle switches on the front panel. Moreover, the 256-byte basic memory was too small to allow the Altair to do much, Salsberg's comments notwithstanding. As a result, all you could really do with the Altair was play with it, and one of its first programs was a game that generated increasingly complicated patterns of lights on the front panel, patterns that had to be duplicated by the players. (The game resembled a popular toy, called Simon, that appeared a few years later.)

What the Altair needed most of all, aside from more memory and peripherals, was a BASIC interpreter. Such an internal program would enable the machine's users (assuming they had a paper-tape reader) to write programs in BASIC, a popular, easy-to-use high-level language, rather than in machine code. As coincidence would have it, Paul Allen, a young programmer who worked outside Boston, happened to be strolling through Harvard Square one day when he noticed the January issue of *Popular Electronics* on a newsstand. A computer hobbyist since junior high school, Allen bought a copy and went on to visit his friend William Gates, a Harvard freshman. Enterprising young men, Allen and Gates phoned Roberts with an offer to write a BASIC interpreter for the Altair. Roberts was interested, and the pair got to work. Six weeks later, Allen flew out to Albuquerque with the interpreter. Roberts bought it, and Allen promptly became MITS's software director. Meanwhile, Gates dropped out of Harvard and went to work as a freelance software writer. Gates and Allen later established the Microsoft Corporation, in Bellevue, Washington, and it is now one of the country's largest software companies.

*William Gates in 1982*

Other people got into the act, too. Although MITS eventually offered 4K memory boards for $150, the first boards didn't work well, and another company, Processor Technology, of Berkeley, California, arose to supply them. Operating out of a garage, Processor Technology was typical of the computer companies that cropped up in the wake of the Altair's appearance. It was small, undercapitalized, and amateurish, but overflowing with optimism and good intentions. It went on to make a personal computer of its own and enjoyed some success; by 1977, the company had about ninety employees and occupied a large building in Emeryville, California, southwest of Berkeley. By that time, however, there were at least thirty personal computer companies, including Apple, IMSAI, Commodore, Vector Graphic, Heathkit, Cromemco, Radio Shack, North Star, and MITS. A highly competitive personal computer industry was springing up, with an infrastructure of its own — trade fairs (the First World Altair Computer Conference, in Albuquerque in March 1976); magazines (*Byte*, in August 1975); and computer shops (The Computer Store, in Los Angeles, in July 1975).

Meanwhile, Edward Roberts, unhappy in his role as manager, decided to sell out. On 22 May 1977, MITS was acquired by the Pertec Computer Corporation (now known as TA Pertec and based in Chatsworth, California), a firm that made disk and tape drives for minicomputers and mainframes. Roberts and MITS's other stockholders received $6.5 million in Pertec stock; Pertec sent in its own management team; and MITS began to collapse. In the first place, MITS no longer monopolized the personal computer market; in fact, IMSAI, whose computer was essentially an enhanced version of the Altair, pulled ahead of MITS with a zealous sales effort that focused on small businesses. Pertec also decided to concentrate on the business market, but the Altair wasn't efficient enough for the needs of small businesses and small businesses weren't ready for personal computers. In the second place, small personal computers with built-in monitors, keyboards, and disk drives were beginning to appear. Easier to use, these machines appealed to the general public, but Pertec had nothing similar. By 1979, both MITS and IMSAI were bankrupt.

*Stephen Wozniak in 1980*

The Altair inspired many hobbyists to design their own computers. One of these tinkerers was an unconventional, self-taught engineer named Stephen G. Wozniak. Woz, as he was known to his friends, had been an avid electronics hobbyist since his youth. Like many of the seminal figures in the history of computers, Woz was the son of an engineer — his father, Francis, helped design satellite guidance systems at the huge Lockheed Missiles & Space Company plant in Sunnyvale, California, not far from Intel and Fairchild Semiconductor. Francis taught his son the fundamentals of electronics and encouraged him to experiment on his own. Woz had a talent for electronics, and he built all sorts of gadgets, including a transistor radio. By the time he was in sixth grade, he had decided to become an electronics engineer.

An unusually intelligent youngster, Woz was an indifferent student. He shone in the few classes that interested him — mathematics and science — and did poorly in the rest. In general, he was bored by school; electronics and, increasingly, computers were his greatest interest, and neither his junior high school nor his high school had much to offer him in either subject. He took to reading computer manuals and programming textbooks on his own, and he soon pulled ahead of his fellow students and even his teachers. When he was thirteen, he built a transistorized calculator that won first prize in a Bay Area science fair. Much as other teenagers pasted up photos of rock stars and other heroes on their bedroom walls, Woz put up pictures of his favorite computer systems. He was drawn to minicomputers most of all, admiring their compactness, accessibility, and inexpensiveness. By the end of high school, Woz knew that he wanted to be a computer engineer.

Lackadaisical about school, Woz didn't give much serious thought to college. On a visit to Colorado, he had seen snow for the first time and had fallen in love with it; so, instead of going to a well-known engineering school, such as MIT or Stanford, he went to the University of Colorado. After a year in Colorado he transferred to De Anza College, a junior college in Cupertino, California, and then he left school altogether, working for a year as a programmer for a small computer company. He gave college another shot in 1971, this time at the University of California at Berkeley, but that didn't work out either, and he dropped out and went to work as an engineer in the calculator division of Hewlett-Packard in Palo Alto. Why study computers when you could make a good living designing them?

In the summer of 1971, when Woz was working as a programmer, a friend introduced him to a quiet, intense, longhaired teenager by the name of Steven P. Jobs. Jobs, who was sixteen years old at the time, lived in nearby Los Altos, where his father was a machinist. Although Woz was five years older, he and Jobs hit it off right away. Like Woz, Jobs was an electronics hobbyist as well as a student at Homestead High School in Cupertino, Woz's alma mater. He was just as bored by school as Woz had been, and just as obsessed by the shadowy by-products of technology — in particular, by a small electronic gadget, known as a blue box, that emitted various tones, enabling the user to take control of a telephone line and make free calls. Woz designed one of his own, and Jobs, in the same collaborative style they would use to develop the Apple computer, obtained the necessary parts and circuit boards for more boxes from local electronic companies. Although it was illegal to use the boxes, Woz and Jobs sold about a hundred and fifty, at $40 to $150 apiece, to friends and acquaintances.

*Steven Jobs in 1983*

After high school, Jobs went to Reed College, in Portland, Oregon, but dropped out during the second semester. He hung around the campus for another year, living in the dorms, attending classes occasionally, and reading a good deal about Eastern religions. He became a vegetarian, subsisting on cereal, partly because it was inexpensive and partly because it entailed a small degree of mortification. Then he returned home and got a job as a video game designer for a rambunctious young firm called Atari. Jobs worked at night, and Woz often came by to play with the company's video games. Within a few months, Jobs had saved enough money to quit his job and fly to India, where he traveled with a friend from Reed until 1974, when his money ran out.

In 1971, Wozniak and a close friend, William Fernandez, built a small 8-bit computer made out of logic ICs. Fernandez (above left) holds the computer in his hand. Right: The single-board computer, known as the Apple I, that launched the Apple Computer Corporation.

The introduction of the Altair had led to the formation of computer clubs all over the country, including one in Silicon Valley known as the Homebrew Computer Club. Woz heard about the group through word of mouth and attended the first meeting, held in an engineer's garage in Menlo Park, near Stanford University, in March 1975. About thirty people showed up, but the group, fueled by the excitement generated by the Altair, expanded rapidly. It soon numbered about five hundred members and held monthly meetings in an auditorium at the Stanford Linear Accelerator Center. These meetings were divided into a "random-access" period, during which the floor was thrown open to anyone who had anything to say, and a "mapping" period, when the audience broke up into small groups devoted to common concerns. Excited by the prospect of a computerized world, Woz was one of Homebrew's most active members.

He started building his own microprocessor-based computer later that year. For $20, he bought a new 8-bit microprocessor, the 6502, designed by a small Silicon Valley company called MOS Technology (now based in Norristown, Pennsylvania, and a part of Commodore Business Machines Inc., the home computer manufacturer). Woz first wrote a BASIC interpreter for the 6502; then he designed the computer itself, laboring mostly at night, after work, for about six months.

The device consisted of a single circuit board with 4K of RAM. Although it wasn't as powerful as Altair's and IMSAI's offerings, it was cheaper and less complicated, and it included circuits that enabled it to be connected directly to a monitor. Woz did most of the work, but Jobs, who was trying to persuade Woz to go into business with him, chipped in with many suggestions.

*The interior of the Apple IIe, an enhanced version of the enormously popular Apple II*

Woz demonstrated the board to an enthusiastic Homebrew audience and then tried to interest Hewlett-Packard, his employer, in making personal computers. However, the company doubted there was much of a market for the machine.

Jobs, however, thought otherwise and began a dogged search for buyers. He found one in Paul Terrell, owner of the newly established Byte Shop stores and a member of Homebrew. Terrell ordered a hundred boards at $500 a piece, and Woz and Jobs set up a partnership — the Apple Computer Company. Brandishing Terrell's order as proof of their financial credibility, the pair obtained the neccessary parts for the boards on thirty-day credit. Scrambling for operating funds, Jobs sold his Volkswagen bus and Woz his Hewlett-Packard programmable calculator, realizing $1,350 altogether. They also borrowed $5,000 from a friend. Then they hired one firm to make the printed circuit boards and another outfit to plug the chips into the boards. Since Woz's single-board computers lacked keyboards, terminals, disk drives, and other peripherals, they could be used only by sophisticated hobbyists — but the Bay Area was full of them. All told, Woz and Jobs sold about 175 boards for $500 apiece, netting about half that sum in profit. (The retail price was a whimsical $666.66.)

The board's success convinced Woz and Jobs that they were on to something. While Woz went on to design a more sophisticated computer, Jobs looked after the business side of the operation. Capital was the most pressing need. Jobs asked Nolan Bushnell, Atari's founder, for some help, and Bushnell sent him to Don Valentine, a venture capitalist who in turn referred him to A. C. Markkula. Markkula had been Intel's marketing manager between 1970 and 1974, when the firm introduced the microproces-

*A. C. Markkula in 1982*

sor and saw its sales begin to take off. Rich with stock options —
a millionaire at thirty-two — Markkula had left the company to
devote more time to the finer things of life. He sometimes helped
his entrepreneurial friends with their business problems, free of
charge. In October 1976, at Valentine's suggestion, Markkula
stopped by the Jobses' garage — Apple's humble distribution center, sales office, and world headquarters.

He liked Jobs and Woz, and he helped them write a business plan. In the course of his work, Markkula realized that the
personal computer industry was on the verge of an enormous
boom; some consulting firms were predicting that personal computer sales would reach several billion dollars by 1982. It seemed
to him that the Apple II — the successor to Woz's single-board
computer — was a first-rate machine, just right for the mass market. With the proper guidance, Apple could become a big company within a few years. So Markkula decided to join Woz and
Jobs, buying a third of the firm for $91,000. He arranged a
$250,000 line of credit for the company with Bank of America,
and raised about $660,000 from several sources, including Arthur
Rock, the venture capitalist who had helped finance Intel, and
Venrock Associates, a Rockefeller family company. Apple now
had the money and management to become a leader in the personal computer industry.

Introduced in 1977, the Apple II proved to be the Volks-
wagen of personal computers. It sold for only $1,195 (with 16K of
RAM and without a monitor) and was ideal for playing video
games; in fact, Woz, who loved to play games himself, had designed the computer with that purpose uppermost in mind. Bol-
stered by an imaginative advertising campaign, the Apple II took
off, and Apple became the fastest-growing company in American
history. The firm's annual sales rose from $775,000 in 1977, its
second year, to $335 million four years later. When Apple went
public in December 1980, it was one of the most successful stock
offerings in Wall Street history. Its stock opened at $22 and had
climbed to $29 by the end of the day, bringing the company's
market value to $1.2 billion. At the opening price, Jobs's shares
were worth $165 million, Woz's $88 million, and Markkula's $154
million. By the end of 1983 — six years after its incorporation —
Apple had almost 4,700 employees and $983 million in sales.

In 1981, IBM introduced its own personal computer, the
PC. Backed by one of the biggest and wealthiest companies in the
world, the machine was an immediate success. In 1981, about
35,000 were sold; in 1983, 800,000; and the IBM PC became the
most popular and influential personal computer. Many manufac-

*Apple's first logo was a drawing of Newton sitting under an apple tree. Apple Computer Corporation's first office consisted of two suites in a modest building in Cupertino, California. Left to right, top: the main office, with Jobs standing, away from the camera, on the right; the research and development lab, with Daniel Kottke, Jobs's traveling companion in India, in the background. Bottom: Mike Scott (left), Apple's first president, and Jobs (right) at their desks in the main office; and the shipping and receiving department.*

turers, hitching a ride on IBM's coattails, came out with low-priced PC-compatible computers, while other firms carved out comfortable niches for themselves as makers of PC-compatible peripherals and software. As a result, the PC has had a stabilizing influence on the youthful personal computer industry, providing a focal point for manufacturers and customers alike. Once an exotic and expensive technical tool, the computer has become an ordinary commodity; like the TV set or the refrigerator, it is a permanent and accepted addition to the technology of life.

# The Lesson of History

I t seems like only yesterday that we lived in a world where computers were rare and their role in our affairs quite minor. Scientists used pencil and paper, and sometimes mechanical calculators, to solve mathematical problems; the Census Bureau counted the population with punch card tabulators; bookkeepers kept track of accounts with the help of adding machines and ledgers; writers tapped away on Underwoods; factory workers produced goods on manual assembly lines; engineers designed machines, planes, and ships with T-squares and drawing boards; and everyone kept time with watches whose hands rotated around a dial. Not anymore. These and a million other tasks have been increasingly given over to computers, and the result has been a radical, fundamental change in the nature of our society.

Almost every human endeavor has benefited from the invention of the computer, a general-purpose information processor whose utility is limited only by our imagination. By manipulating vast amounts of data at high speed, the computer has enabled us to solve scientific, technical, financial, and administrative problems that used to be far beyond our practical ability. The computer is the intellectual equivalent of the steam engine, amplifying the power of our minds much as the steam engine — the great tool of the Industrial Revolution — multiplied the power of our muscles. No wonder the computer, made ever more compact and inexpensive by the continuing development of the IC, has spread so rapidly through the United States, Europe, and Japan. Forty years ago, there wasn't a single computer in the entire world; thirty years ago, there were some 250 in the United States; twenty years ago, there were 24,000; today, there are millions; tomorrow, there will be tens of millions.

Clearly, the computer is one of the most influential inventions of the twentieth century — indeed, of all time. However, we should resist the impulse to single it out as the most important invention of our century. The author of a recent book on computers suggests that "the three most important inventions of the twentieth century are the atomic bomb, the computer, and the

A close-up of a high-speed 64K RAM from IBM. A sixteen-bit word can be retrieved from the chip in sixteen to twenty billionths of a second, three to nineteen times faster than a typical 64K RAM. The section of the chip shown here is a sense amplifier, a unit that detects and amplifies the information in the chip's storage cells.

transistor" — a statement that conveniently ignores the airplane, rocket, satellite, integrated circuit, microprocessor (the computer writ small), birth-control pill, penicillin, television, and radio. Is the computer more important than the airplane? The pill? The rocket? Has any invention exercised greater influence than television? Our world would be a distinctly different place without any of these innovations, and there is little point in debating their relative significance.

In light of the computer's utility and pervasiveness, however, it seems as if we have entered a new age and, not surprisingly, writers are falling over each other in the rush to proclaim the dawn of what has variously been described as the Computer Revolution, the Microelectronics Age, the Electronic Revolution, the Information Society, or (god save us!) the Micro Millennium. But the proclamation of a new epoch ought be heard with a measure of skepticism, and it is worth remembering that the advent of any major technology inspires utopian sentiments. Strictly speaking, electronic technology has undergone several enormous advances since the invention of the vacuum tube. For example, the microprocessor made it possible to install computers in the tiniest devices; programmable gadgets of every sort, including personal computers, were the result. As an expression of progress in the field of electronics, the term "Electronic Revolution" seems appropriate. But is it appropriate to hail the second half of the twentieth century — which still has a few years to run, after all — as the beginning of the Micro Millennium?

In the past, such pronouncements have turned out to be wildly off the mark. Listen to what one writer, J. A. Etzler, said about the steam engine in 1842:

> Fellow men! I promise to show the means of creating a paradise within ten years, where everything desirable for human life may be had by every man in superabundance, without labor, and without pay; where the whole face of nature shall be changed into the most beautiful of forms, and man may live in the most magnificent palaces, in all imaginable refinements of luxury, and in the most delightful gardens; where he may accomplish, without labor, in one year, more than hitherto could be done in thousands of years.

Here is another writer, Joseph K. Hart, heralding the future of electricity in 1924:

> Centralization has claimed everything for a century: the results are apparent on every hand. But the reign of steam approaches

its end: a new stage in the industrial revolution comes on. Electric power, breaking away from its servitude to steam, is becoming independent. Electricity is a decentralizing form of power: it runs over distributing lines and subdivides to all the minutiae of life and need. Working with it, men may feel the thrill of control and freedom once again.

And this is what Marshall McLuhan wrote about electronics in 1964:

> The electric age of servomechanisms suddenly releases men from the mechanical and specialist servitude of the preceding machine age. As the machine and the motorcar released the horse and projected it onto the plane of entertainment, so does automation with men. We are suddenly threatened with a liberation that taxes our inner resources of self-employment and imaginative participation in society.

Only forty years old, the computer is still in its infancy. Some day in the distant future, a team of scientists and engineers, headed by a visionary as great as Babbage, might succeed in creating an intelligent computer whose reasoning and creative powers match or exceed our own. Yet, no matter how smart we manage to make it, the computer will never be a panacea. It is a tool, a fabulous tool, but nothing more, and we shouldn't invest it with all our hopes and dreams for the future.

# APPENDIX:
# THE FBI DOSSIER OF
# JOHN WILLIAM MAUCHLY

In addition to its financial and marketing dilemmas, J. Presper
Eckert and John Mauchly's company had another, much more in-
sidious problem — the FBI and military intelligence suspected
that the firm was infiltrated by Communists and Communist sym-
pathizers. In early 1948, the firm, then called the Electronic Control Company, was disqualified from receiving classified material.
As a result, the outfit couldn't be considered for several sizable
military contracts that might have enabled it to stay afloat, including a $2 million deal to build a computer for the Navy's Pacific
Missile Test Center at Point Mugu in Southern California. The
firm fell deeper into debt, and Eckert and Mauchly eventually had
to sell out to Remington Rand.

      It is common knowledge among historians that Eckert and
Mauchly's company, and Mauchly in particular, had serious security problems, yet the exact nature of those problems has been obscure. Documents were scarce and memories vague. In February
1984, however, I applied for Mauchly's FBI dossier under the
Freedom of Information Act, and the file — about 125 pages altogether — was released in May. It was heavily censored, primarily
to conceal the identities of other people. Nevertheless, it is full of
revealing information. Along with twelve letters from Mauchly's
private papers, loaned to me by his widow, Kathleen Mauchly,
and interviews with Eckert and Mrs. Mauchly, the file provides a
compelling portrait of a company — the first computer company
— caught in the treacherous crosswinds of the Cold War.

      The following is a summary of Mauchly's security prob-
lems and the investigations that caused them.

In 1947 and 1948, Eckert and Mauchly's little firm had two military contracts. One was a subcontract from Northrop Aircraft
Company for the construction of BINAC; the other was a small
contract from the Army Signal Corps for electronic cryptographic
equipment for the Army Security Agency. Both projects were top
secret, but Eckert, Mauchly, and their engineers, most of whom

had also worked on ENIAC, were given the necessary security
clearances. (The clearance hierarchy runs from *confidential* to *restricted* to *secret* to *top secret*, with a few even more exclusive
realms beyond that.) Those clearances apparently were temporary
— Mauchly's dossier doesn't say who granted them and Eckert
doesn't remember — pending a security investigation by the appropriate military and civilian agencies.

In early 1948, the Army's Intelligence Division investigated
Eckert and Mauchly's firm, and it didn't like what it found. The
company had applied for clearances for nine people, including
Eckert and Mauchly, and the Army concluded that five of them —
Mauchly; his secretary, Dorothy K. Shisler; and three engineers,
Albert A. Auerbach, Robert F. Shaw, and Charles B. Sheppard —
had "subversive tendencies or connections." And what were those
tendencies or connections? All information relating to Shisler and
the engineers was censored from Mauchly's dossier, but the Army
had this to say about Mauchly:

> Mauchly was a member of the Philadelphia branch of the
> American Association of Scientific Workers, an organization
> formed by the Communist Party as a front to influence legisla-
> tion restricting the free exchange of information relative to
> atomic energy. [Three lines censored.] Mauchly was legally
> married and the father of two children. In August 1946,
> Mauchly's wife was mysteriously drowned while both were
> moonlight bathing in Wildwood, N.J.

In the eyes of the Army, this was damning stuff. As one of
the FBI documents in Mauchly's dossier explained, the Association of Scientific Workers "was cited by the California Committee
of Un-American Activities [*sic*] as an organization 'included
among the Communist Fronts reported' at the WIN-THE-PEACE
CONFERENCE in Washington, D.C., from April 5 through 7,
1946." Bad enough but, the Army insinuated, Mauchly also may
have been involved in the death of his first wife — a farfetched
suggestion that never again appears in the dossier. Mary Mauchly's drowning was a tragic accident, and no one, including the
New Jersey police, suspected foul play.

The Army's investigation had two consequences. First, in
February or March 1948 the Air Force ordered Northrop to with-
hold classified material from the company, a decision that had
little or no effect on the BINAC project, which was already well
underway. Second, on 6 October Army Intelligence asked the FBI
to conduct "a complaint type investigation" of Mauchly and other
suspects. It's not clear why the Army believed that an additional

investigation was necessary, but it probably wanted the FBI to corroborate its findings.

In any event, the FBI, acting on the Army's request for an investigation, went to work. On 17 October, the FBI ordered the agency's Philadelphia bureau to investigate Mauchly, Shisler, and the engineers. The FBI was in a hurry, and the bureau was given a month to submit a report. Other bureaus — in New York City; Baltimore; Newark; and Norfolk, Virginia — were also enlisted in the effort. Two Philadelphia agents were assigned to the case full-time, interviewing Mauchly's colleagues, friends, and neighbors. Their fifteen-page report, submitted to Washington on 18 November, cleared Mauchly of misconduct or disloyalty. The report describes many responses similar to the one given by a former colleague at Ursinus College in Collegeville, Pennsylvania.

> Dr. MAUCHLY was described by [censored] as being very eccentric. However, [censored] declared he knew of no subversive tendencies, connections or activities on the part of Dr. MAUCHLY, whom he had always regarded as a loyal and patriotic individual. He knew of no reason why he should not be allowed to handle matters of trust for the government.

There was only one suspicious bit of information (although other material may have been censored):

> In May, 1947, [censored], of known reliability, advised that the name of JOHN W. MAUCHLY, Moore School, University of Pennsylvania, appeared on a list of individuals who signed a petition distributed by the ASSOCIATION OF PHILADELPHIA SCIENTISTS, urging the President and the House and Senate Military Affairs Committee to adopt laws which would provide for the civilian control of atomic energy and the elimination of military control.

The agent hadn't seen the petition, which had been signed by about 980 scientists, but was only passing on the words of an informant "of known reliability." Nevertheless, the disclosure was regarded as a sign of Mauchly's untrustworthiness. (The Association of Philadelphia Scientists was affiliated with the American Association of Scientific Workers, and both organizations were affiliated with the American Association for the Advancement of Science.) On 31 January 1950, the Army's Philadelphia Ordnance District sent a terse letter to the Eckert-Mauchly Computer Corporation, as it was now called, informing it "that the Department of the Army has denied security clearance for your firm and particularly the two individuals John W. Mauchly and Robert Findley

Shaw." If the company wished, the Ordnance District said, it could appeal to the Industrial Employment Review Board in Washington, D.C.

The letter was opened by George V. Eltgroth, the company's corporate counsel. By that time, the Northrop and Signal Corps projects had been completed, the firm wasn't doing any classified work, and Eckert and Mauchly were busy trying to keep the company afloat. Eltgroth didn't bother to tell Mauchly about the letter, and Mauchly didn't learn about the denial of clearance until late August. By then, the company had been bought by Remington Rand, the Korean War had begun, and the firm was hoping to sell computers to the military. So Mauchly wrote to the Industrial Employment Review Board on 15 September, asking for an explanation for the denial and requesting an appeal. On 27 November, the board responded,

> You were denied access to classified military information because reports of investigation purport to show that:
>
> a. You have held membership in organizations alleged to be Communist-dominated and Communist front organizations.
> b. You have been closely and sympathetically associated with a known member of the Communist Party.

On 8 January 1951, Mauchly and his attorney, Frank C. Sterck, an assistant general counsel at Remington Rand, traveled to Washington for a hearing before the review board. Mauchly and Sterck thought they had an open-and-shut case and didn't bring any witnesses or introduce any evidence. Why? On 8 August 1949, Mauchly had received a letter from the Provost Marshal of the Air Force, in Dayton, Ohio, granting him a top secret clearance — a clearance that, the Provost Marshal wrote, also applied to all Army and Navy contracts. Mauchly and Sterck assumed that because of a bureaucratic mix-up the Philadelphia Ordnance District, which had sent the clearance denial notice, simply had not been informed of the Provost Marshal's action. Since the Provost Marshal's office outranked the Ordnance District, Mauchly and his attorney were confident that the review board would rule in their favor.

But the panel upheld the denial. At the suggestion of Remington Rand, Mauchly resigned as president of his company on 8 March 1951. He withdrew from the firm's activities — it was building UNIVAC at the time — and spent the next two years working at a Remington Rand office in another part of Philadelphia, as director of programming research. Except for official cere-

monies, such as the unveiling of UNIVAC in March 1951, he
stayed away from the computer company's offices. Despite his retreat, he and Eckert consulted with each other frequently, and
Mauchly accepted his tribulations with fortitude and resignation.
He left the matter to his lawyers and went about his work and life
as usual, rarely mentioning his security problem. Most of his associates were quite sympathetic.

In the spring of 1951, while Mauchly was appealing the
ruling, the FBI decided to investigate him again. In a 3 May memo
from the Philadelphia bureau to FBI headquarters, an agent
writes:

> [Censored] related that the captioned individuals, all of whom
> are presently or have been working on this Computer as elec-
> tronic engineers, are believed to be Communistically inclined.
> [Censored] could offer no specific facts to substantiate this
> statement. . . .
>
> In view of the information supplied by [censored; apparently
> the informant mentioned above] as well as the background of
> the captioned individuals, and their detailed knowledge of the
> Computer Project, it is felt that additional investigation should
> be conducted, bringing their activities up to date, to determine
> if they should be considered for inclusion in the Security
> Index.

Washington agreed, and the investigation was reopened. It
went slowly; its priority apparently was low. On 5 February 1952,
an FBI agent interviewed Mauchly for fifty-five minutes. Mauchly,
according to the agent's report, filed six days later, was "cooperative throughout." First, he defended his colleagues, saying

> that he did not believe any of the four persons mentioned
> above [apparently Shisler and the three engineers] were Com-
> munists or that they would be intentionally disloyal to this
> country. He said he regards them as "intellectually honest,"
> that is, that they say what they believe, even though that is the
> same thing the Communists are preaching.

Then Mauchly defended himself:

> MAUCHLY volunteered the information that he felt he had been
> an unfortunate victim of circumstances in his own trouble of
> security clearance. He said the Employees [sic] Review Board
> confronted him with the assertion that he once signed a peti-
> tion distributed by the Association of Philadelphia Scientists,
> local council of the American Association of Scientific Work-
> ers, urging civilian control of atomic energy. The Board also

told him that he was regarded as being a member of that organization. Dr. MAUCHLY explained that he once attended a scientific meeting, sponsorship not recalled and, desiring certain scientific pamphlets, had signed a card indicating this desire. He does not recall actually turning in the $1 he believes was required to get these pamphlets. This act, nevertheless, according to MAUCHLY, evidently made him a member of the Association of Philadelphia Scientists in the minds of the officials of the organization, if not in his own mind.

MAUCHLY also related that he had once been a member of Consumers' Research in the early 1940s when one faction within this organization broke off to form Consumers' Union. He, MAUCHLY, went with Consumers' Union and remained a member until an Army officer friend warned him the organization was Communist infiltrated. He then withdrew.

It is noted that the Consumers' Union was cited as a Communist front organization by the House Committee on Un-American Activities in its report of 3/29/44 . . .

Not surprisingly, the FBI's second investigation failed to turn up new revelations. Meanwhile, Mauchly continued to press for his vindication. On 3 December 1952, the Industrial Employment Review Board reconsidered its ruling and granted him a restricted clearance. Six years later, the Secretary of the Army, on behalf of all the services, upgraded his clearance to secret. After an eight-year ordeal, Mauchly, an innocent victim of anti-Communist hysteria, had finally been restored to a position of trust.

—

# CHRONOLOGY OF THE HISTORY OF COMPUTERS

| | |
|---|---|
| 3000 B.C. | The abacus is developed in Babylonia. |
| A.D. 700–900 | Europeans begin using Hindu-Arabic math. |
| 1600 | Hindu-Arabic math is in common use throughout Europe. |
| 1614 | John Napier introduces logarithms. |
| 1617 | Napier invents rods. |
| 1623 | Wilhelm Schickard invents the mechanical calculator. |
| 1630–1633 | William Oughtred and Richard Delamain introduce the slide rule. |
| 1644–1645 | Blaise Pascal completes his calculator. |
| 1672–1674 | Leibniz builds his first calculator. |
| 1801 | Joseph-Marie Jacquard develops a loom programmed by punched tape. |
| 1820 | The Arithmometer, the first commercial calculator, is introduced. |
| 1823 | Charles Babbage begins the Difference Engine project. |
| 1834 | Babbage starts designing the Analytical Engine. |
| 1847 | George Boole publishes *The Mathematical Analysis of Logic*. |
| 1853 | Pehr and Edvard Scheutz complete their Tabulating Machine. |
| 1854 | Boole publishes *The Laws of Thought*. |
| 1875 | Frank Baldwin opens a workshop in Philadelphia, inaugurating the American calculator industry. |
| 1876–1878 | Baron Kelvin builds his harmonic analyzer and tide predictor machines. |
| 1878 | Ramon Verea patents a calculator capable of direct multiplication and division. |
| 1885 | Dorr Felt devises the Comptometer, a key-driven adding and subtracting calculator. |
| 1889 | Felt's Comptograph, containing a built-in printer, is introduced. |

1890    Herman Hollerith's punch cards and tabulating equipment are used in the U.S. Census.

1892    William S. Burroughs introduces an adder-subtracter with a superior printer.

1893    The Millionaire, the first efficient four-function calculator, is invented.

1900–1910    Mechanical calculators become commonplace.

1906    Lee De Forest devises a three-electrode tube, or triode.

1910–1913    Bertrand Russell and Alfred North Whitehead publish *Principia Mathematica*.

1911    Hollerith Tabulating Machine Company merges into Computing-Tabulating-Recording Corporation (CTR).

1914    Thomas Watson, Sr., joins CTR.

1919    W. H. Eccles and F. W. Jordan publish a paper on flip-flop circuits.

1924    CTR becomes International Business Machines Corporation (IBM).

1930    Vannevar Bush completes his differential analyzer, stimulating international interest in analog computing.

1937    Alan Turing publishes "On Computable Numbers."

1938    Konrad Zuse finishes his Z1, the first binary calculating machine.

    Claude Shannon publishes "A Symbolic Analysis of Relay and Switching Circuits."

1939    Bell Labs builds the Complex Number Calculator.

1941    Zuse assembles the Z3, the first electromechanical general-purpose program-controlled calculator.

1942    John V. Atanasoff and Clifford Berry's electronic calculating machine, one of the first calculating devices with tubes, goes into operation.

1943    IBM-Harvard Mark I is completed.

    First Colossus code-breaking machine is installed at Bletchley Park.

1944    J. Presper Eckert and John W. Mauchly conceive of the stored-program computer.

1945    ENIAC, the first fully functional electronic calculator, goes into operation in November.

    John von Neumann writes "First Draft of Report on the EDVAC."

IBM becomes the largest business machine manufacturer in the United States.

1946     Arthur Burks, Herman Goldstine, and von Neumann write "Preliminary Discussion of the Logical Design of an Electronic Computing Instrument."

Von Neumann starts a computer project at the Institute for Advanced Study.

Eckert and Mauchly establish the Electronic Control Company, America's first computer manufacturer.

1947     Bell Labs invents the point-contact transistor.

1948     IBM assembles the SSEC electromechanical computer, which runs a stored program on 27 January.

Manchester University's Mark I prototype runs the first fully electronic stored program on 21 June.

1949     EDSAC, the first full-scale electronic stored-program computer, begins operating at Cambridge University in June.

BINAC, the first stored-program computer in America, is tested in August.

1950     Remington Rand buys the Eckert-Mauchly Computer Corporation.

1951     The Ferranti Mark I, the first commercially manufactured computer, is installed at Manchester University in February.

The first UNIVAC is delivered to the Census Bureau in March.

Whirlwind, the first real-time computer, is completed.

William Shockley invents the junction transistor.

Grace Hopper conceives of an internal program known as a compiler.

1952     Thomas Watson, Jr., becomes president of IBM.

UNIVAC successfully predicts the outcome of the presidential election.

1953     IBM delivers the 701, its first electronic computer, to Los Alamos in March.

MIT conducts a successful full-scale test of Jay W. Forrester's magnetic-core memory.

1954     IBM introduces the 650 medium-size computer in December.

1955     Remington Rand merges with Sperry Corp., forming Sperry Rand.

Shockley establishes a semiconductor company in Mountain View, California.

1956    John McCarthy, an MIT computer scientist, coins the phrase "artificial intelligence."

1957    IBM introduces FORTRAN, the first high-level computer language.

Philco Corporation introduces the Philco 2000, the first commercially available transistorized computer.

1958    The first SAGE direction center goes into operation at McGuire Air Force Base in New Jersey.

Jack Kilby builds an integrated circuit (IC) at Texas Instruments in Dallas.

Jean Hoerni devises the planar process for making transistors.

1959    Kurt Lehovec designs an IC whose components are isolated with pn junctions.

Robert Noyce invents a planar IC, paving the way for the mass manufacture of reliable and efficient ICs.

1961    MIT develops the first computer time-sharing system.

Texas Instruments builds the first IC computer.

1963    The Digital Equipment Corporation introduces the minicomputer.

The Bell Punch Company, a British firm, offers electronic calculators using discrete components.

1964    IBM unveils the System/360, the first family of computers.

1968    Noyce and Gordon Moore establish Intel in Santa Clara, California.

Intel introduces the first 1K random-access memory (RAM).

1971    Intel invents the microprocessor.

Mass-produced pocket calculators are introduced in the U.S.

1973    The ENIAC patent is invalidated.

IC computers become commonplace.

1974    An article describing the construction of a "personal minicomputer" appears in *Radio-Electronics*.

1975    The Altair computer premières in *Popular Electronics*, inaugurating the personal computer industry.

1977    The Apple II is introduced.

1981    IBM enters the personal computer market with the PC.

1984    IBM develops a one-million bit RAM.

# BIBLIOGRAPHY
# AND NOTES

If you would like to dig deeper into the history of computers, the following bibliography will serve as a guide. The entries have been arranged by chapter and include both technical and general works. Only major sources have been listed.

The historiography of computers possesses an excellent academic journal — *Annals of the History of Computing*, a quarterly published by the American Federation of Information Processing Societies, Arlington, Virginia, and edited by a distinguished board of computer scientists and historians. Started in 1979, the *Annals* (as it hereafter will be referred to) is a cross between a scholarly journal and a memoir, and learned technical treatises run back to back with chatty reminiscences by computer pioneers. The *Annals* is the single most important source of information on the history of computers, but the journal's contributors tend to concentrate on a relatively small number of historical issues — the Atanasoff-Mauchly debate, ENIAC, Babbage, Whirlwind, and so on. Surprisingly, the *Annals* has yet to run an article on integrated circuits, minicomputers, or personal computers.

In addition to the *Annals*, the historiography of computers has two excellent anthologies — *A History of Computing in the Twentieth Century*, edited by N. Metropolis, J. Howlett, and Gian-Carlo Rota (New York: Academic Press, 1980); and *The Origins of Digital Computers*, edited by Brian Randell (New York: Springer-Verlag, 1982). Both volumes are treasure troves of original historical material; for instance, Randell's contains Atanasoff's 1940 grant proposal for a computing machine as well as Mauchly's 1942 memo on the construction of a high-speed electronic calculator. It also contains a 131-page annotated bibliography on the history of computers (an updated version of a bibliography that Randell compiled for the October 1979 issue of the *Annals*).

If you would rather avoid the rigors of original source material, there are at least two other books (in English, anyway) on the history of computers — R. Moreau's *The Computer Comes of Age: The People, the Hardware, and the Software* (Cambridge, Mass.: MIT Press, 1984); and Herman H. Goldstine's *The Computer from Pascal to von Neumann* (Princeton, N.J.: Princeton

University Press, 1980). Moreau is the director of scientific development for IBM France, and his book reflects his first-hand knowledge of computers, particularly IBM's. Moreau's book isn't forbiddingly technical, and it's well organized and well written. Goldstine's work, on the other hand, is rather tough going, and the narrative ends in the early 1950s; but it's full of illuminating technical details. Goldstine was the Army officer who got the ENIAC project going, and he played an important role in the early history of computers.

# Chapter 1

## Bibliography

Bell, Eric Temple. *Men of Mathematics.* New York: Simon & Schuster, 1937. (Chapters on Pascal, Leibniz, and George Boole.)

Bishop, Morris. *Pascal: The Life of Genius.* New York: Reynal & Hitchcock, 1936.

Cajori, Florian. *A History of Mathematics.* New York: Macmillan, 1919.

"Calculating Machine by Wilhelm Schickard: Operating Instructions." (A twelve-page pamphlet.) Stuttgart: IBM Deutschland GmbH. Undated (1965?).

Delamain, Richard. Translated extract from *Grammelogia*, 1630. In Smith, *A Source Book*, pp. 156–159.

Eves, Howard. *An Introduction to the History of Mathematics.* New York: Holt, Rinehart and Winston, 1964.

Flad, Jean-Paul. *Les Trois Premières Machines à Calculer: Schickard (1623) — Pascal (1642) — Leibniz (1673).* In *La Conference au Palais de la Découverte*, no. D93. Paris: Université de Paris, 1963.

Glaisher, James Whitbread Lee. "Napier, John." *Encyclopaedia Britannica*, 11th ed., vol. 19, pp. 171–175.

Heath, F. G. "Origins of the Binary Code." *Scientific American*, August 1972, p. 76.

Hofmann, Joseph E. *Leibniz in Paris 1672–1676: His Growth to Mathematical Maturity.* Cambridge: Cambridge University Press, 1974.

Horsburgh, Ellice Martin, ed. *Modern Instruments and Methods of Calculations: A Handbook of the Napier Tercentenary Celebration Exhibition.* London: G. Bell and Sons, 1914.

Kline, Morris. *Mathematical Thought from Ancient to Modern Times.* Oxford: Oxford University Press, 1972.

Kreiling, Frederick C. "Leibniz." *Scientific American*, May 1968, p. 95.

Leibniz, Gottfried. Translated extract of *Machina arithmetica.* In Smith, *A Source Book*, pp. 173–181.

Locke, Leland L. "The Contributions of Leibniz to the Art of Mechanical Calculation." *Scripta Mathematica* 1 (June 1933): 315–321.

Napier, John. Translated extracts from *Mirifici logarithmorum canonis constructio*, 1619; and from *Rabdologiae*, 1617. In Smith, *A Source Book*, pp. 149–155.

Oughtred, William. Translated extracts from *Circles of Proportion*, 1630. In Smith, *A Source Book*, pp. 160–164.

"Oughtred, William." *Encyclopaedia Britannica*, 11th ed., vol. 20, p. 378.

Pascal, Blaise. Translation of "Advertisement: Necessary to those who have curiosity to see the Arithmetic Machine, and to operate it." In Smith, *A Source Book*, pp. 165–172.

Payen, Jacques. "Les Exemplaires Conservés de la Machine de Pascal." *Revue d'Histoire des Sciences et de Leurs Applications* 16 (April 1963): 139–160.

Price, Derek de Solla. "An Ancient Greek Computer." *Scientific American*, June 1959, p. 60.

———. *Gears from the Greeks: The Antikythera Mechanism — A Calendar Computer from ca. 80 B.C.* New York: Science History Publications, 1975.

Pullan, J. M. *The History of the Abacus.* New York: Praeger, 1969.

Seck, Friedrich, ed. *Wilhelm Schickard 1592–1635: Astronom — Geograph — Orientalist — Erfinder der Rechenmaschine.* Tübingen, West Germany: J. C. B. Mohr (Paul Siebeck), 1978.

Smith, David Eugene. *History of Mathematics.* 2 vols. New York: Dover Publications, 1958.

———, ed. *A Source Book in Mathematics.* New York: McGraw-Hill, 1929.

———, and Karpinski, Louis. *The Hindu-Arabic Numerals.* Boston: Ginn and Company, 1911.

Steinmann, Jean. *Pascal.* New York: Harcourt, Brace & World, 1962.

Taton, René. "Sur l'Invention de la Machine Arithmetique." *Revue d'Histoire des Sciences et de Leurs Applications* 16 (April 1963): 139–160.

von Freytag Loringhöff, Baron Bruno. "Die Erste Rechenmaschine: Tübingen 1623." *Humanismus und Technik* 9 (20 April 1964): 45–55.

———. "Wilhelm Schickard und seine Rechenmaschine von 1623." In *350 Jahre Rechenmaschinen*, edited by Martin Graef, pp. 11–20. Munich: Carl Hanser Verlag, 1973.

Williams, M. R. "From Napier to Lucas: The Use of Napier's Bones in Calculating Instruments." *Annals* 5 (July 1983): 279–296.

## Notes

3 "There is no greater mistake": Knuth, Donald E. *The Art of Computer Programming*, vol. 2, 2nd ed. (Reading, Mass.: Addison-Wesley, 1981), p. 178.

"I submit to the public": Smith, *A Source Book*, p. 166.

8 "hereby the simple of this Iland": *Encyclopaedia Britannica*, 11th ed., vol. 19, p. 172.

"When Merchiston first published": Bell, *Men of Mathematics*, p. 526.

16 "thin, garrulous, and bad-tempered":
*Dictionary of Scientific Biography*, vol. 7,
p. 289.

18 Schickard's letters translated by Horst Salzwedel, based on extracts in Seck, *Wilhelm
Schickard*, pp. 289–290. The accuracy of
the translations was verified by von Freytag
Loringhöff in a 6 April 1984 letter to the
author.

24 "The calculating machine was born of filial
love": P. Guth in *Le Figaro Littéraire*, 12
July 1947, as quoted in Steinmann, *Pascal*,
p. 28.

28 Dalibray's sonnet: Steinmann, *Pascal*, p. 32.
Pascal's broadside: Ibid., p. 29.

30 "greatly excited by the division": Ruth Lydia
Saw, *Leibniz* (New York: Penguin Books,
1954), pp. 9–10.

31 "When, several years ago": Smith, *A Source
Book*, p. 173–174.

## Chapter 2

## Bibliography

*Annals of the Dudley Observatory*, vol. 1. Albany,
N.Y.: Weed, Parsons and Company, 1866. pp.
116–126.

Archibald, R. C. "P. G. Scheutz, Publicist, Author,
Scientific Mechanician, and Edvard Scheutz,
Engineer — Biography and Bibliography."
*Mathematical Tables and Other Aids to Compu-
tation* 2 (October 1947): 238–245.

Babbage, Charles. *Passages from the Life of a Philosopher*. 1864. Reprint. New York: Augustus M.
Kelley, 1969.

Babbage, Henry Prevost, ed. *Babbage's Calculating
Engines, Being a Collection of Papers Relating
to Them, Their History and Construction*. 1889.
Reprint. Los Angeles: Tomash Publishers, 1983.

Baxandall, D. *Calculating Machines and Instruments*. 1926. Revised by Jane Pugh. London:
Science Museum, 1975.

Bromley, Allan G. "Charles Babbage's Analytical
Engine." *Annals* 4 (July 1982): 196–217.

Chase, George C. "History of Mechanical Computing Machinery." *Annals* 2 (July 1980): 198–226.

Clerke, A. M. "Babbage, Charles." *Dictionary of
National Biography*, vol. 2, pp. 304–306.

*Defence of Dr. Gould by the Scientific Council of
the Dudley Observatory*. Albany, N.Y.: Weed,
Parsons and Company, 1858.

Horsburgh, Ellice Martin, ed. *Modern Instruments
and Methods of Calculations: A Handbook of*

*the Napier Tercentenary Celebration Exhibition*.
London: G. Bell and Sons, 1914.

Huskey, Velma R., and Huskey, Harry D. "Lady
Lovelace and Charles Babbage." *Annals* 2 (October 1980): 299–329.

Hyman, Anthony. *Charles Babbage: Pioneer of the
Computer*. Princeton, N.J.: Princeton University
Press, 1983.

Last, J. "Digital Calculating Machines." *The Char-
tered Mechanical Engineer* 9 (December 1962):
572–579.

Lovelace, Augusta Ada. "Sketch of the Analytical
Engine Invented by Charles Babbage, by L. F.
Menabrea, of Turin, Officer of the Military Engi-
neers, With notes upon the Memoir by the
Translator." 1843. In Morrison, *Charles Bab-
bage*, pp. 225–297.

Margerison, T. A. "Computers." In *A History of
Technology*, edited by Trevor I. Williams, vol. 7,
pt. 2, pp. 1150–1203. Oxford: Clarendon Press,
1978.

Morrison, Philip and Emily, eds. *Charles Babbage
and His Calculating Engines*. New York: Dover
Publications, 1961.

*Statement of the Trustees of the Dudley Observa-
tory*. Albany, N.Y.: Van Benthuysen, 1858.

Usher, A. P. *A History of Mechanical Inventions*.
2nd ed. Cambridge, Mass.: Harvard University
Press, 1954.

Williams, M. R. "The Difference Engines." *The
Computer Journal* 19 (February 1976): 82–89.

## Notes

37 "One evening I was sitting": Babbage, *Passages*, p. 42.

40 "I wish to God these calculations": Morrison,
*Charles Babbage*, p. xiv.

43 "Mr. Babbage has displayed great talent": Hyman, *Charles Babbage*, p. 52.
"I had some conversations": Ibid.

44 "get up every morning": Babbage, *Passages*,
p.19.

46 "the principles of pure *D*-ism": Morrison,
*Charles Babbage*, p. 66.

53 "I remember a funny dinner": Hyman,
*Charles Babbage*, p. 179.
"My Lords cannot but express": Ibid., p. 130.
"The drawings and parts": Ibid., p. 132.

54 "What shall we do to get rid": Ibid., pp. 190–
191.
"I have . . . been compelled": Ibid., p. 134.

57 "Inventors are so seldom found": Ibid., p.
240.

59 "The *constructor* of the *navy*": Ibid., p. 241.

64 "We may say most aptly": Morrison, *Charles
Babbage*, p. 252.

66 "In the first room I saw": Horsburgh, *Modern Instruments and Methods of Calculations*, pp. 19–21.

## Chapter 3

### Bibliography

"An Improved Calculating Machine." *Scientific American*, 27 October 1888, p. 265. (An article on Felt's Comptometer.)

Austrian, Geoffrey D. *Herman Hollerith: Forgotten Giant of Information Processing*. New York: Columbia University Press, 1982.

Broadbent, T. A. A. "Russell, Bertrand." *Dictionary of Scientific Biography*, vol. 12, pp. 9–17.

"Burroughs, William Seward." *National Cyclopaedia of American Biography*, vol. 27, pp. 383–384.

"Bush, Vannevar." *Current Biography, 1947*, pp. 80–82.

Bush, Vannevar. *Pieces of the Action*. New York: William Morrow, 1970.

Cerruzi, Paul. *Reckoners: The Prehistory of the Digital Computer, from Relays to the Stored Program Concept, 1935–1945*. Westport, Conn.: Greenwood Press, 1983. (Sections on Howard Aiken and the Mark I, George Stibitz and the Bell Labs calculators, and ENIAC.)

Crossley, J. N., et al. *What Is Mathematical Logic?* Oxford: Oxford University Press, 1979.

Desmonde, William H., and Berkling, Klaus J. "The Zuse Z3: German Predecessor of the Mark I." *Datamation* 9 (September 1966): 30–31.

Eccles, W. H., and Jordan, F. W. "A Trigger Relay Utilizing Three-Electrode Thermionic Vacuum Tubes." *Radio Review*, 1919. Reprinted in Swartzlander, *Computer Design Development*, pp. 298–300.

"Felt, Dorr Eugene." *National Cyclopaedia of American Biography*, vol. 40, pp. 23–24.

Gardner, Martin. "Logic Machines." *Scientific American*, March 1952, p. 68.

———. *Logic Machines and Diagrams*. New York: McGraw-Hill, 1958.

Gore, John K. "Apparatus for Sorting Cards and Compiling Statistics." U.S. Patent No. 518,240, 17 April 1894.

Hollerith, Herman. "An Electric Tabulating System." 1889. In Randell, *Origins of Digital Computers*, pp. 133–143.

Hollerith, Virginia. "Biographical Sketch of Herman Hollerith." *Isis* 62 (1971): 69–78.

Jevons, William Stanley. "Boole, George." *Ency-clopaedia Britannica*, 11th ed., vol. 4, pp. 235–236.

Kelvin, William Thomson, 1st Baron. *Mathematical and Physical Papers*. 6 vols. Cambridge: Cambridge University Press, 1911.

Lyndon, Roger C. "The Zuse Computer." *Mathematical Tables and Other Aids to Calculation* 2 (October 1947): 355–359.

Metropolis, N.; Howlett, J.; and Rota, Gian-Carlo, eds. *A History of Computing in the Twentieth Century*. New York: Academic Press, 1980.

Paullin, Charles O. "Burroughs, William Seward." *Dictionary of American Biography*, vol. 11, supp. 1, pp. 138–139.

Pfeiffer, John E. "Symbolic Logic." *Scientific American*, December 1950, p. 22.

Randell, Brian, ed. *The Origins of Digital Computers*. New York: Springer-Verlag, 1982.

Schreyer, Helmut. "Technical Computing Machines." 1939. In Randell, *Origins of Digital Computers*, pp. 170–173.

Spahr, G. W. "Store-Keeping by Machinery: A Description of the System in Operation at the Frog and Switch Department of the Pennsylvania Steel Co." *The Frog Shop Digest* 3 (March 1912): 8–11. Photocopy. Bethlehem, Pa.: Public Relations Department, Bethlehem Steel Company, 1983.

Speiser, A. P. "The Relay Calculator Z4." *Annals* 3 (July 1980): 242–245.

Swartzlander, Earl E., Jr. *Computer Design Development: Principal Papers*. Rochelle Park, N.Y.: Hayden Book Co., 1976.

Truesdell, Leon E. *The Development of Punch Card Tabulation in the Bureau of the Census, 1890–1940*. Washington, D.C.: U.S. Government Printing Office, 1965.

Turck, Joseph A. V. *Origin of Modern Calculating Machines*. 1921. Reprint. New York: Arno Press, 1972.

Venn, John. "Boole, George." *Dictionary of National Biography*, vol. 5, pp. 369–370.

Willcox, Walter F. "Billings, John Shaw." *Dictionary of American Biography*, vol. 1, pt. 2, pp. 266–269.

———. "Hollerith, Herman." *Dictionary of American Biography*, vol. 11, supp. 1, pp. 415–416.

Wilson, Norman H. "Letter to H. R. Russell, Office Machines Research, Inc., 8 Nov. 1937, on Gore Sorter." Photocopy. Newark, N.J.: Public Relations Department, Prudential Insurance Company of America, 1983.

Zuse, Konrad. "Method for Automatic Execution of Calculations with the Aid of Computers." 1936. In Randell, *Origins of Digital Computers*, pp. 163–169.

———. "The Outline of a Computer Development

from Mechanics to Electronics." In Randell, *Origins of Digital Computers*, pp. 175–190.

———. "Some Remarks on the History of Computing in Germany." In Metropolis et al., *A History of Computing*, pp. 611–627.

## Notes

69  "Herman Hollerith is a man": Austrian, *Herman Hollerith*, p. 339.

    "I was a student in civil engineering": Zuse, "Some Remarks," p. 611.

71  "One Sunday evening, at Dr. Billings' ": Truesdell, *The Development of Punch Card Tabulation*, p. 31.

73  "I was traveling in the West": Austrian, *Herman Hollerith*, p. 15.

84  "brass for brain": Kelvin, *Papers*, vol. 6, p. 272.

86  "I was trying to solve": Bush, *Pieces of the Action*, p. 161.

91  "This is the work of a real *thinker*": Hyman, *Charles Babbage*, p. 244.

94  "In 1939, due to the perfectly private state": Zuse, "Some Remarks," p. 612.

# Chapter 4

## Bibliography

Aiken, Howard. "Proposed Automatic Calculating Machine." 1937. In Randell, *Origins of Digital Computers*, pp. 195–201.

———, and Hopper, Grace M. "The Automatic Sequence Controlled Calculator." 1946. In Randell, *Origins of Digital Computers*, pp. 203–222.

"Aiken, Howard." *Current Biography*, 1947, pp. 5–7.

Atanasoff, John V. "Advent of Electronic Digital Computing." *Annals* 6 (July 1984): 229–282.

———. "Computing Machine for the Solution of Large Systems of Linear Algebraic Equations." 1940. In Randell, *Origins of Digital Computers*, pp. 315–335.

———. "Comment by J. V. Atanasoff." *Annals* 3 (October 1981): 390.

Brainerd, John G. "Genesis of the ENIAC." *Technology and Culture* 17 (July 1976): 482–488.

Burks, Arthur W. "Who Invented the General-Purpose Electronic Computer?" Transcript of talk in Rackham Lecture Hall, University of Michigan, 2 April 1974. Photocopy. Arthur Burks, Ann Arbor, Mich., 1983.

———, and Burks, Alice R. "The ENIAC: First General-Purpose Electronic Computer." *Annals* 3 (October 1981): 310–391.

"Firing Tables for 155-mm. Gun, M1917, M1917A1, and M1918M1; Firing Shell, H.E., MK.III." 1933. Photocopy. Washington, D.C.: Department of the Army, 1983.

Gardner, W. David. "Will the Inventor of the First Digital Computer Please Stand Up?" *Datamation* 20 (February 1974): 84–90.

Goldstine, Herman, and Goldstine, Adele. "The Electronic Numerical Integrator and Computer (ENIAC)." *Mathematical Tables and Other Aids to Calculation* 2 (January 1946): 97–110.

Loveday, Evelyn. "George Stibitz and the Bell Labs Relay Computers." *Datamation* 23 (September 1977): 80–85.

Mauchly, John W. "The Use of High-Speed Vacuum Tube Devices for Calculating." In Randell, *Origins of Digital Computers*, pp. 355–358.

Metropolis, N.; Howlett, J.; and Rota, Gian-Carlo, eds. *A History of Computing in the Twentieth Century*. New York: Academic Press, 1980.

Oettinger, Anthony G. "Retiring Computer Pioneer: Howard Aiken." *Communications of the ACM* 5 (June 1962): 298–299.

Randell, Brian, ed. *The Origins of Digital Computers*. New York: Springer-Verlag, 1982.

Shannon, Claude E. "A Symbolic Analysis of Relay and Switching Circuits." 1938. Reprinted in Swartzlander, *Computer Design Development*, pp. 3–24.

Shurkin, Joel. *Engines of the Mind: A History of the Computer*. New York: W. W. Norton, 1984.

Stern, Nancy. *From ENIAC to UNIVAC: An Appraisal of the Eckert-Mauchly Computers*. Bedford, Mass.: Digital Press, 1981.

Stibitz, George. "Computer." 1940. In Randell, *Origins of Digital Computers*, pp. 247–252.

———. "Early Computers." In Metropolis et al., *A History of Computing*, pp. 479–483.

———, as told to Loveday, Evelyn. "The Relay Computers at Bell Labs." *Datamation* 13 (1967): April, pp. 35–44; May, pp. 45–49.

Swartzlander, Earl E., Jr. *Computer Design Development: Principal Papers*. Rochelle Park, N.Y.: Hayden Book Co., 1976.

War Department, Bureau of Public Relations. Five news releases on the development, operation, and application of ENIAC. 15 February 1946. Photocopy. Philadelphia: Archives, University of Pennsylvania, 1983.

Wulforst, Harry. *Breakthrough to the Computer Age*. New York: Charles Scribner's Sons, 1982.

## Notes

99  "I explained what was to be done": Burks, "Who Invented the General-Purpose Electronic Computer?" p. 8.

"to start what I thought of": Stibitz, "The Relay Computers," April 1967, p. 35.

100 "I had observed": Ibid.

106 "like a roomful of ladies knitting": Jeremy Bernstein, *The Analytical Engine* (New York: Random House, 1963), p. 64.

110 "In the specific case of sidewise firing": Wulforst, *Breakthrough*, p. 54.

111 "As already stated, the electronic computor": Mauchly, "The Use of High-Speed Vacuum Tube Devices," p. 356.

119 "As time goes on, I expect to get": Burks and Burks, "The ENIAC: First General-Purpose Electronic Computer," p. 332.

131 "The complexity of these problems": Stern, *From ENIAC to UNIVAC*, p. 63.

## Chapter 5

### Bibliography

Bigelow, Julian. "Computer Development at the Institute for Advanced Study." In Metropolis et al., *A History of Computing*, pp. 291–310.

Burks, Arthur W. "From ENIAC to the Stored-Program Computer: Two Revolutions in Computers." In Metropolis et al., *A History of Computing*, pp. 311–344.

Burks, Arthur W.; Goldstine, Herman H.; and von Neumann, John. "Preliminary Discussion of the Logical Design of an Electronic Computing Instrument." 1946. Reprinted in Swartzlander, *Computer Design Development*, pp. 221–259.

Campbell-Kelly, Martin. "Programming the Manchester Mark I." *Annals* 2 (April 1980): 130–168.

Goldstine, Herman H. *The Computer from Pascal to von Neumann*. Princeton, N.J.: Princeton University Press, 1980.

Heims, Steve J. *John von Neumann and Norbert Weiner: From Mathematics to the Technologies of Life and Death*. Cambridge, Mass.: The MIT Press, 1980.

Hodges, Andrew. *Alan Turing: The Enigma*. New York: Simon and Schuster, 1983.

Hofstadter, Douglas R. *Gödel, Escher, Bach: An Eternal Golden Braid*. New York: Basic Books, 1979.

Kemeny, John G. "Man Viewed as a Machine." *Scientific American*, April 1955, p. 58.

Lavington, Simon. *Early British Computers*. Bedford, Mass.: Digital Press, 1980.

Mauchly, John W. "Amending the ENIAC Story." *Datamation* 25 (October 1979): 217–219.

———. "Preparation of Problems for EDVAC-Type Machines." 1947. In Randell, *Origins of Digital Computers*, pp. 393–397.

Metropolis, N.; Howlett, J.; and Rota, Gian-Carlo, eds. *A History of Computing in the Twentieth Century*. New York: Academic Press, 1980.

Metropolis, N., and Worlton, J. "A Trilogy of Errors in the History of Computing." *Annals* 2 (January 1980): 49–59.

Randell, Brian. "The Colossus." In Metropolis et al., *A History of Computing*, pp. 47–92.

———, ed. *The Origins of Digital Computers*. New York: Springer-Verlag, 1982.

Stern, Nancy. *From ENIAC to UNIVAC: An Appraisal of the Eckert-Mauchly Computers*. Bedford, Mass.: Digital Press, 1981.

Swartzlander, Earl E., Jr. *Computer Design Development: Principal Papers*. Rochelle Park, N.Y.: Hayden Book Co., 1976.

Ulam, S. M. "John von Neumann, 1903–1957." *Bulletin of the American Mathematical Society*. 1958. Reprinted in *Annals* 4 (April 1982): 157–181.

von Neumann, John. "First Draft of a Report on the EDVAC." 1945. Reprinted in Stern, *From ENIAC to UNIVAC*, pp. 177–246.

Wilkes, M. V., and Renwick, W. "The EDSAC." In Randell, *Origins of Digital Computers*, pp. 417–421.

Wulforst, Harry. *Breakthrough to the Computer Age*. New York: Charles Scribner's Sons, 1982.

### Notes

133 "Tell me, Walter": Wulforst, *Breakthrough*, p. 163. Fuldheim was the station's evening news anchor, and the interview took place on 16 October 1952. (Wulforst letter to the author, 23 May 1984.)

135 "No attempt has been made to make provision": Stern, *From ENIAC to UNIVAC*, p. 75.

136 "when along came von Neumann": Goldstine, *The Computer from Pascal to von Neumann*, p. 182.

137 "We started with our basic ideas": Mauchly, "Amending the ENIAC Story," p. 217. "Like a child with a new toy": Ibid.

138 "It was, I think, a pretty sad spectacle": Stern, *From ENIAC to UNIVAC*, p. 23.

145 "gross indecency": Hodges, *Alan Turing*, p. 458. Turing's crime was "Gross Indecency contrary to Section 11 of the Criminal Law Amendment Act 1885."

149 "When [the machine was] first built": Campbell-Kelly, "Programming the Mark I," p. 134. See also Hodges, *Alan Turing*, p. 385.

151 "assign his rights in the patent": Stern, *From ENIAC to UNIVAC*, p. 159.

"Under this view the University": Ibid., pp. 49–50.

156 "There will never be enough problems": Ibid., p. 111.
158 "I find it difficult to say much": Ibid., p. 105.
160 "BINAC seemed to operate well": Ibid., p. 128.
164 "The trouble with machines": "The Machine Vote," *Newsweek*, 17 November 1952, p. 64.

## Chapter 6

### Bibliography

Belden, Thomas and Marva. *The Lengthening Shadow: The Life of Thomas J. Watson.* Boston: Little, Brown, 1962.

Drucker, Peter F. "Thomas Watson's Principles of Modern Management." *Esquire*, December 1983, p. 194.

Engelbourg, Saul. *International Business Machines: A Business History.* New York: Arno Press, 1976.

Fishman, Katherine Davis. *The Computer Establishment.* New York: McGraw-Hill, 1981.

Greenwald, John. "The Colossus That Works." *Time*, 11 July 1983, p. 44.

Hurd, Cuthbert C. "Computer Development at IBM." In Metropolis et al., *A History of Computing*, pp. 389–418.

———. "Early Computers at IBM." *Annals* 3 (April 1981): 163–182.

Metropolis, N.; Howlett, J.; and Rota, Gian-Carlo, eds. *A History of Computing in the Twentieth Century.* New York: Academic Press, 1980.

*Moody's Industrial Manual,* 1930–1940.

Phelps, Byron E. "Early Electronic Computer Developments at IBM." *Annals* 2 (July 1980): 253–269.

Rodgers, William. *Think: A Biography of the Watsons and I.B.M.* New York: Stein & Day, 1969.

Sheean, Robert. "Tom Jr.'s I.B.M." *Fortune*, September 1956, p. 113.

Sobel, Robert. *IBM: Colossus in Transition.* New York: Times Books, 1981.

"Special Issue: IBM 701," *Annals* 5 (April 1983): passim.

Wulforst, Harry. *Breakthrough to the Computer Age.* New York: Charles Scribner's Sons, 1982.

### Notes

167 "Clothes don't make the man": Sobel, *IBM*, p. 33.

"Pack your todays with effort": Ibid., p. 36.
"You cannot be a success": Ibid., p. 55.
"We have different ideas": Ibid.
169 "They say money isn't everything": Ibid., p. 33.
171 "It is the men who are willing": Ibid., p. 26.
179 "Mr. Watson is the man": Ibid., p. 57.
180 "Our products are known": Greenwald, "The Colossus That Works," p. 46.
"When IBM was under the old man": Fishman, *The Computer Establishment*, p. 57.
185 "The company is in the family": Sobel, *IBM*, p. 112.
186 "The thing that I am looking forward to": Ibid., pp. 113–114.
"There is a reason for my success": Fishman, *The Computer Establishment*, p. 51.
"Frankly I can hardly wait to begin": Sobel, *IBM*, p. 115.
187 "He had a large desk": Ibid., p. 102.
188 "If Aiken and my father": Fishman, *The Computer Establishment*, p. 36.
191 "It dawned on us": Ibid., p. 40.
"Because they could not imagine": Hurd, "Early Computers," p. 166.
193 "lay out the department": Wulforst, *Breakthrough*, p. 174.

## Chapter 7

### Bibliography

Backus, John. "The History of FORTRAN I, II, and III," *Annals* 1 (July 1979): 21–37.

Bello, Francis. "The War of the Computers." *Fortune*, October 1959, p. 128.

Boehm, George A. "The Next Generation of Computers." *Fortune*, March 1959, p. 132.

Burck, Gilbert. " 'On Line' in 'Real Time,' " *Fortune*, April 1964, p. 141.

Evans, Christopher. "Conversation: Jay W. Forrester." *Annals* 5 (July 1983): 297–301.

Everett, Robert R., ed. "Special Issue: SAGE (Semi-Automatic Ground Environment)." *Annals* 5 (October 1983).

———. "Whirlwind." In Metropolis et al., *A History of Computing*, pp. 365–384.

Fishman, Katherine Davis. *The Computer Establishment.* New York: McGraw-Hill, 1981.

*Honeywell, Inc. v. Sperry Rand Corp. and Illinois Scientific Developments, Inc.,* U.S. District Court, District of Minnesota, Fourth Division, Civil Action File No. 4–67 Civ. 138. October 19, 1973. *Findings of Fact, Conclusions of Law and Order of Judgement.*

Hurd, Cuthbert C. "Early Computers at IBM." *Annals* 3 (April 1981): 163–182.

Knuth, Donald E., and Pardo, Luis Trabb. "The Early Development of Programming Languages." In Metropolis et al., *A History of Computing*, pp. 197–273.

Lee, John A. N., and Tropp, Henry S., eds. "Special Issue: FORTRAN's Twenty-Fifth Anniversary." *Annals* 6 (January 1984).

Metropolis, N.; Howlett, J.; and Rota, Gian-Carlo, eds. *A History of Computing in the Twentieth Century.* New York: Academic Press, 1980.

Pfeiffer, John. "Machines That Man Can Talk With." *Fortune*, May 1964, p. 153.

Redmond, Kent C., and Smith, Thomas M. *Project Whirlwind: The History of the Pioneer Computer.* Bedford, Mass.: Digital Press, 1980.

Rosen, Saul. "Programming Systems and Languages: A Historical Survey." *Proceedings of the Spring Joint Computing Conference, 1964*, pp. 1–16.

Sammet, Jean E. *Programming: History and Fundamentals.* Englewood Cliffs, N.J.: Prentice-Hall, 1969.

Saxenian, Hrand. "Programming for Whirlwind I." Report R-196, 11 June 1951, Electronic Computer Division, Servomechanisms Laboratory, MIT. Photocopy. Cambridge, Mass.: MIT Archives.

"Sperry Rand: Still Merging." *Fortune*, March 1960, p. 125.

Van Deusen, Edmund L. "The Two-Plus-Two of Sperry Rand." *Fortune*, August 1955, p. 88.

## Notes

196 "This is not the age": "Hogben." J. M. and M. J. Cohen. *The Penguin Dictionary of Modern Quotations.* 2nd ed. (New York: Penguin Books, 1980), s.v.

"Is it progress": "Lec." Ibid., s.v.

197 "a physicist's dream": Redmond and Smith, *Project Whirlwind*, p. 7.

"Jay . . . talked to a number of people": Everett, "Whirlwind," pp. 365–366.

198 "Bob Everett was relaxed": Redmond and Smith, *Project Whirlwind*, p. 135.

201 "I was reading a technical journal": Evans, "Conversation," pp. 298–299.

206 "The buildings of the direction centers": Everett, ed. "Special Issue: SAGE," p. 390.

209 "The opposition within IBM": Hurd, "Early Computers," p. 172.

"The market forecast procedure": Ibid.

214 "Can a machine translate": Backus, "The History of FORTRAN," p. 23.

"Automatic programming, tried and tested":

*Journal of the ACM*, vol. 2 (1955), p. 291.

"This was in the days": Knuth and Pardo, "Programming Languages," p. 239.

215 "We simply made up the language": Backus, "The History of FORTRAN," p. 24.

"The pace of debugging": Ibid., p. 29.

216 "Like most of the early hardware": Rosen, "Programming Systems and Languages," p. 4.

219 "At IBM, Bibby would press": Fishman, *The Computer Establishment*, p. 46.

222 "did not themselves first invent": *Findings of Fact*, sec. 3, pt. 1, par. 3.

## Chapter 8

## Bibliography

"Advanced New Line of Solid Circuit Semiconductor Networks Offered by Texas Instruments for Immediate Space-Age Equipment Applications." News release, 19 October 1973. Photocopy. Dallas, Tex.: Public Relations Department, Texas Instruments, 1984.

Augarten, Stan. *State of the Art: A Photographic History of the Integrated Circuit.* New York: Ticknor & Fields, 1983.

Braun, Ernest, and Macdonald, Stuart. *Revolution in Miniature: The History and Impact of Semiconductor Electronics.* 2nd ed. Cambridge: Cambridge University Press, 1982.

Burck, Gilbert. "The 'Assault' on Fortress IBM." *Fortune*, June 1964, p. 112.

Dean, K. J., and White, G. "The Semiconductor Story." *Wireless World* 79 (1973): January, pp. 2–5; February, pp. 65–69; March, pp. 137–140; April, pp. 169–173.

Dummer, G. W. A. *Electronic Inventions and Discoveries.* 2nd ed. Oxford: Pergamon Press, 1978.

———. "Lost Opportunities of UK's Pioneering Work on ICs." *Electrons* (18 March 1980): 4–5.

Eimbinder, Jerry. "History of the Semiconductor Industry." *Circuit News.* Reprint for the Signetics Corp., Sunnyvale, Calif. Undated.

"Going After the Leader." *Business Week*, 12 December 1964, p. 122.

Haanstra, John W. et al. "Processor Products—Final Report of SPREAD Task Group, December 28, 1961," *Annals* 5 (January 1983): 6–26.

Hansen, Dirk. *The New Alchemists.* Boston: Little, Brown, 1983.

Harris, William B. "The Battle of the Components." *Fortune*, May 1957, p. 135.

Hoerni, J. A. "Method of Manufacturing Semiconductor Devices." U.S. Patent 3,025,589, 20 March 1962.

"How to Get a Bright Idea." *The Economist,* 27 December 1980, p. 59. (Portraits of Kilby, Noyce, and Hoff.)

Kilby, Jack S. "Invention of the Integrated Circuit." *IEEE Transactions on Electron Devices* 23 (July 1976): 648–654.

———. "Miniaturized Electronic Circuits." U.S. Patent 3,138,743, 23 June 1964.

Lehovec, Kurt. "Invention of p-n Junction Isolation in Integrated Circuits." *IEEE Transactions on Electron Devices* 25 (April 1978): 495–496.

———. "Multiple Semiconductor Assembly." U.S. Patent 3,029,366, 10 April 1962.

Noyce, Robert. "Semiconductor Device-And-Lead Structure." U.S. Patent 2,981,877, 25 April 1961.

———, et al. "Microelectronics" issue, *Scientific American,* September 1977.

Shockley, William. "The Path to the Conception of the Junction Transistor." *IEEE Transactions on Electron Devices* 23 (July 1976): 597–620.

"Solid Circuit Semiconductor Network Computer, 6.3 Cubic Inches in Size, Is Demonstrated in Operation by U.S. Air Force and Texas Instruments." News release, 19 October 1961. Photocopy. Dallas, Tex.: Public Relations Department, Texas Instruments, 1984.

"Solid-State Circuits Used to Build 10 oz. General-Purpose Computer." *Aviation Week and Space Technology,* 30 October 1961, p. 81.

"Transistors: Growing Up Fast." *Business Week,* 5 February 1955, p. 86.

Weiner, Charles. "How the Transistor Emerged." *IEEE Spectrum* 10 (January 1973): 24–35.

Wise, T. A. "IBM's $5,000,000,000 Gamble." *Fortune,* September 1966, p. 118.

———. "The Rocky Road to the Marketplace." *Fortune,* October 1966, p. 138.

Wolf, Thomas. "The Tinkerings of Robert Noyce." *Esquire,* December 1983, p. 346.

Wolff, Michael F. "The Genesis of the Integrated Circuit." *IEEE Spectrum* 13 (August 1976): 45–53.

## Notes

225  "If you take a bale of hay": Wolf, "The Tinkerings of Robert Noyce," p. 356.

227  "I cannot overemphasize": Weiner, "How the Transistor Emerged," p. 31.

228  "This circuit was actually spoken over": Ibid., p. 25.

231  "With the advent of the transistor": Dummer, *Electronic Inventions,* p. 128.

"Dummer was preaching": Alan Gibson, quoted in Braun and Macdonald, *Revolution in Miniature,* p. 94.

233  "These attempts [at miniaturization]": Noyce et al., *Scientific American,* p. 4.

234  "the development of a semiconductor": Hansen, *The New Alchemists,* p. 96.

235  "At that time, radio was still": Wolff, "The Genesis of the Integrated Circuit," p. 47.

238  "This shaping concept": Kilby, "Miniaturized Electronic Circuits," column 2, line 25.

"It is possible . . . to achieve": Ibid., column 7, line 20.

242  "The idea was shamelessly simple": Author interview with Lehovec, June 1983.

243  "When this [the planar process]": Wolff, "The Genesis of the Integrated Circuit," p. 51.

245  "There was a lot of work": Robert Lloyd, quoted in Hansen, *The New Alchemists,* p. 104.

248  "It was roughly as though": Wise, "IBM's $5,000,000,000 Gamble," p. 119.

## Chapter 9

### Bibliography

"The Age of Altair." (Twenty-page product brochure.) Albuquerque, N.M.: Micro Instrumentation and Telemetry Systems, 1975. Jim Bybee, Albuquerque, N.M., 1984.

Augarten, Stan. *State of the Art: A Photographic History of the Integrated Circuit.* New York: Ticknor & Fields, 1983.

———. "Ted Hoff: Engineer's Engineer." *Peninsula Times-Tribune,* 29 March 1983, B-5.

"The Big-Time Beckons Minicomputers." *Business Week,* 30 January 1971, p. 32.

Bylinsky, Gene. "Here Comes the Second Computer Revolution." *Fortune,* November 1975, p. 134.

Ciotti, Paul. "Revenge of the Nerds." *California,* July 1982, p. 72.

Fishman, Katherine Davis. *The Computer Establishment.* New York: McGraw-Hill, 1981.

Freiberger, Paul, and Swaine, Michael. *Fire in the Valley: The Making of the Personal Computer.* Berkeley, Calif.: Osborne/McGraw-Hill, 1984.

Greenwald, John. "D-Day for the Home Computer." *Time,* 7 November 1983, p. 76.

Heiserman, David L. "Minicomputers — What They Are and What They Do." *Popular Electronics,* June 1972, p. 32.

Hilts, Philip J. *Scientific Temperaments: Three Lives in Contemporary Science.* New York: Simon & Schuster, 1984. (Includes a biography of John McCarthy, one of the inventors of time-sharing.)

"How Apple Will Keep Growth Going." *Business Week*, 8 February 1982, p. 66.

"In Cooperative Project Called LOCAL: Five Massachusetts Schools Pioneer Computer Education." *Educational Media*, March 1970.

"Jobs, Steven." *Current Biography*, 1983, pp. 204–207.

Kemeny, John. *Man and the Computer*. New York: Charles Scribner's Sons, 1972.

Kuzela, Lab. "Building Computer Is as Easy as Apple Pie." *Industry Week*, 9 June 1980, p. 80.

"MITS, Inc.: Offering Circular." 6 November 1973. Hyder & Co., underwriter, and The First National Bank in Albuquerque, transfer agent. Jim Bybee, Albuquerque, N.M., 1984.

Noyce, Robert N., and Hoff, Marcian E., Jr., "A History of Microprocessor Development at Intel." *IEEE Micro*, 1981. Reprint AR-173. Santa Clara, Calif.: Intel Corporation.

Nulty, Peter. "Apple's Bid to Stay in the Big Time." *Fortune* 7 February 1983, p. 36.

Roberts, H. Edward, and Yates, William. "Altair 8800: The Most Powerful Minicomputer Project Ever Presented — Can Be Built for Under $400." *Popular Electronics*, January–February 1975, p. 33; p. 58.

Singer, Hal, ed. *Mark-8 User Group Newsletter*. vol. 1, nos. 1, 2, 4. Lompoc, California, 1974. Photocopy. Jonathan Titus, Blacksburg, Va., 1984.

Sklarewitz, Norman. "Born to Grow." *Inc.*, April 1979, p. 53.

"Surviving a Microcomputer Shift." *Business Week*, 16 April 1979. Reprint. Cupertino, Calif.: Public Relations Department, Apple Computer.

"Swimming Upstream to Computer Success." *Business Week*, 21 September 1968, p. 152.

"Time Sharing Zooms Through the Ceiling." *Business Week*, 22 June 1968, p. 121.

Titus, Jonathan. "Build the Mark-8: Your Personal Computer." *Radio Electronics*, July 1974, p. 29.

———. *Computer!* New York: Gernsback Publications, 1974.

## Notes

253 "No one saw [them] . . . coming": Bradbury, foreword to Augarten, *State of the Art*, p. iii.

"For the first two decades": Kemeny, *Man and the Computer*, p. 21.

256 "When IBM started to build": Fishman, *The Computer Establishment*, p. 211.

258 "This may sound trivial": "Swimming Upstream." *Business Week*, p. 153.

262 "When my washing machine breaks": Stan Mazor, as quoted in Augarten, "Ted Hoff," B-5.

273 "For many years": *Popular Electronics* (January 1975): 4.

## Epilogue

### Bibliography

Evans, Christopher. *The Micro Millennium*. New York: Viking Press, 1979.

Forester, Tom, ed. *The Microelectronics Revolution: The Complete Guide to the New Technology and Its Impact on Society*. Cambridge, Mass.: MIT Press, 1981.

McLuhan, Marshall. *Understanding Media: The Extensions of Man*. New York: McGraw-Hill, 1964.

Osborne, Adam. *Running Wild: The Next Industrial Revolution*. Berkeley, Calif.: Osborne/McGraw-Hill, 1979.

Shurkin, Joel. *Engines of the Mind: A History of the Computer*. New York: W. W. Norton, 1984.

Van Deusen, Edmund L. "The Coming Victory Over Paper." *Fortune*, October 1956, p. 130.

Winner, Langdon. "Mythinformation in the High-Tech Era." *IEEE Spectrum* 21 (June 1984), p. 90.

### Notes

283 "the three most important inventions": Shurkin, *Engines of the Mind*, p. 9.

284 "Fellow men!": Winner, *Mythinformation*, p. 91.

"Centralization has claimed everything": Ibid.

285 "The electric age of servomechanisms": McLuhan, *Understanding Media*, pp. 357–358.

### Interviews

The following people were interviewed for this book: David Ahl; John V. Atanasoff; John Backus; John G. Brainerd; Arthur and Alice Burks; J. Presper Eckert, Jr.; Harry J. Gray; Jean Hoerni; Marcian E. Hoff; Cuthbert C. Hurd; Stephen A. Kallis, Jr.; A. C. Markkula; Kathleen Mauchly; Stan Mazor; Forrest Mims III; Edward Roberts; Jonathan Titus; Stephen Wozniak.

# ACKNOWLEDGMENTS

More than most books, this one was a cooperative effort, and I am grateful to the dozens of people who helped me, whether with advice, photographs, or historical material. I can't list all of their names here, but I would like to single out some of them for special mention.

I had the good fortune to work with an unusually dedicated and intelligent group of editors and designers at Ticknor & Fields and Houghton Mifflin. Every one of them gave above and beyond the call of duty: Katrina Kenison, my editor; Laurie Parsons, the photo researcher; Helena Bentz and Janice Byers, the manuscript editors; Cope Cumpston, the book designer; and Louise Noble, who designed the cover. Each one deserves a literary distinguished-service cross with clusters for hard work, talent, and dedication.

Several people, knowledgeable about one or another period of the history of computers, read portions of the manuscript, and I am indebted to them. They were Arthur W. Burks, and his wife, Alice, both of whom worked on ENIAC; Paul E. Ceruzzi, an excellent historian and the author of *Reckoners*; Bill Fernandez, Apple's first employee; Bruno Baron von Freytag Löringhoff, who reconstructed Schickard's calculator; Forrest Mims III, one of the founders of MITS and a prolific writer on electronics and computers; A. C. Markkula, one of the founders of Apple Computer; and Allan Schiffman, an engineer for the Fairchild Camera & Instrument Corporation. I also read a portion of the manuscript over the phone to John Backus, the chief author of FORTRAN. If, despite all the advice I received, there are any errors in the book, I am the one to blame.

The public relations business is often maligned and rarely praised, but almost all of the PR representatives with whom my photo researcher and I dealt were wonderfully helpful. I'd like to thank Erika Volger of Apple Computer; David R. Curry of Burroughs; Stephen A. Kallis, Jr., of Digital; John C. Reilly and Sue Ann Bailey of IBM; Howard High of Intel; Edward L. Galvin of MITRE; R. K. Kramer of NCR; George Eager of Princeton University; Richard A. Mathisen of Prudential Insurance; Michael Maynard and Michael Heck of Sperry; Richard Perdue of Texas

Instruments; and Francesca Chapman of the University of Pennsylvania.

I am especially grateful to several photo archivists for their help: Mary E. Williams of the Bristol Record Office, who supplied us with the photographs of the Bristol rent rolls in Chapter 1; William J. Wisheart of the Computer Museum, Boston; Armand J. Dionne and Richard MacDonald of the Cruft Photographic Laboratory at Harvard; Jane Bradshaw, Jane S. M. Bowen, and Sue Mossman of the Science Museum, London, who patiently responded to our many photo orders; and Dr. Uta C. Mertzbach of the Smithsonian Institution, who answered our numerous requests for pictures.

Finally, I'd like to thank some of the people who helped me even though it wasn't their jobs to do so: Geoffrey D. Austrian of IBM; Paul Bird, who obtained the color photos of the Pascaline; James Bybee, formerly of MITS; G. W. A. Dummer, who contributed the Tinkertoy and micromodule photos; I. Bernard Cohen of Harvard; Robert J. Deroski of Deroski Consolidated Enterprises, Cutchogue, New York, who took the color photo of the Antikythera mechanism; Bill Fernandez, who provided the shots of Apple's first office; Harry J. Gray of the Moore School, who supplied the photos of EDVAC; Daniel Leeson of IBM; Forrest Mims III, who took the pictures of the Altair and the cover of *Popular Electronics*; Byron Phelps of IBM; Horst Salzwedel, who translated several German papers on Schickard for me; Keith W. Smillie of the University of Alberta; Charlotte Wilkes of the Dublin, Georgia, *Courier Herald*, who took the photo of Edward Roberts; and M. R. Williams of the University of Calgary.

# INDEX

# PHOTO CREDITS